"THIS IS
THE AMERICAN FORCES NETWORK"

"THIS IS
THE AMERICAN FORCES NETWORK"

The Anglo-American Battle of the Air Waves
in World War II

Patrick Morley

Westport, Connecticut
London

Library of Congress Cataloging-in-Publication Data

Morley, Patrick.
   "This is the American Forces Network" : the Anglo–American battle of the air waves in World War II / Patrick Morley.
      p. cm.
   Includes bibliographical references and index.
   ISBN 0-275-96901-0 (alk. paper)
   1. American Forces Network—History. 2. Radio broadcasting—Great Britain—History. I. Title.
PN1991.3.G7 M67 2001
384.54′06′573—dc21   00-032622

British Library Cataloguing in Publication Data is available.

Library of Congress Catalog Card Number: 00-032622

ISBN: 0-275-96901-0

First published in 2001

Praeger Publishers, 88 Post Road West, Westport, CT 06881
An imprint of Greenwood Publishing Group, Inc.
www.praeger.com

Printed in the United States of America

The paper used in this book complies with the
Permanent Paper Standard issued by the National
Information Standards Organization (Z39.48-1984).

10 9 8 7 6 5 4 3 2 1

Copyright Acknowledgments

Extracts from BBC radio broadcast of 8 June 1953 and from BBC documents relating to the AFN, the AEFP, and other related topics reproduced by permission of the BBC Written Archives Centre.

Extracts from Trent Christman, *Brass Button Broadcasters* (Turner Publishing, 1993), reproduced by permission. Copyright Turner Publishing, 1993.

The Stars and Stripes is a registered trademark of the National Tribune Corporation and is used with their permission.

Every reasonable effort has been made to trace the owners of copyright materials in this book, but in the case of Maurice Gorham, *Sound and Fury* (Percival Marshall, 1948) this has proven impossible. The author and publisher will be glad to receive information leading to more complete acknowledgments in subsequent printings of the book, and in the meantime extend their apologies for this omission.

Contents

Acknowledgments   vii

Abbreviations   ix

Preface   xi

Introduction   xiii

CHAPTER ONE
The Reason Why   1

CHAPTER TWO
Battle Is Joined   11

CHAPTER THREE
AFN on the Air   22

CHAPTER FOUR
Programs and Personalities   32

CHAPTER FIVE
BBC and AFN   46

CHAPTER SIX
Forces Broadcasting   58

CHAPTER SEVEN
"The Greatest Radio Show in History"   69

CHAPTER EIGHT
AEFP Birth Pangs   80

CHAPTER NINE
AEFP "Politics and Intrigue"   93

CHAPTER TEN
"The Best Entertainment Program Ever"   104

CHAPTER ELEVEN
AFN on the Road to Berlin   118

CHAPTER TWELVE
AFN Postwar   127

POSTSCRIPT
Afterthoughts and Memories   138

Appendix I: Transmitters   151

Appendix II: AFN Program Schedules   156

A Note on the Principal Sources Used   160

Index   167

Photo essay follows page 68.

Acknowledgments

A great many people have helped me in writing this book, some with factual contributions and recordings of old radio programs, many with recollections, others with encouragement. I must express my thanks to Jacqueline Kavanagh, the BBC Written Archivist, and I am particularly grateful to Sue Hiranandani and Marget Horne (formerly Margaret Hubble) and Harry Mackenzie, who encouraged me to continue when I was very much inclined to give up. I also owe a debt of gratitude to Trevor Hill, a former BBC colleague, for all his good advice, especially over the draft manuscript. Others to whom I am indebted in one way or another are David Ades (of the Robert Farnon Society), Tony Adkins, Jill Balcon (Mrs C. Day-Lewis), Peter Ball, Dennis Barrow, Roger Bickerton (founder of the Vintange Record Programme Collectors Circle), Dennis Bigwood, Rex Boys, A. L. Bray, Mary Cadogan, Mike Carey, Mark Chamberlain, John Charman, Michael Conway (of the 1940 Association), Roy Cooke, Alan Davies, Gerry Didymus, Brian Dyson, Andrew Emmerson (editor of *Radio Days*), Alasdair Fenton, D. Filer, D. L. Fleming, Thomas Forrester, Dave Gallop, John Gardiner, Geoff Gardner, B. Gastrell, Peter Good, the late Benny Green, Kathleen Hall, Michael Highton, Sunil Hiranandani, Eric Hitchcock, Con Holland-Skinner, Bob Holness, Audrey Johnson, Brian Johnson, Charles King, Richard March (of the Glenn Miller Society), Derek Maidment, L. J. Le Moignon, John Momber, Colin Morgan (former owner and editor of *In Tune*), Norman Morrison, Bryan Ough, Ray Pallett (editor of *Memory Lane*), Fred Passey, David Ponting, David Price, Neil Ridley, Paul Rentle, Gillian Reynolds,

David Savage, Bill Slater, Graeme Stevenson (editor of *Tune into Yesterday*), Ray Todd, Michael F. Tyson, Mike Waring, Raymond Welch-Bartram, Don Wicks, and Allan G. Williams. The author is most grateful to the American Forces Network in Frankfurt and to John Provan for providing many of the photographs used in this volume. The latter also kindly loaned me the AFN logos. The photograph of GI Jill and Bing Crosby was the personal gift of Jill herself (Martha Wilkerson) only a short while before she died. In Germany I owe a particular debt to Guenter Lulay and Gregor Prumbs for all their willing help and advice and the invaluable gift of AFN recordings from the late 1940s and early 1950s, and also to Mark White, for many years "Mr AFN Berlin." Thanks, too, to Christian Muermann for his audiotapes and recollections. In the United States and Canada, a special "thank you" to Trent Christman and Marty Halperin, who have been so helpful in so many ways, and also Syl Binkin, Frank Bresee, Mike Biel (for his valuable guidance on recording techniques and history), Ken Dunnagan, Robert J. Harlan, Art Malham, Allen J. Moratz, Roy Neal, Loyd Sigmon, Gary Terrell (for his collection of AFN recordings), and Phillip Wedge.

Abbreviations

ABC	American Broadcasting Company
ABSIE	American Broadcasting Station in Europe
AEFP	Allied Expeditionary Forces Programme
AES	American Expeditionary Station
AFN	American Forces Network
AFRS	Armed Forces Radio Service
BBC	British Broadcasting Corporation
BFN	British Forces Network
CBS	Columbia Broadcasting System
DG	Director-General (BBC)
DDG	Deputy Director-General (BBC)
DPP	Director of Programme Planning (BBC)
ETO	European Theater of Operations
ETOUSA	European Theater of Operations, U.S. Army
FCC	Federal Communications Commission
GI	Government Issue
ITMA	*It's That Man Again*
NAD	North American Director (BBC)
NBC	National Broadcasting Company
OWI	Office of War Information

SHAEF	Supreme Headquarters, Allied Expeditionary Force
SHAPE	Supreme Headquarters, Allied Powers Europe
SOS	Services of Supply (U.S. Army)
USO	United Service Organizations
WAC	Women's Army Corps
WRNS	Women's Royal Naval Service

Preface

This book started off as a radio broadcast. It began in 1995 during the celebrations to mark the 50th anniversary of the end of World War II. It struck me that no one had so much as mentioned one organization that had done a lot to brighten our lives during those drab wartime years in Britain—AFN, the American Forces Network. It had a big audience among British listeners, myself included. So why not a radio program paying tribute to those DJs of long ago?

In the end, the project fell through. But by that time I had heard from a number of listeners who remembered AFN with pleasure and affection. I also made contact with several former AFN staff members. I even heard from two engineers with the BBC, the British Broadcasting Corporation, who had helped to wire AFN's wartime studios. So as there was no book published in England chronicling the station's war years, I decided to fill the gap.

I was a teenager during the war, an absorbed spectator of great events. I lived through a few air raids, went to the movies endlessly, and listened all the time to "the wireless"—as we called the radio then. I liked the BBC, but I liked AFN better. I loved the music and I loved the comedy shows, especially Jack Benny and Bob Hope. It is for the music above all else that almost everyone remembers AFN—that, and the relaxed, easy chatter of their announcers, who endeared themselves to us all with their jokes and their friendly talk. Sadly, they have all gone now, but there are many of us who still remember them. This book is a tribute and a belated thank you to all of them.

Introduction

It was the Anglo-American alliance that won World War II. Even the Soviet Union would not have been able to defeat Hitler single-handed, certainly not without the support of the "arsenal of democracy." And it is inconceivable that the United States would have come to the aid of Communist Russia without the involvement of Britain, whose unconquered territory was vital as a launch pad against Nazi-occupied Europe. So the "uneasy alliance," as it is often referred to, was crucial for victory.

As a result, it has been the subject of a great deal of scrutiny. Most of this has dealt with its military or political aspects or with the social and personal relationships arising from the war. One aspect of the alliance, however, has not received the attention it deserves, and it is the aim of the present book to fill this gap.

Uneasy the alliance often was. The disharmony was most evident in the military field, and whole volumes have been written about it. And it was the military who were partly responsible for the problems in the relationship between what was then the world's leading broadcasting organization—the British Broadcasting Corporation—and a fledgling American forces radio network.

By the middle of the war, the standing of the BBC had never been greater. All Britain and much of Nazi-occupied Europe listened to its news broadcasts.[1] Yet at this high point in its history, the BBC spent months in an extraordinary attempt to stifle at birth a broadcasting service intended only for homesick American troops, the American Forces Network.

Within a year of losing that battle, the BBC was again at daggers drawn with the Americans over the setting up of another forces broadcasting service. This time Churchill himself was called on to intervene, at the pressing request of General Eisenhower. So the difficulties that accompanied AFN's birth epitomize the tensions that beset the Anglo-American alliance as a whole. The story of how AFN came into being, and of the later problems affecting the D-Day broadcasting service, throw light on how two English-speaking but often divergent allies were able to resolve their differences.

Sometimes feathers were ruffled. There were acrimonious exchanges. The Old World might look down its nose at the New, while the New chafed in exasperation at the set patterns of the Old. But generally each tolerated the other, and at a personal level relations were often warm and friendly. In the last resort, whatever their differences (and there were many), the relationship worked—because it had to. So the way the two broadcasting organizations worked together for two-and-a-half years is a reflection in microcosm of the Anglo-American alliance in the wider sphere.

But AFN was not about alliances or politics or high strategy. It was about entertainment, about providing its listeners with the best in popular music, comedy, and sport. So any account of AFN must reflect those aspects of its work, which to those who listened were all that mattered. Much of its output came from the Armed Forces Radio Service (AFRS), the most remarkable entertainment organization created by the war. And that, too, will figure in the pages that follow.

Behind the microphone, the relations between Americans and British were politically significant, though the general public was unaware of this. What came out of the microphone was just as important in a different way, because it helped to form the attitudes to the United States of the station's British listeners, of whom in time there were many. Those twin aspects of the Anglo-American alliance are what this book sets out to examine.

NOTE

1. For an authoritative view of the effect of the BBC's wartime broadcasts on the morale of occupied Europe, see Asa Briggs, *History of Broadcasting in the United Kingdom*, Vol. III: *The War of Words* (Oxford University Press, 1970), pp. 11–12.

ONE

The Reason Why

The American Forces Network came into existence in 1943. It was the largest of the network of U.S. military broadcasting stations that sprang up in the war. The BBC later described it as "a unique feature" of the broadcasting history of Britain.[1]

By early 1942 Britain had been earmarked as the springboard for the vast Allied army that was to reconquer Nazi-occupied Europe. AFN was set up to cater for the thousands of U.S. servicemen who were in Britain for that invasion and for the air offensive against Hitler's Germany. The first contingent of American servicemen landed in the United Kingdom as early as January 1942, less than two months after the United States had entered the war. By the middle of that year, U.S. troops were beginning to pour into Britain and continued to do so in steadily increasing numbers, building up to their wartime peak of one-and-a-half million.[2]

Many had never even left home before, never mind traveling thousands of miles to a foreign country, across an ocean menaced by enemy U-boats. They were not merely in a strange land far from home—they were in a country that was suffering from the effects of three years of total war. In wartime Britain, there was a shortage of almost everything that made life worth living. What was not actually rationed was hard to get, with factories almost totally devoted to turning out war weapons, not consumer goods. The GIs saw for themselves the widespread devastation caused by German bombing. If they traveled by rail, they had to go on trains that were always overcrowded and frequently delayed because of air raids or priority freight trains carrying military supplies.

And they experienced at first hand the depressing effect of the total blackout imposed everywhere at night, so different from the far less effective "brownouts" back in the States.[3]

It is hardly surprising, then, that the U.S. servicemen missed America and all things American. Not that they went short of anything. In their military bases, they were insulated from the privations of everyday life in Britain. Although they were aware of the bombing, most had no conception of the difficulties and shortages that had to be coped with every day by the ordinary British family. They would have been surprised at the viewpoint of a member of Britain's Women's Royal Naval Service (WRNS), the "Wrens," who sometimes breakfasted at an American mess after a night watch at the U.S. naval base in Londonderry, Northern Ireland. She describes the contrast with the frugal daily fare that was the lot of most Britons:

[In the American mess] bacon and egg, sausages, tomatoes could be had on any day. . . . my bacon would be cooked exactly as I ordered. My eggs were either sunny side up, easy over, or whatever way I preferred. There were many types of cereal and tinned fruit to start with and piles of toast with butter and any preserve. I thought of my family at home, their one egg a week and their whole week's bacon ration that would have provided just one American breakfast.[4]

With the Americans, she wrote, "there was no shortage of food, no shortage of drink: just no shortages." But if the American forces could expect the kind of food and other home comforts they got back in the United States, there were other things that were not so easily available. They particularly missed the sort of radio programs they had come to take for granted back home. They were used to listening to the radio a lot, but the output of Britain's only broadcasting service, the BBC, was not to their taste. One American writer described it unkindly—and unjustly—as "the dust bowl of the airwaves."[5] And he went on to say: "There is much displeasure, even among the British, at its choice of programs," a comment that ignored the fact that no broadcasting organization has ever earned the universal approval of its audience.

Certainly, though, the American GIs complained loud and long about the BBC. They found the music dull, the humor alien, the announcers stiff and unfriendly. The BBC was aware of the problem. One official went so far as to put on record this damning comment: "All information is unanimous that American troops consider the BBC's programs lousy."[6] They didn't even like the news, which was presented in a sober, serious manner quite unlike the style and pace of the American announcers. The obvious answer was for the Americans to have a radio network all to themselves.

The BBC, it must be said, had not ignored the presence in its midst of the growing army of Americans. Early in the war, it had set up its own Forces Programme for British troops at home and overseas. This radical departure from the pattern of British broadcasting had started, ironically, for British forces overseas who (like the Americans now) had wanted to hear radio programs from home. They were the men of the British Expeditionary Force stationed in France in 1940. They wished to hear comedy and popular music: there were even calls for "more Bing Crosby." And so, under pressure from the military authorities, the BBC obliged and started up a whole new broadcasting channel. It even went so far as to relax its firm "Sundays are serious" policy, which frowned on light entertainment on the Lord's Day. That was an indication of how the war was compelling the corporation to rethink entrenched attitudes, though one wonders whether it would have done the same if the listeners involved had not been members of the forces.

As it was, the new service was heard clearly in England and soon became so popular with the civilian population that after the British Army had been driven out of France by the Germans the Forces Programme became an established part of the broadcasting scene in Britain. Indeed, it proved to be more popular than the Home Service, which was the name given to the main BBC radio channel; this provided a diet of serious talks, plays, and music, which was not to everyone's taste.[7]

With the American troops now clamoring for their own radio service, the BBC felt obliged in the interest of Anglo-American relations to make concessions to their allies. The Forces Programme already included regular items for troops from the British Dominions, especially the Canadians and the Australians. So, after some heart-searching, the BBC introduced a number of American programs into its output. Jack Benny was heard regularly by British listeners, as was Bob Hope. The BBC did rather well out of it financially. One official noted that Jack Benny's show cost $12,000 to produce, but the BBC was getting it for only £15 (then about $60).[8] In the late summer of 1942, an American sport bulletin was introduced; it was only on for five minutes a day except on Sundays, when it ran for ten minutes. What British listeners thought of hearing on their own radio programs reports on what to them were such incomprehensibly arcane sports as baseball and American football has not been recorded.

More was to follow. By now, the BBC was going to some trouble to try to please their military visitors. *Command Performance*, which became one of the most popular American wartime programs, is a case in point. One of the early editions was recorded from a shortwave broadcast so that the corporation's hierarchy could get an idea of what they might be letting themselves—and the BBC radio audience—in for. The audition, which is what it was in effect, was clearly a success. Arrangements were made with the American authorities for the BBC to rebroadcast the program on a regular basis. Recordings on disc were flown across the Atlantic by military aircraft—"the bomber run." And just in case the bomber failed to arrive, the shortwave broadcasts were recorded as a standby.

All did not go smoothly, however. A BBC official noted that although on the whole the material in the American programs was "quite clean," certain artists' dialogue needed editing. Among those who had to be "cleaned up" were Robert Benchley, Frank Morgan, and Al Jolson. This censoring caused some dismay in America when the news filtered back across the Atlantic, and cables flew back and forth until agreement about editing was reached.[9]

Before long, as well as *Command Performance* and a similar program, *Mail Call*, British listeners were getting a weekly diet of Bob Hope, Jack Benny, Charlie McCarthy, and other American entertainers—so much so that there was growing concern within the corporation about what was seen as the "Americanization" of output. The head of the BBC, the director-general (DG), William Haley, expressed the view that "it is essential to ensure that the use of American broadcasts . . . such as Bob Hope, Jack Benny and other programmes does not become a Franken-stein."[10] Conversely, another member of the BBC hierarchy gave it as his opinion that if any hundred British troops were asked to choose their own records, 90 percent of them would opt for American material.[11]

All the same, whatever the rank and file of the forces may have felt, there were many British listeners who agreed with the head of the BBC. They were happy with the BBC as it was and saw nothing greatly to admire in the American programs—which illustrates one of the dilem-mas the corporation faced in trying to please everyone.

All its best efforts, however, were nowhere enough to satisfy the homesick GIs. Apart from their dislike of the tone of the BBC's programs and announcers, there was another problem for the American authori-ties. German stations could be picked up easily in England, and the U.S. commanders had no wish for their men to listen to Axis propaganda. Its insidious effects had been demonstrated in Britain by the reaction to the broadcasts of the notorious "Lord Haw-Haw," the pseudonym given to William Joyce, a leading supporter of the Fascist movement in Britain before the war, who just before the outbreak of hostilities had gone to live in Germany.

Joyce broadcast regularly to Britain, and the BBC's listener research department estimated that in the early stages of the war over a quarter of the population tuned in to him.[12] By many he was regarded as a joke, with his familiar "This is Jairmany calling," delivered in what was perceived as a parody of an upper-class accent, hence the title Lord Haw-Haw. Nevertheless, it would be unwise to dismiss Joyce altogether. He was a beguiling broadcaster, and, exaggerated though his claims were, there was often an element of truth in them. Furthermore, his subversive social message struck a chord with a certain group of his listeners.

Certainly, the British authorities, including the BBC, did not regard him as a joke and took steps to counter his sometimes plausible propaganda claims, even going so far as to rearrange program schedules to provide their own listeners with a worthwhile alternative and dissuade them from tuning in to him. All the same, there were those who felt that the official reaction to Joyce was exaggerated. The British audience may have listened to him during the so-called "phony war," though even then few took him seriously. But, once France had fallen and Britain had its back to the wall, attitudes to Lord Haw-Haw changed markedly, and his listening audience plummeted.

He continued broadcasting throughout the war but making little impression. This was confirmed by the U.S. Intelligence Service, which monitored Joyce later in the war. In a memo dated 25 March 1944, it noted that he had attracted a "fairly considerable following" earlier in the war and mentioned references in his broadcasts to locations or happenings that appeared to indicate a real knowledge of events in Britain. But the memo goes on to say: "With the passage of time, however, these broadcasts have been steadily more inaccurate, apparently due at least in part, to a lack of firsthand information about conditions in Great Britain. Joyce has lost his originality and has become merely another Berlin broadcaster following the usual German propaganda line."[13]

There was some surprise, therefore, that the British Government pursued him so relentlessly at the end of the war, determined on hanging him even though he was American-born. The fact that he had used a British passport to get to Germany was considered sufficient reason to claim that the man born in Brooklyn owed allegiance to the Crown.[14] When he was sentenced to death, there was considerable disquiet in the legal profession, and there were appeals to the King from members of the public asking for clemency, but he was hanged nonetheless. His execution was in marked contrast to the fate that met the American traitor "Axis Sally," of whom more later.

A BBC official who toured British bases in France in 1940, before that country surrendered to the Germans, wrote that Lord Haw-Haw was as popular with the troops there as with the public back home.[15] Later in the war, similar concern was expressed about the popularity of German broadcasts to the Middle East. There, the British troops were spending more of their leisure time than their commanders approved listening to

German broadcasts. The BBC man in Cairo reported that the authorities there were perturbed because "there are definite signs that enemy propaganda in radio programmes is beginning to have its effects."

He went on to say:

Dissatisfaction with BBC programmes among the troops is practically universal and the number and bitterness of their complaints is a serious matter. . . . Practically all our troops in the Middle East habitually listen to Axis radio in preference to the BBC. This is partly because such stations as Belgrade are better heard here than our own short waves. But men repeatedly tune in to the B.B.C. then switch over to the Germans or Italy in disgust.[16]

If British troops far from home took such a jaundiced view of their own radio service, it is hardly surprising that the GIs felt the same. This was all the more so since the Britons' experience and expectations of what radio could provide did not compare with that of the Americans, with a multitude of radio stations to choose from back home.

As far as the British troops were concerned, it was not only that the Axis radio broadcasts could be received more clearly than the BBC shortwave transmissions. The men took a poor view apparently of "all the talk" on the BBC. "If they tune in to a BBC music programme they know they won't get more than a few minutes without someone starting talking or a chat programme taking over," the same official in Cairo noted.

So what did the British troops want? The BBC man summed it up thus: "Cut the talk. Cut all the explanations and excuses. Give us straight music, snappy variety and hard honest-to-God news." And that went for the officers as well as the men.

The emphasis was on music, lots of it, and that is what the British Army in the Middle East got—not from their own radio network, but from their enemies', the Germans. One piece of music in particular made a huge impact: Lale Andersen's famous rendering of **Lilli Marlene**, beamed from powerful transmitters in Nazi-occupied Belgrade, was the favorite song not only of Rommel's Afrika Korps but of the British Eighth Army, too.

The Americans had no intention of letting their troops follow suit. If anyone was going to bewitch them, it would be someone of the likes of Dinah Shore, not some foreign siren. In the end it proved to be Marlene Dietrich. Being German-born, she was in a sense a foreign siren, but her career in Hollywood presumably gave her the right American credentials.

She recorded an English-language version of the song with lyrics written by a British songwriter[17] at the behest of no less a person than Winston Churchill. He was very much alive to the danger of letting the Germans get away with it musically. And despite the huge pressures of

being the prime minister, minister of defence, and leader of the Conservative Party, all in the middle of a world war, Churchill never lost
sight of what was popular and what was important for morale, especially of the fighting services. He was aware that the "Desert Rats," as
the British Army in Egypt was affectionately called,[18] had fallen for **Lilli
Marlene**. So through a BBC intermediary he persuaded one of the most
popular young British singers of the day, Anne Shelton, to record the
specially written English version of the song. It became an instant hit
and sold over a million copies.[19]

Lilli Marlene (in German, Lili Marleen) was probably the only song of
World War II which achieved widespread popularity with the fighting
men of both sides. The words came from a poem written by a young
German poet who had been conscripted into the army during World
War I. A volume of his poetry was published in 1937, and the words
appealed to a German songwriter, who set it to music. It was recorded
by Lale Andersen just before the war began, but the song did not really
take off until 1941 when the Germans beamed it to their troops in the
Western Desert.[20]

Ironically, the German broadcaster credited with introducing it to
Allied service listeners was an American, Mildred Gillars. She had gone
to Germany in the 1920s as a music student and later worked as a
teacher of English. Gillars was still there when war broke out, and she
began broadcasting propaganda for the Nazis, persuaded, she said, by
her lover, an official in the German Foreign Ministry. Later in the war
she broadcast to American troops, who liked her jazz records and chris-
tened her "Axis Sally." After the war, she was put on trial for treason
but, in contrast to Lord Haw-Haw, escaped with a term of imprisonment, from which she was released after twelve years.[21]

Clearly, then, the American troops did tune in to German radio. After
all, like their British counterparts in the Middle East, they appreciated
Lilli Marlene too—and Axis Sally's jazz as well. But by all accounts the
propaganda elements of German broadcasts left them unmoved. "They
suffered no ill effects," one report said. "The propaganda is weak and
almost pitiful."[22] It is interesting to speculate on why, unlike the British
troops, the Americans were apparently unaffected. The answer perhaps
lies in national attitudes and the length of time the British had been
exposed to the influence of Axis broadcasts at a point in the war when
the Germans were all-victorious. The morale of an army that has suffered a long series of defeats, as the British had, is bound to suffer,
making its troops susceptible to the suggestive elements even of the
most obvious propaganda. The Americans, on the other hand, were
fresh to the war, full of a confident optimism untempered by even
the notion of defeat. Small wonder they paid no attention to what
Dr. Goebbels and his minions had to say.

Nevertheless, the U.S. authorities were alert to the potential dangers. Indeed, the morale factor, allied to the grumbles of the troops about missing the sort of radio programs they were used to, had already been anticipated by those in charge, in particular Eisenhower himself. It was in June of 1942 that General Dwight D. Eisenhower had been appointed commander in chief of the European Theater of Operations (ETO). He was a leader who set great store by morale. "Morale is the greatest single factor in successful war," he was to write later. "In any long . . . campaign morale will always suffer unless all ranks thoroughly believe that their commanders are concerned first and always with the welfare of the troops who do the fighting."[23]

So important did he consider it that he was the first general to order regular research surveys of the morale and needs of his troops—in effect, opinion polls of what the army was thinking.[24] Clearly, the broadcasting problem was an important morale factor with a huge army waiting for months to go into action. One of Eisenhower's first acts was to hold a meeting with some of his senior aides to discuss the setting up of a broadcasting service dedicated to the American troops. He had already talked the idea over with General George C. Marshall, the Army chief of staff in Washington, who was very much in favor.[25]

Marshall's role in recognizing the importance of setting up broadcasting stations for American troops overseas and his involvement in their establishment will be dealt with later. But for now it is enough to say that he and Eisenhower were at one on the issue and recognized its importance. They both agreed that as far as their troops in Britain were concerned, they should have as nearly as possible the same kind of radio service as they got at home. It is one thing, however, to agree something needs to be done and another actually to do it. General Eisenhower was soon to find out it was not going to be all plain sailing. Before long, he ran into resistance from the one organization whose help he needed more than any other: Britain's broadcasting service, the BBC.

NOTES

1. BBC Written Archives Centre, R34/909/1 (DPP memo, 27 January 1944). Previous writers have used the abbreviation BBCWAC for these, and the present writer has adopted the same system, as the Archives are referred to frequently.

2. Roland G. Ruppenthal, *Logistical Support of the Armies* (1953) part of the *Official History of the U.S. Army in World War II* (Center of Military History, 1953), quoted by David Reynolds, *Rich Relations: The American Occupation of Britain 1943–45* (Harper-Collins, 1995).

3. (i) Officially known as dimouts, the limited American lighting restrictions applied mainly to coastal cities, where the bright glare of the lights illuminated merchant ships and made them easy targets for German U-boats. The dimout was tried in other areas when German (or later Japanese) air attacks were thought likely, but a

total blackout, such as was essential in Britain, was never contemplated. (ii) The impact of U.S. troops on Britain and vice versa has been chronicled at length. Among the two most detailed accounts are Reynolds, *Rich Relations*, and Juliet Gardner, *Over Here: The GIs in Wartime Britain* (Collins & Brown, 1992).

4. Audrey Johnson, *Do March in Step Girls: A Wren's Story* (privately printed 1997).

5. A draft copy of an article entitled "GI Network," written for the *Saturday Evening Post*, by Cecil Carnes, one of the few contemporary articles about AFN; now in the BBC Written Archives, R34/907 [hereafter *Saturday Evening Post*].

6. BBCWAC, R34/912/1. This is the record (by R. W. P. Cockburn, Assistant, Listener Research) of a frank and interesting discussion that the BBC's Director of Programme Planning had at U.S. Army HQ, 24 July 1942, with a Colonel Ramey and a Major Curry. After quoting the view that Americans considered BBC programs lousy, the record added comfortingly that this "should not be taken as too disheartening." The listening habits of U.S. troops were gone into (midday meal times, then the peak period from 7:30 p.m. to 9:30 p.m. with lights out earlier than in the British army). It was also noted that American troops "very badly want baseball and in the winter football results" and that these should not merely be the bare scores but "a brief sketch of the high spots of the day's play, presented by an American in the American manner."

7. BBCWAC (*BBC Year Book 1943*, p. 97), quoted by Briggs, *History*, Vol. III, pp. 139–140.

8. BBCWAC, R47/111/1 (DPP memo, 29 July 1942).

9. Ibid. (Basil Adams memo, 24 July 1942).

10. BBCWAC, E109 (DG memo, 16 August 1944).

11. BBCWAC (Norman Collins memo, 19 April 1944), quoted by Briggs, *History*, Vol. III, p. 568.

12. BBCWAC (Head of Listener Research R. J. E. Silvey memo, 17 November 1939), quoted by Briggs, *History*, Vol. III, p. 148.

13. Public Record Office, London SHAEF files, WO 219/7 (U.S. Intelligence memo, 25 March 1944).

14. J. W. Hall (ed.), *The Trial of William Joyce. Notable British Trials Series* (Wm Hodge & Co, 1946); C. E. Bechhofer Roberts, *The Trial of William Joyce. Old Bailey Trial Series* (Jarrold, 1946).

15. BBCWAC (Home Board Minutes, 29 March 1940), quoted by Briggs, *History*, p. 141.

16. BBCWAC, R34/118 (memo, 29 July 1942), and R34/912/1 (memo, 24 July 1942), quoted by Reynolds, *Rich Relations*, p. 166.

17. The song writer was Tommie Connor, the author of, among many others, **The Biggest Aspidistra in the World,** a tune popular with British listeners as rendered in a broad Lancashire accent by Gracie Fields. Source: Frank E. Huggett, *Goodnight Sweetheart* (W. H. Allen, 1979).

18. Strictly, only the British 7th Armoured Division was the Desert Rats, so called because its official formation insignia was a jerboa, more colloquially the desert rat, a creature noted for its speed and ability to survive. But in the public mind, the whole of the Eighth Army in North Africa came to be associated with the term.

19. The Lilli Marlene story has been the subject of various works. Among the most useful are Huggett, *Goodnight Sweetheart*, Louis L. Snyder, *Encyclopaedia of the Third Reich* (McGraw-Hill, 1976), and Thomas Parrish (ed.), *Encyclopaedia of World War II* (Secker & Warburg, 1978).

20. Huggett, *Goodnight Sweetheart*; Snyder, *Encyclopaedia*.

21. Snyder, *Encyclopaedia*; Parrish, *Encyclopaedia*.

22. *Saturday Evening Post*.

23. Gen. Eisenhower, *Crusade in Europe* (Heinemann, 1948), p. 231.

24. Reynolds, *Rich Relations*, pp. 168–169.

25. U.S. Army Broadcasting Service information sheet on the history of AFN, July 1994.

TWO

Battle Is Joined

The *BBC Year Book for 1944* contained this brief account of the setting up of the American Forces Network:

During 1943, the United States military authorities asked the BBC, as a special war-time measure, to provide facilities which would enable American troops in Britain to be served by a radio programme more of the kind to which they are accustomed than was possible within the scope of the BBC Home Service and Forces programme. Realising the importance of a scheme which would help to make the American servicemen more at home in a strange land and which would give the US leaders an opportunity of talking directly to the men, the BBC readily co-operated, though the new service meant for the duration a departure from the principles on which it has always operated. . . . Reception of BBC programmes is in no way affected by this novel form of lend-lease.[1]

A succinct and accurate statement—but one that gives a blandly misleading impression of a power struggle that went on for several months. The fact that it was conducted in a civilized and restrained way (for that is the BBC's style) does not alter the determination with which it was carried on by both sides.

The precise genesis of the American Forces Network is not entirely clear. The official (American) version is that "early in the summer of 1942 plans were discussed by General Marshall, General Eisenhower, General Hughes and representatives of the Office of War Information

[OWI] with reference [to setting up AFN]. To avoid placing the United States Army in a position of political responsibility it was decided that OWI should act as the American . . . negotiating agent." But things had started moving well before the summer, so the decision to let the OWI do the donkey work was presumably taken because its people knew all about broadcasting whereas the army were stumbling in the dark, as will soon emerge.[2]

The BBC got the first hint of what was afoot as early as February 1942, only three weeks after the arrival of the first Americans in Belfast. A Major Whitney, of the U.S. Army, went to see the head of the BBC, the director-general, at the suggestion of the British Minister of Information, who had been approached by the American military authorities.[3] Why a more senior officer was not chosen for the task is not clear, but the head of the BBC afforded him a courteous hearing. Whitney explained that the U.S. Army wanted to provide programs for their troops in Northern Ireland and asked for the BBC's help in how best this could be achieved.

At first, the Americans suggested that perhaps the BBC could insert special programs that would appeal to the troops in their normal domestic broadcasts. The answer was "No" since, understandably, "we could not insert an appreciable amount of special American items in the Home programme."[4] Added to this, for technical reasons the transmitter used for Northern Ireland also served other parts of Britain, so that references to U.S. troops in the province would simply have made no sense to listeners elsewhere.[5]

The next thought was for the Americans to use some of their own military transmitters to put out the sort of material they had in mind. Wavelengths were an immediate problem since the airwaves in Europe were crowded and any low-powered signal, such as was envisaged, was liable to be drowned out or alternatively interfere with BBC local output. There was another technical problem: The BBC transmitters were liable to be closed down at any time by RAF Fighter Command when the presence of German aircraft was suspected within a certain radius of the transmitter, since they acted as a homing signal for enemy planes.[6]

Soon after the initial approach, the BBC met a senior official from the U.S. embassy in London, Morris Gilbert, to put the discussions on a formal basis. It soon emerged that the Americans had no very precise idea of what they intended (small wonder, therefore, that the OWI's expertise was required before long). A BBC note of the meeting reported that it was understood that "the programme material would consist largely of recordings obtained from America and pick ups from American short-wave stations."[7] The latter would need a receiving station in Britain and landlines to a studio center. That in turn meant the setting up of a studio dedicated to the American broadcasts.

The BBC engineers came up with various ideas about meeting the transmitter requirements, the most favored of which was the provision of several scattered low-powered stations, which could all use the same frequency and so not give the same navigational aid to enemy aircraft as one high-powered transmitter would. An additional bonus was that the stations would be easily portable and could therefore be moved if the location of the U.S. base being served was changed.[8]

There was no mention in the recorded note of the meeting of any BBC reservations about the proposals. But in an internal memorandum from the Assistant Controller, Engineering, marked "SECRET" (and with a written annotation, "Very Urgent"), two warning notes were sounded. One indicated that although at the moment the Americans were talking only about Northern Ireland, the same facilities might apply to "any other part of the British Isles where large bodies of American troops may be stationed." And the memo went on to say: "If the number of American troops in Great Britain increases substantially, proposals for other groups of transmitters in other areas may become an embarrassment, particularly having regard to our attitude to a similar request from the Poles."[9]

This was a reference to the Polish forces-in-exile which had a substantial number of men in Britain, as did the Belgian army. Both were keen to be able to broadcast to their men, who, unlike the Americans, were totally deprived of broadcasts in their own language since the transmitters in their own countries put out only what the Nazis allowed them to. They had a good case, therefore, for their own broadcasting service, as did other Allied governments in exile. They had pressed the BBC hard, but the corporation had refused to give way.

The American initiative was known at first only to those at the top level in the BBC. But news began to leak out when the U.S. military in Northern Ireland made informal inquiries of local BBC engineers about the availability of wavelengths and whether any transmitter they might put up would interfere with domestic services. When the BBC head of broadcasting in Northern Ireland finally learned what was afoot, he expressed surprise that there was talk of "gramophone recordings, because as you know in the USA canned music of every description is practically banned by the broadcasting authorities on the ground that no one will listen to records."[10] He therefore deduced that live programs would be required, which meant he would have to provide the studio and other facilities needed.

He was clearly not happy about that and, as the news began to filter round the BBC, neither were others in positions of authority. Their concern, not to say consternation, is evident in the memos that began to flow up and down the corridors of Broadcasting House, the headquarters of the BBC. The problems it would cause with Britain's other allies were emphasized again by one executive: "If we let the Americans have their own network, there will be pressure from other allied nations to have their own stations," he pointed out. "What more do the Americans want?" was the tone taken by another member of the BBC hierarchy, who emphasized how many American programs there were already on the domestic radio output in Britain. "Undesirable American separatism" summed up yet a different viewpoint.

Underlying all these attitudes was the (publicly) unspoken fear about the effect the American proposals might have on the BBC's unique position as the only authorized broadcasting organization in Britain.

The BBC had a total monopoly then of all broadcasting in the United Kingdom. It operated under a Royal Charter and still owed much to the Reithian principle of public-service broadcasting. This did not mean it eschewed entertainment: far from it. But there was much greater emphasis on culture, on informing and educating the listener, in the broadest sense, than in a commercial broadcasting organization. And, of course, there was no advertising of any kind. The corporation's finances relied not on income from advertisements, but on a license fee levied by the government on everyone who owned a wireless set.

For that reason, the BBC was worried that any breach of its cherished monopoly might set a precedent for commercial stations after the war. One senior corporation official wrote, in a document marked "CONFIDEN-TIAL," that he regarded this as the key objection to the American proposal:

The whole scheme is so alien to the tradition and practice of broadcasting in this country that to enumerate at this stage all the possible anxieties that may arise can only lead to wasted days and sleepless nights. I put forward, however, one consideration which, to my mind, transcends in importance any [other]. . . . It is not unlikely that various parties who are interested in seeing a highly commercialised set up for British broadcasting after the war, may point to the American Forces Network as an example of a normal commercial chain and the programs it can produce, with accompanying disparagement of BBC output.[11]

Small wonder, then, that the BBC set such store by its monopoly and had no wish to have it broken, even by a forces station broadcasting to a limited audience. It gradually became apparent that that was what the Americans were after: a broadcasting station all of their own.

There was no public inkling of any of this until, as so often is the case, a newspaper brought it all into the open. On 4 October 1942, the *Sunday Express* newspaper published a story under the heading: "US Radio Station for Britain." The report that followed said plans were being discussed for the setting up of a U.S. broadcasting station in Britain to provide special programs and home news for the thousands of American troops over here. Programs, it said, will be presented "in the American manner." It continued: "There have been complaints that there is a shortage of 'home town' news in British programmes and newspapers and the U.S. authorities, while recognizing that, with the present small newspapers [usually only four pages because of the shortage of newsprint] this is unavoidable, feel that the morale of their troops will benefit if they can know what is going on at home." And it added significantly: "The programmes will, of course, be heard by British listeners who tune in to the correct wavelength."

The U.S. authorities in Britain issued an immediate statement, and shortly afterward the British minister of information made a short announcement in the House of Commons. Both statements were intended to dampen any speculation and to reassure the BBC and those members of the listening public who might fear the airwaves in Britain were to be filled with American programs.

The American statement, issued by the Office of War Information, was not as frank as it might have been. "There is no question of setting up a United States broadcasting station in Britain if one understands the expression to mean radio transmission facilities comparable to those used by the BBC in Britain," it said, ignoring the fact that no one had suggested that anything so ambitious was what was intended.

As to programs being presented "in the American manner," the statement went on to say that "although some familiar American programs would be presented, as well as feature news of American interest only, in no way would such projected facilities be confined to programs in the American manner." Which neatly evaded the real point the *Sunday Express* story was making—that it was the style of presentation that would be American, which in fact is precisely what happened.

Regarding British listeners being able to hear the broadcasts, the OWI statement had this explanation to offer: "If and when special facilities are provided for American troops (by no means a firm conclusion) they may consist of (a) telephone links to the canteens or mess halls (b) and/ or extremely small transmitters limited to a radius of about five miles. While this radius might permit some British listeners in troop areas to tune in, it will be understood readily that the numbers of certain listeners would be limited by technical considerations."

The statement went on to say that the suggestion that programs would be heard by British listeners was therefore "somewhat misleading." But no more misleading than the statement itself, since in the event the newspaper was proved to be absolutely right.[12]

The statement made in the British House of Commons by the minister of information, Brendan Bracken, was shorter but no less economical with the truth:

Discussions are taking place between the BBC and the US Office of War Information, with the object of securing the best possible provision of broadcasts for American troops in this country. It is not proposed to set up a separate American broadcasting station, but it is hoped to provide additional facilities which would enable the needs of American troop concentrations to be more fully served than is possible within the scope of the BBC's regular Home and Forces programmes.[13]

The fiction that there was to be no separate American broadcasting station was continued to the very end, for the political reasons already indicated. AFN was not to be regarded as a precedent for the future, because it was really an adjunct of the BBC. That way of describing it suited the corporation, and as long as the Americans got what they wanted they did not greatly care how it was described.

The statement made in the House of Commons was the result of questions raised with the government by members of Parliament who shared the BBC's worries that the American Troop Network (as it was being described at that stage) would open the way for commercial broadcasting after the war. They, like much of the population, had a great regard and respect for the BBC and had no wish to see it seriously threatened by a commercial undertaking. On-air advertising was anathema to most British listeners then (and to many still is). The proposed American station was being seen as the thin end of the wedge, and now that the matter was out in the open, the BBC was marshaling its arguments against the idea.

It had to tread warily. Anglo-American cooperation was crucial to winning the war—everyone accepted that. Which meant that the BBC was faced with a real dilemma. It did not want AFN, but it must be seen, in not wanting it, as acting from the best and most practical motives. In the end, it knew it would probably have to give way, but if it could be done in a watered-down, fudged fashion, then so much the better.

In an internal document, the corporation summarized its objections under eight main headings (though it was careful to put nothing on paper about the breach of its monopoly and the threat from commercial broadcasting). The document put it thus. "The following red lights have been shown:"

1. difficulties likely to arise with other Allied governments;
2. problems of policy and censorship;
3. dangers of separatism;
4. technical complications;
5. complications if Americans began outside broadcasts on a large scale;
6. the problems of what would be a new program service running parallel with the BBC;

7. problems with CBS (Columbia Broadcasting System);
8. diversion of scarce equipment.[14]

The first four were the most important and will be dealt with at some length. The last four were, in effect, variations on the same theme, apart from the reference to CBS. This was the BBC's (as it proved, unfounded) fear that since two senior CBS producers had come over to work with the OWI they might soon be producing special programs for the "troop network." Was it advisable to help the OWI to start a program-producing organization in Britain? If that came about, then CBS in America might turn to that organization in future for features about life in Britain, rather than the BBC, as at present. In the event, it turned out that the two producers were not to be involved directly in broadcasting at all. In fact, one of them was Guy della Cioppa who was appointed the OWI's assistant head of broadcasting in Britain and was one of the chief negotiators with the BBC. But it is an indication of how paranoid the corporation was about the projected Forces network.[15]

The BBC's concerns about the technical problems were, by contrast, well founded. The corporation was desperately short of equipment because of the war, and many of its experienced engineering staff had been called into the forces. Those remaining were hard pressed, and to be asked to assist in establishing a new broadcasting service was a real headache, especially if, as proved to be the case, the Americans wanted BBC help to set up regular outside broadcasts, which can only be done with a good deal of technical preparation. The air waves, as has been indicated, were crowded, and finding frequencies for the troop network was not at all straightforward.

The problem of Allied governments-in-exile being unhappy about the priority given to the Americans has already been referred to. It is reasonable to speculate that they resented the fact that a nation which had only just entered a war they had been fighting for three years, and whose troops all spoke English, the language of the BBC, was likely to be given what they had been demanding since 1940 but had been refused. Language apart, the nation with most to complain about was Canada, which by the end of 1942 had 300,000 troops in Britain, far more than the Americans at that time. They had had to be content with a few token programs for their men in the BBC's domestic output.

Two obvious factors ensured that the Americans were far more likely to be given the priority denied to others. First, in immediate terms they were able to provide the money and the equipment for the broadcasting setup, which other Allied nations could not. Second, in the broader field their material contribution to the Allied war effort was so much greater than all the other nations that it gave them a powerful political leverage.

The BBC's trump card in the attempt to stifle the troop network at birth was the question of separatism, since this struck a chord with a good many influential people in Britain, including the American ambassador himself. The argument is well summed up by the BBC's director of programme planning (DPP), Godfrey Adams, in a long memorandum on the subject to the director-general. It reflects not only his own opinion but views that were widely held in Britain at the time:

The American Army authorities are anxious to have everything over here of their own—their own equipment, of course; their own food, their own sports kit to play their own games and so forth. In a word, pretty well all they require from this country is a piece of land to camp on until the second front opens. This is not an unnatural attitude, but together with their views about serving under a British Commander-in-Chief, it does reflect to some extent their evaluation of our own army and its record in this war. If, now, they have their own broadcasting transmitters this separatism will be carried a stage further.

He goes on to say that one of the main purposes of the BBC's Forces Programme should be to integrate and bind together all the Allied troops stationed in Britain. From the point of view of promoting good relations between the two countries he thinks it ironical that when the BBC in America was doing its best to persuade the U.S. networks to broadcast programs carrying the message of Britain to the American people, "we should have perhaps more than half a million American youth in this country [it was actually a good deal less at the time] with elaborate arrangements to ensure that they need not listen to British programs."

He makes the point that

a very different view to that of the American military people is held in certain civilian quarters, notably, I believe, by Mr. Winant [John G. Winant, the U.S. ambassador to Britain]. In their view, which is shared by our own War Office, there are dangers in this separatist attitude and it would be wise that the Americans over here should be encouraged, to some extent, to absorb something of our way of life, learn to play our games and so forth.

He concludes by saying that in any plans to set up an American forces network these considerations should be kept well in mind.[16]

Interestingly, his view was shared by the head of the BBC's North American Service, Maurice Gorham, who was a firm believer in Anglo-American friendship and cooperation. He was to write later that he thought that setting up AFN was part of a mistaken policy from the Americans' own point of view:

To my mind their troops, especially those who were here for a long time, were too much insulated from the British people. They already had almost everything laid on in their own camps—their own daily newspaper, their own movies, their own food and every sort of American amenity stocked in the PX. The one thing they did not have . . . was liquor, and for that they had to go to the local pubs. Coming from an environment so scrupulously American, they had nothing in common with the people they met there: they had not eaten the same food, read the same news, or even heard the same radio; they had no common ground. That seemed to me to be one reason why they so often seemed to treat Britain as an occupied country rather than an ally.[17]

Strong views from a man who was later to work closely with the Americans in another broadcasting setup spawned by the war, the Allied Expeditionary Forces Programme, of which much more will be heard later.

The BBC's concerns about the danger of the Americans setting up what was virtually a separate state within the United Kingdom were shared in government and political circles. The Americans had already been granted powers by Parliament (under the United States of America Visiting Forces Act 1942) to try their own servicemen who committed offenses in Britain quite separately from the English legal system. They even imposed the death penalty for offenses that were not capital crimes in England, such as rape. Some eighteen American servicemen (twelve black and six white) were actually executed in Britain for rape. Such trials aroused widespread misgivings, none more so than the case of a black GI, Leroy Henry.

Henry was accused of having raped a British woman at knifepoint in a village on the outskirts of the Georgian city of Bath. He did not deny intercourse but said he had met the woman by arrangement and had had sex for £1. It was the third time he had paid her for having intercourse, but on this occasion she had demanded £2 afterwards, saying she would cause trouble if he did not pay up. Although no knife was ever found and the woman's story had a number of inconsistencies, the GI was sentenced to death at a court-martial in May 1944. When the case was reported in the British press, there was a public outcry. The mayor of Bath and over 30,000 local residents signed a petition calling for the sentence to be reviewed, the implication being that the woman was no better than a prostitute and was well known locally for consorting with black Americans for money. A mass-circulation tabloid newspaper, the *Daily Mirror*, started a campaign for a review of the verdict. Coming as it did at the time of the D-Day invasion, the case was a considerable embarrassment to the U.S. authorities, and General Eisenhower acted quickly to quash the findings of the court-martial and order the GI's release.[18]

Significantly, when a few months later another American serviceman was accused, with a teenage British girl, of murder (the so-called "Cleft Chin" murder case), the U.S. authorities waived their right to try him. He appeared before a British judge and jury and was convicted and sentenced to death, along with the girl. Ironically, he was hanged, but the girl was not.[19]

Although the trials quoted occurred later, there had been a number of similar cases which reinforced the BBC's concerns about separatism and produced some sympathy in Whitehall. There were influential people who held a different viewpoint, among them a member of Churchill's government, Hugh Dalton. He thought that animosity between white and black Americans might cause so much trouble in the streets and pubs that it would be better to separate them from the British completely in their own special zones.[20] But, in general, among those whose views counted, the feeling was against separatism and in favor of integration. The problem was to convince the U.S. military authorities. They were perfectly well aware that all those homesick young Americans were more interested in their favorite radio shows than any amount of lofty notions about Allied unity and learning about the British life-style.

Nevertheless, the BBC persisted. No doubt it saw to it that behind the scenes its point of view was pressed on those who mattered. Senior American officers were as prone to wine and dine in the right places in London as others in authority, and it would have been surprising if some persuasive lobbying did not take place. If so, it failed to produce the desired results.[21]

Gradually, the BBC resistance was worn down, though for a time hopes were still pinned on expanding the number of American programs in domestic output. One senior official emphasized that four popular U.S. programs were being heard on the BBC every week, Bob Hope, Jack Benny, *Command Performance*, and *Mail Call*. "A generous allowance, I think," was his comment.[22] Regular concerts from American bases were broadcast in the BBC's Forces Programme; American army talent was used in a variety of programs; there were special broadcasts for the visits of such American stars as Martha Raye and Edward G. Robinson; both Independence Day and Thanksgiving were marked by the BBC; and, of course, there was the daily sport bulletin. No one could say the BBC wasn't trying, so much so that at a management meeting it was suggested that more should be done to let the American troops know what delights awaited them on the BBC.[23]

But it was all in vain. A note from the director-general in January 1943 confirmed that it was "pretty definite that the Americans were going ahead with their scheme."[24] It was now a matter of accepting the inevitable and getting the best possible deal from the Americans.

NOTES

1. BBCWAC (*BBC Year Book 1944*).

2. BBCWAC, R34/907/1 (Colonel C. H. Gurney and Captain John Hayes memo, "This Is AFN," 1 November 1943).

3. Ibid. (DG Minutes, 18 February 1942).

4. Ibid. (Assistant Controller Engineering memo, 14 February 1942).

5. Ibid. (DG letter to M. Gilbert, 17 February 1942).

6. Ibid. NOTE: For a detailed account of how the BBC coped with the requirements of Fighter Command while ensuring its listeners still got a signal, see Edward Pawley, *BBC Engineering 1922-1972* (BBC Publications 1972), pp 215–222. While most BBC transmitters could act as an unintentional homing device for German bombers, the reverse could apply. The BBC television transmitter at Alexandra Palace in North London (closed for the duration for domestic TV programs) was pressed into service to jam the Luftwaffe's beam radar system guiding bombers to their targets in southern England. The inside story of Operation Domino (referred to by Winston Churchill as "the Battle of the Beams") is told by former BBC engineer Wilfred Pafford in *Let's Hear It for the Backroom Boys* (privately printed, 1998).

7. BBCWAC, R34/907/1 (DG letter to M. Gilbert, 17 February 1942).

8. Ibid. (Assistant Controller Engineering memo).

9. Ibid.

10. Ibid. (Northern Ireland Director memo, 28 April 1942).

11. Ibid. (DPP memo, 27 April 1943 [*sic*]).

12. BBCWAC, R34/907/1 (Statement by Brewster Morgan, OWI, 4 October 1942).

13. Ibid. (House of Commons statement, quoted in undated memorandum on American Troop Network).

14. Ibid.

15. Ibid. (North American Director memo, 17 May 1943).

16. Ibid. (DPP memo to DG, 31 July 1942).

17. Maurice Gorham, *Sound and Fury* (Percival Marshall, 1948), p. 134.

18. Contemporary newspaper accounts; Reynolds, *Rich Relations*, pp. 234–237; James Belsey and Helen Reid, *West at War* (Redcliffe Press, 1990). The case was the subject of a play, *The Life and Death of a "Buffalo" Soldier*, produced at the Bristol Old Vic in 1995 (*Western Daily Press*, 5 May 1995).

19. C. E. Bechhofer Roberts, *Trial of Jones and Hulten. Old Bailey Trials Series* (Jarrold, 1945); R. Alwyn Raymond, *The Cleft Chin Murder* (Claud Morris, 1945); Steve Jones, *When the Lights Went Down: Crime in Wartime London* (Wicked Publications, 1945) (also contains useful material on the seedier aspects of GIs' behavior in the British capital).

20. Ben Pimlott (ed.), *The Second World War Diary of Hugh Dalton 1940–45* (Jonathan Cape, 1986), p. 463.

21. Gorham, *Sound and Fury* (the author frequently refers to socializing at London restaurants and clubs with senior American officers).

22. BBCWAC, R34/907/1 (DPP memo to DG, 22 December 1942).

23. Ibid. (Programme Planning Minutes, 17 July 1942).

24. Ibid. (DG memo, 15 January 1943).

THREE

AFN on the Air

The BBC had never had any real chance of preventing the Americans from having some kind of broadcasting service of their own. The idea that they would be satisfied with a handful of programs on the domestic channels was unrealistic from the start. But because, as has been noted, the U.S. military authorities had no real idea of precisely what they wanted (hardly surprising, since they were soldiers not broadcasters), the corporation had reasonable hopes of some kind of shared broadcasting service, in which it would be at least equal partners and, hopefully, to some extent call the tune. That hope vanished with the arrival in Britain of Brewster Morgan, of the Office of War Information.[1]

The OWI was one of three organizations that had its fingers in the AFN pie. The others were the War Department in Washington, through the Radio Division of the Bureau of Public Relations (which, surprisingly perhaps, was responsible for launching the highly successful program, *Command Performance*), and the fledgling Armed Forces Radio Service, of which more later.

The OWI had been set up by President Roosevelt in June 1942 under the control of Elmer Davis, one of the most highly regarded newscasters of his day. Its task was the directing of war propaganda and the official flow of information. Its functions therefore overlapped those of several other organizations, and this was to lead to some friction on occasion as far as AFN was concerned. But generally the OWI came to be regarded as one of the more successful and efficient of the multitude of government agencies spawned by the war.[2]

The OWI played a key role in the setting up of AFN, partly because it was footing the bill and providing essential equipment but much more because of the bargaining efforts of Brewster Morgan, the chief of broadcasting. He was sent to England to pave the way and work out the details of how the new network could come into being. He listened to the various ideas being put forward, gathered together all the disparate strands, and on 1 November 1942 delivered a report setting out detailed proposals to General Eisenhower. A few days later he was given the go ahead. In the discussions that followed, he proved a skilled and resourceful negotiator.[3]

Morgan's approach was as tactful as it was persuasive. He was prepared to make a number of concessions if it got the Americans what they wanted. In particular, he proffered the BBC a particularly tempting morsel. All programs on the "troop network" (including the top U.S. shows) would be offered to the corporation *first* for broadcasting in Britain. And the BBC would also have first choice when it came to the big American stars who were expected to cross the Atlantic to entertain the troops and appear on the new network. It was a generous gesture and typifies the spirit of the discussions. Morgan and his negotiating team realized they were asking a lot of the BBC and were prepared to bend over backward to please it and achieve their goal.

They now issued a "statement of intention" under Morgan's name which confirmed the offer of first choice of top shows and stars.[4] It emphasized that the new network would operate as an auxiliary service of the BBC. It would carry a substantial number of BBC programs and operate "in harmony with the general best interests of broadcasting" in the United Kingdom. The BBC wrote to say it regarded the statement as "extremely generous and satisfactory" and "there should now be no possibility of any embarrassments arising when the Troop Network comes into operation."[5] It also reminded the Americans that an office was being kept available for them at Broadcasting House for use at any time.

There were still a good many practical details remaining to be resolved. The Home Office—the British government department responsible for broadcasting and also legal matters—had already formally reminded the BBC that arrangements needed to be made about security, control over program content, and copyright.

The arrangements for censorship, to make sure that nothing was broadcast which could be of help to the enemy, followed the same lines as those adopted by the BBC. Instead of having government censors checking its broadcasts, the corporation appointed its own officials to act as censors of all broadcast output. They were fully briefed by the Ministry of Information, received all the daily lists of what was security-sensitive, and were able to refer to the ministry direct in case of doubt. It had worked well since the war began, and the Americans were happy to follow suit.[6]

As far as program content was concerned, the Americans agreed to abide by the same program restrictions as the BBC, including restrictions on questionable lyrics. There was even a promise that BBC policy on the performance of jazz versions of the classics and musical compositions by enemy composers would be observed. In the news field, the two broadcasting organizations would speak with one voice, though the corporation's news department had reservations about the arrangements, reservations which, as will emerge later, proved well founded.

The Americans accepted that they must comply with British copyright law, which in some respects was far stricter than in the United States. In fact, the new network had the blanket permission of all the American commercial phonograph companies to broadcast commercial discs, and in Britain the Performing Rights Society had given them approval, pending formal negotiations, to use all the music it controlled. Finally, the Americans agreed to indemnify the BBC against legal actions for defamation and other matters arising from American forces broadcasts.

The BBC had already been given an assurance on the important matter of commercial advertising in programs from the United States. By order of the U.S. government, all commercials were to be removed from recordings of radio broadcasts before they were sent to the troops overseas. So the corporation need have no fears on that score.

On the technical side, the BBC was to provide a studio, the landlines to carry the output to the transmitters (which would be provided and erected by the U.S. Army), and the broadcasting frequencies, as well as the necessary engineering staff.

The BBC was still concerned about its listeners. Whatever might be said about the Americans' low-powered transmitters, it would not be possible to stop home listeners tuning in to them. The corporation was not keen on the possibility of losing even part of its audience to a station which could call on the top American entertainers and the leading comedy shows. Nor did it want its domestic services interfered with by the American broadcasts. So it laid down that there should be no transmitters in the London area and none near large centers of population, except in special circumstances.

A final meeting was held at Broadcasting House in London on 21 June 1943 at which the main American representative was Guy della Cioppa, the former CBS producer who was now assistant head of OWI in Britain. Like Brewster Morgan, he had played an important role in the negotiations and clearly had the grasp of detail that was essential for success. After disposing of a number of legal and copyright points, it was agreed that the new service would be named the American Forces Network, rather than the American Troop Network, to indicate that it embraced all arms of the United States Forces. And it was settled that AFN would go on the air on 4 July 1943.[7]

All that then remained was for the BBC to waive its monopoly of broadcasting in the United Kingdom. Formal operating agreements were signed between the OWI and the corporation, while the Wireless Telegraphy Board, which controlled broadcasting frequencies in Britain, gave its authority for AFN to use the frequencies allotted to it, broadcasting hours having been agreed previously.

The BBC accepted defeat gracefully and was unstinting in the technical and other help it now gave to the new station. "The BBC," an American journalist wrote," became the helpful big brother to the new GI network."[8] The whole exercise was a significant example of the way in which initial—and fundamental—differences between the two allies could be resolved, given goodwill and give-and-take between the two sides. So, after all the difficulties and arguments, the stage was set for AFN to go ahead with its plans to get on the air. Before that could happen, a great deal of work had to be done in a short period of time. The two most pressing needs were to assemble the necessary staff and to set up the transmitter network.

General Eisenhower had approved the appointment on 25 June 1943 of a nine-man board of governors, which included seven senior army officers as well as Brewster Morgan. A representative of the BBC was also invited to sit in on a smaller group which actually ran the new station.[9] The man put in charge of AFN was Lieutenant Colonel Charles H. Gurney, who in civilian life had owned and operated a radio station in South Dakota, a far cry from the broadcasting world of Europe and the political minefield that was the BBC. [10]

Gurney's deputy was appointed at a meeting early in 1943 in the London office of Lieutenant General Jacob Devers, acting head of the European Theater of Operations. After presenting a group of officers with Brewster Morgan's report, he turned to a young captain who was there because of his radio experience and said: "See this part about a radio network?" "Yes, sir." "Well, start one." And so Captain John S. Hayes (one day to be the U.S. ambassador to Switzerland) was given the task of setting up a complete radio network from scratch within a few short months. That, at any rate, is the somewhat colorful version of AFN's genesis given in a U.S. Army publicity sheet.[11]

Hayes was formerly assistant to the vice-president of a major network outlet (WOR-Mutual), so the politics of broadcasting was nothing new to him. He was described by a contemporary as a "stocky, aggressive New Yorker" and was the author of *Both Sides of the Microphone*, a textbook on broadcasting.[12]

On Captain Hayes, with Colonel Gurney as his immediate superior, fell much of the immediate day-to-day responsibility for setting up the new network. His brief was straightforward enough: "The mission of the American Forces Network is to present radio programs of a character familiar to, and desired by, American military personnel in the United Kingdom." It was emphasized that AFN "is in no sense a competitor of the British Broadcasting Corporation but, rather, an auxiliary American service of the BBC, designed to lift some of the wartime burden from that organization."

His official briefing went on: "The objectives of the American Forces Network are threefold: first to broadcast American entertainment; secondly, continually to co-operate with training, educational and religious projects of the Army; and, thirdly, to assist the American soldier and sailor in adjusting himself to his new environment in the United Kingdom, fostering a mutual understanding between himself and his British comrades."[13]

The requirement that AFN should provide a broadcasting service as near as possible to what the forces would get at home sounded simple enough. But Captain Hayes's determination to do just that led to problems once the new station was on the air. The OWI, which was supplying most of the equipment and some of the personnel, was in the business of broadcasting propaganda about America's role in the war. AFN was trying to bring American servicemen the voice of home, not the voice of government. Clashes were inevitable. But Hayes was a strongly independent figure, and he held firm. He laid it down as his cardinal principle that "American personnel in the European theater should never be subjected to any broadcast over AFN that might be construed as propaganda." AFN staff would control all commentary, news analysis, and hard news in such a way that its service listeners would not come to the conclusion "that the American Forces Network was being used as a propaganda arm of the Government."[14]

His first priority was to get AFN up and running with the small team put at his disposal: four officers and thirteen enlisted men. Considering there were supposed to be two men at each transmitter, it was not over-generous.[15]

To install the transmitters, the OWI called on the U.S. Army Signal Corps. A former engineer with Station KMPC in Los Angeles was given an immediate commission and was sent to England shortly afterwards. Captain Loyd Sigmon sailed for Britain with a team of sixteen radio engineers under his command. But the moment they landed, not having any written orders, they were all speedily hijacked by other units, keen to make use of their expertise. By the time Sigmon learned what his task was, they had been scattered all over the country, and it took some time to reassemble them.

Sigmon had only a few short weeks to get the transmitters operational before the start date of 4 July. However, he later recalled, it was not a difficult task, once all his men were together again, because each transmitter came as a complete package. An initial batch of twenty-eight had been ordered by the OWI and specially manufactured by the TWT Company of Los Angeles. They proved so successful that an order was placed for another twenty-five. The package consisted of a 50-watt transmitter, the antenna, and all the associated equipment. Sigmon, who had been in radio since the 1920s, was used to dealing with powerful 50,000-watt transmitters and was taken aback to be faced with something so completely different. However, he said his biggest problem was finding a satisfactory site on or near each base on which to locate the transmitter.[16]

Ultimately, the aim was to have a network of transmitters in those regions where it was planned to house the greatest number of American servicemen. These were the west of England, where at their peak there were over half a million Americans; southern England (another 500,000); East Anglia, home of the Eighth Air Force (200,000), northwest England (100,000); and Northern Ireland (75,000). The largest single concentration was in the county of Wiltshire, which already housed some of the British Army's biggest barracks and where Salisbury Plain was almost entirely turned over to the military. The county eventually had over 137,000 U.S. servicemen stationed in it, getting on for half of the entire peacetime civilian population.[17]

Because the BBC had insisted that there should be no transmitters in the London area, the Americans had to find a way around the problem. In the end, they decided to wire up the American Red Cross and other clubs in the capital catering for American personnel, as well as some U.S. quarters and office buildings in the city, so that AFN's output was piped direct to listeners through a network of loudspeakers.

Apart from the famous Rainbow Corner in Piccadilly, which was open twenty-four hours a day, there were eventually a dozen locations in the capital offering a slice of America for the homesick GIs (and gals) who flocked to London on leave. They provided sleeping accommodation (bed and breakfast was 50 cents) and U.S.-style meals, too, by the thousand. AFN made sure they got U.S.-style radio as well, though as some were former hotels wiring them all up was no simple job.[18]

Altogether, some seventy-five locations in the London area were wired to receive AFN, and a similar service was eventually provided at fifty-eight U.S. air bases throughout the country. In addition, twenty BBC premises were able to have their own direct feed of AFN output.[19]

So Loyd Sigmon and his team had good reason to feel pleased with their efforts. When his job with AFN was completed, he was made responsible for setting up a special radio circuit so that President Roosevelt and Winston Churchill could talk to each other at all hours of the day or night. This was a back-up to the transatlantic telephone cable, and Sigmon recalls that on one occasion sun spots severely interfered with reception. He was taken to task by the general in charge of communications, who was no engineer and was not prepared to accept that a heavenly body 93 million miles away could interfere with signals on earth. Sigmon was ordered to make sure it never happened again![20]

Meanwhile, another team of engineers was hard at work preparing the premises made available by the BBC. AFN's first London studio was at 11 Carlos Place, just off Grosvenor Square, home of the U.S. Embassy. It was a basic setup: a small studio, a control room, two turntables, and the distribution amplifiers and other equipment needed to feed the signal to the transmitters and the London public-address system. But it was perfectly adequate and was in fact the studio from which Ed Murrow broadcast his famous "This Is London" commentaries to listeners back in the United States.[21]

While all this engineering work was going on, program schedules were being drawn up. The hours of broadcasting were limited: to start with, just under five hours a day during the week, longer at the weekend. AFN had a wealth of material to call on. From America there was the output of the main radio networks, recorded by the Special Service Division of the War Department (later to become the AFRS) with the commercials deleted, then sent overseas by plane or ship for re-broadcast. These included such favorites as Jack Benny, Bob Hope, Kate Smith, Charlie McCarthy, the Lone Ranger, and many others. Then there were the programs produced by the Special Service Division for the forces overseas and not normally heard in the United States. Among these were *Command Performance, Mail Call*, and *Jubilee*. There were also live shortwave broadcasts, mostly commentaries on sporting events, which were picked up by the BBC's powerful receivers and fed to the AFN studio.

BBC programs available to the new network, apart from news bulletins, included some British comedy shows (not, as a rule, popular with the Americans), orchestral music, and also British dance bands, as well as such documentaries as *Into Battle* and *Weekly War Commentary*. Finally, there were the programs AFN produced from its own resources, though these had to be built up gradually over a period of several months. Among them were record-request shows, which were among the most popular (apart from broadcasts of U.S. forces sporting events in Britain), and programs which made use of the talent of the troops stationed in the United Kingdom.[22]

So there was no shortage of choice. The only problem was finding the military personnel with the experience to handle all this material. The air bases and army camps springing up all over Britain were scoured for those men who had worked in the broadcasting field before being drafted. One of the most popular DJs, a radio announcer before he had been called up for the forces, was discovered as a lowly private, peeling potatoes in an army camp. He was only too glad to be recruited by AFN. When it went on the air, AFN was still so short of personnel that it had to rely on *Stars and Stripes*, the daily newspaper for the American troops in the ETO, to staff its newsroom. (*Stars and Stripes*, incidentally, was printed in London by The Times newspaper, another example of Anglo-American cooperation.)

As opening day neared, the BBC, the OWI, and the U.S. Army arranged a press conference so that the listening public in Britain would be aware of what was going on, especially after the rumors that had appeared in the newspapers. Arrangements were also made for the *Radio Times* (the BBC's weekly program magazine) to carry "a paragraph or two" about AFN. And a statement was issued giving an assurance that the new radio facilities would be available only over limited areas and "there will be no interference with the reception in these areas of BBC programmes." The statement added that "for security reasons it is obviously not possible to say in what parts of the country these programmes will be heard, but the transmitters provided are of very low power."

An internal BBC memorandum notes that before the press conference took place, a small committee should consider the "number of very ticklish questions" arising so they would be prepared to meet "any awkward posers" from the journalists present. In the event, no reports exist of any such awkward questions being put. It was also decided that after the station was safely on the air, there would be a formal ceremony a few days later involving various VIPs.[23]

On the day before the new station went on the air, AFN was front-page news in *Stars and Stripes*. Under the heading "ETO Radio Network on Air Sunday," it told U.S. troops what to expect.

A "back home" radio program, designed to provide US forces in the ETO with American-slanted broadcasts will get under way tomorrow at 5.45 p.m. Shows recorded in the United States for troop broadcasts, Stars and Stripes news bulletins and special features will be presented. . . . The American Forces Network, through a complicated system of landlines and regional transmitters, will reach a limited number of US troops at first. Eventually it is expected that every American station and camp in the United Kingdom will be able to hear the program as the service will be extended further each month.[24]

The *Stars and Stripes* was at pains to emphasize that the new station was operating with the cooperation of the British Broadcasting Corporation and added: "The new service marks the first time Britain has granted broadcasting facilities on its home territory to an allied nation." And once again an assurance was given that there would be no interference with BBC programs.

To *Stars and Stripes* we owe the schedule of the first day's broadcasting:

Sunday 4 July 1943: **5.45 p.m.** Program summary and network opening; **6 p.m.** News (BBC); **6.15 p.m.** Harry James & His Orchestra; **6.30 p.m.** Transatlantic Call People to People; **7.5 p.m.** Bing Crosby Music Hall; **7.30 p.m.** Front Line Theater. Robert Young and Joan Bennett in "Mr and Mrs Smith" with guest stars Ralph Bellamy, Gene Krupa and A. Q. Bryan; **8 p.m.** Anglo-American service from St. Paul's Cathedral, London and Washington Cathedral; **8.40 p.m.** Charlie McCarthy and Edgar Bergen with Ray Noble and His Orchestra, Don Ameche and Bert Lahr; **9 p.m.** News (BBC); **9.15 p.m.** Dinah Shore Show; **9.30 p.m.** Independence Day program; **10.15 p.m.** "Final Edition" late world, sport and army news presented by Stars and Stripes; **10.20 p.m.** Artie Shaw and His Orchestra; **10.30 p.m.** Sign Off.

It was appropriately on 4 July 1943, American Independence Day, that the American Forces Network began broadcasting in the United Kingdom. As it happened, preparations were so well advanced it could have gone on the air earlier, but it was decided to wait for the auspicious date. The **Star-Spangled Banner** was played, then the first voice to be heard on the new network was that of Brewster Morgan, the OWI head in Britain, who had played such a key role in the negotiations with the BBC.

And in his opening announcement he made sure the corporation got the credit that was due. "This is the American Forces Network operating in the United Kingdom with the co-operation of the British Broadcasting Corporation. We are now signing on and presenting programs of interest to America's Overseas Forces in the European Theater of Operations."

Waiting at the microphone, nervously flipping a silver-dollar good-luck piece, was Corporal Syl Binkin, of St. Louis. As the opening announcement ended, he put the coin down, took a deep breath, and started telling his listeners what they would soon be hearing. AFN was finally on the air.[25]

NOTES

1. Morgan had been sent to Britain by Murray Brophy (head of the War Department's Office of Coordinator of Information), who had discussed the requirements for a forces broadcasting service in Britain with General Marshall and, separately, with Colonel Tom Lewis, head of the Armed Forces Radio Service, which eventually became AFN's "parent company" (see chapter 6).

2. *Encyclopaedia of World War II.*

3. *History of AFRTS 1942–92*, produced for the American Forces Information Service and the Armed Forces Radio and Television Service under the imprint of the Depart-

ment of Defense [hereafter *History of AFRTS*]; Trent Christman, *Brass Button Broadcasters* (Turner Publishing, 1993).

4. BBCWAC, R34/907 (Statement issued by OWI, 2 March 1943).

5. Ibid. (DPP memo, 5 March 1943).

6. Maurice Gorham, *Broadcasting: Sound and Television since 1900* (Andrew Dakers, 1952).

7. BBCWAC, R34/907/1 (Minutes of contractual meeting, 21 June 1943).

8. *Saturday Evening Post.*

9. BBCWAC, R34/907/1 (Gurney–Hayes memo, "This Is AFN"). The nine-man board consisted of the chief of special services, SOS (Services of Supply); the chief of administration SOS: the chief signal officer ETOUSA, the public relations officer ETOUSA, the radio officer and the press officer from the ETOUSA Public Relations Office; the radio officer, Special Service Division: the chief of broadcasting for Britain, OWI, and the OWI chief of engineering.

10. *Saturday Evening Post.*

11. Undated Army Broadcasting Service information sheet.

12. *Saturday Evening Post.*

13. BBCWAC, R34/907 (Gurney–Hayes memo).

14. *History of AFRTS*, p. 41.

15. The BBC was supplied with a list of the names of AFN's staff and their duties, some of which overlapped (BBCWAC, R34/907). The Network's "founding members" were: Lt. Col. Charles H. Gurney, Capt. John S. Hayes, First Lt. Irving Reis, 2nd Lt. G. K. Hodenfield; Staff Sgt. Hamilton Whitman, Sgt. Donald H. Robinson, Corporal Ford Kennedy, Corporal John Vrotsos, Corporal Charlie Capps, T/5 Karl Hoffenberg, T/5 Arthur Freeman, T/5 John McNamara, and Privates John Kerr, Syl Binkin, Warren Bryan, Richard McLaughlin and Matthew Smith. By the end of the war their numbers had grown to over 300 (see chapter 11).

16. Interview with author; *History of AFRTS*, p. 40.

17. Ruppenthal, quoted by Reynolds, *Rich Relations.*

18. Reynolds, *Rich Relations*, p. 155; Gardner, *Over Here*, p. 96. See also Appendix I.

19. Theodore S. DeLay, *An Historical Study of the Armed Forces Radio Service to 1946* (privately printed, 1951).

20. Interview with author.

21. *History of AFRTS*, p. 41; Christman, *Brass Button Broadcasters*, p. 40. (For those who like to know these things, AFN's telephone number was GROsvenor 4111.)

22. BBCWAC, R34/907/1 (Gurney–Hayes memo).

23. Ibid. (Director of Publicity, 21 June 1943).

24. *Stars and Stripes*, 3 July 1943. The *Stars and Stripes*, published daily in Europe during the war (and since), is a quite different publication from the veterans' newspaper in the United States. In 1942, as "a patriotic gesture" after an approach from the White House, the publishers, the National Tribune Corporation, granted the War Department a license to use the name for a newspaper for the troops, without charge, on the understanding that it did not circulate in the United States and carried no advertising. One of its best-remembered features was the series of front-line cartoons by Sergeant Bill Mauldin, whose earthily realistic humor went down particularly well with the men at the sharp end of the war.

25. *Saturday Evening Post.* In an interview with the author, Syl Binkin (then in his 80s) says he does not specifically remember tossing the silver dollar, "but I probably did." He does recall that the studio was full of VIPs for the opening. He says Captain Hayes may have been a tough negotiator but he was "a great guy to work with."

FOUR

Programs and Personalities

AFN went on the air with seven transmitters. But it expanded at so rapid a rate that within a year there were over fifty of them scattered the length and breadth of the British Isles. They were to be found as far apart as Upper Ballinderry in Northern Ireland and Barnstaple in the West Country county of Devon. Quiet villages like Shrivenham on the Berkshire/Wiltshire border, Goxhill in rural Lincolnshire, and Horsham St. Faith in the heart of East Anglia, all found themselves with an American aerial array on their doorsteps.[1]

The expansion of AFN needed to be rapid, with U.S. personnel pouring into Britain by the thousand. American camps sprang up, as it seemed to the local residents, almost overnight. In Eastern England, flattish country designated as the site of a great assembly of air bases, a remarkable building program was put in hand. It was planned to construct over 100 air bases within a year, so that on average a new one was started every three days. East Anglia was transformed, in effect, into one vast airfield, with thousands of acres of farmland requisitioned for the purpose. In the county of Norfolk alone, 100,000 acres were swallowed up by the demands of the Eighth Air Force.[2]

And every one of those bases either had AFN piped into its loudspeaker system or had its own transmitter, on the base or at a site close by. The figures show the rate of expansion. In less than two months, the original seven had grown to twelve. By November there were thirty, and by the following February a total of fifty-four. Every transmitter had to be approved not only by the BBC but by the Wireless Telegraphy Board (roughly the equivalent of the Federal Communications Commission, FCC, in the United States). But despite the paperwork involved there was little delay in giving the go-ahead to each new station. Sometimes, the Americans understandably jumped the gun and had the transmitter up and running before formal permission had been given. The files contain several letters of apology from the Americans for being over-hasty. The pace was so rapid that before long it was agreed that line-feeds not involving the erection of transmitters, usually to bomber air bases, could go ahead without formal approval.[3]

Although the BBC had indicated it was not happy at the idea of transmitters in densely populated areas, or in the London region, exceptions were regularly made. AFN wanted a transmitter at Oxford, to service two large military hospitals in the area as well as a nearby air base. They realized there would be "considerable coverage of the civilian population but are hopeful the BBC will take the view that this may be regarded as a special case." It was. So too was a transmitter in Bournemouth, a South Coast resort noted for a wealth of conservative residents. The BBC wryly commented: "We fear there may be complaints from listeners to the BBC Home Service. If the interference proves considerable we shall have to consider what steps should be taken to ameliorate it." Another transmitter was approved at Bovingdon, even though it was only twelve miles from the outskirts of northwest London. The headquarters of the U.S. Army Air Force, some fifteen miles from the capital, settled for landlines from the studio to the HQ's internal loudspeaker system. Clearly, there was a great deal of give-and-take and a willing readiness on the BBC's part to give all the help it could.[4]

At first, the new network could only sustain broadcasting from 5.45 p.m. until 10.30 p.m each weekday evening. It stayed on the air slightly longer on Saturdays and most of the day on Sundays, opening up at 8 a.m. But gradually the schedules were expanded, first (from September) to include the period from 11 a.m. to 2 p.m.—"chow time," which gave rise to a record-request program with the memorable title *Concert for Chowhounds.* Eventually AFN was putting out programs nineteen hours a day.

To begin with, AFN was allotted two frequencies (1402 and 1420 kilocycles or 213.9 and 211.3 meters).[5] Later, the number of frequencies was increased to five (the additional ones being 1375, 1411, and 1447 kilocycles or 218.1, 212.6, and 207.3 meters). Many listeners are sure they also heard AFN on 240 meters, a more accessible wavelength in Britain. If so, it was certainly unofficial and would make AFN the first pirate station in the United Kingdom. True, the Americans did take liberties on occasion, but it seems unlikely they would offend their British hosts by operating on an unauthorized frequency. Added to which, the BBC engineers kept a close ear on what AFN was doing, and such a flagrant breach of the agreement would hardly have gone unrecorded.[6] What is on record is that some of the stations interfered with each other's transmissions, a fact to which the BBC promptly drew AFN's attention. In one case quoted, they were well over thirty miles apart, so clearly their signals were reaching far beyond the base area.[7]

It was hardly surprising, then, that it was not only the personnel at the U.S. bases who were hearing AFN loud and clear. Right at the beginning, the BBC's own engineers had estimated that at least 5 percent of the listening audience would be able to receive the new station. And very soon, the corporation's fears were realized. British listeners began tuning in, as well as American forces. Indeed, Loyd Sigmon, the U.S. Army engineer who supervised the installation of the transmitters, said he would drive around the countryside and hear AFN's programs clearly through the open windows of local homes.[8]

As far as can be judged today, AFN's British audience was a young one. Certainly, many teenagers listened avidly. One listener, now in his late 60s, recalls: "Every clued-up boy at our school listened to the Top Ten each week and knew who was singing what. We were just as knowledgeable as any teenage pop fan now." He remembers that those Top Ten selections fueled the perpetual feud between those who regarded Bing Crosby as simply the best and the supporters of Frank Sinatra, then moving to the peak of his early singing fame.[9]

The British musician and writer Benny Green was a teenager during the war. He says AFN was a revelation:

It was the kind of music we just never heard on the BBC. For the first time, instead of listening to second-rate British imitations of the big bands, we were getting the real thing.

One wartime servicewoman echoes his viewpoint:

What we appreciated about AFN was that they played the music we loved to dance to. The BBC had dance music but it just wasn't the same.[10]

And two other comments from what was then the younger generation:

As a teenager during the war and a lover of Big Band music, I spent hours tuned in to the record shows on AFN whose presenters I found so refreshingly different, compared to our own staid BBC people.[11]

That from a listener in Oxfordshire. This is from a teenage girl growing up in the northern seaside resort of Blackpool:

I was at a girls' school in Blackpool during those years and it was one of our main topics of conversation. We used to discuss the previous day's programs, our favourite presenters and the various bands and singers. I think we found it all so glamorous and of course the standard of music was so high that we enjoyed almost all the music. . . . I remember insisting on New Year's Eve that I couldn't possibly go to bed as AFN was staying open through the night.[12]

For some of the slightly older British listeners, AFN struck a different chord. "It reminded us," one says, "of Radio Luxembourg which we loved to listen to." Radio Luxembourg was a commercial station on the Continent, which had ceased broadcasting when war broke out, though it was later taken over by the Germans after the invasion of Luxembourg. Before the war, it had had a wide following in Britain. Significantly, the BBC had made determined efforts to make life difficult for that lively popular rival as well.[13]

AFN's presentation style was a reminder of those prewar broadcasts. It was not long before the words "This Is the American Forces Network" came to be accepted as a guarantee of the very best in American popular music and radio entertainment by many thousands of British radio listeners, both civilian and military. And this despite the fact that, paradoxically, they were in a sense eavesdroppers since the programs they listened to with such enjoyment were not intended for them at all. Now, after 50 years, the team of American announcers is still remembered with pleasure. "They were so lively and jokey but still very professional."[14]

The name most frequently recalled is Corporal (later Sergeant) Johnny Kerr. He presented a popular request show called *Duffle Bag*, whose signature tune was Tommy Dorsey's **Opus One**. Typical of his relaxed style was the day he announced he was about to spin a particular record, "but I can't—Monaghan's just walked into the studio and sat on it."

That was Corporal George Monaghan, another great favorite. He presented *On the Record*, with another Tommy Dorsey number, **What Is This Thing Called Love**, as his signature tune. He introduced his program by promising "Here comes the program that's got a beat in every jump," and as one listener recalls, "He was fond of reminding us that Saturday night is the loneliest night of the week."

They were appreciated by the professionals, too. *Sound Wave* magazine had this to say about them:

Those AFN *Off the Record* and *Duffle Bag* sessions are object lessons in the way "canned" programs should be presented. Corporal Monaghan and Sergeant Johnny Kerr, the brilliant disc jockeys on those airings, are really good. Oh! for a half hour with these wizard comperes on a "Forces" evening spot, showcasing British bands and vocalists. They'd have the listeners rooting in a big way.[15]

It should be noted that *Off the Record* was the original title of Monaghan's program, but, like Kerr with *Duffle Bag*, he changed it because, as he usually announced, "It's strictly *on* the Record."

Monaghan and Kerr were typical of the announcers who made such an impact on English listeners. Young, relaxed, and confident, radio was everything to them. A BBC broadcaster who worked with them described them as "likeable, lively young men, full of life."

Monaghan had been in broadcasting since 1938 and presented a record program on Station WTHT in Hartford, Connecticut, his home state. "My ideal broadcast is being left alone in the studio with a bunch of records and improvising the script and the running order as I go along," he told a journalist writing about AFN. "Easy and homely is how I like it: makes the boys hearing you feel you're with them, not some stuffed shirt talking at them from the remote distance" (a dig, perhaps, at the style of some of the BBC announcers of the time).

Johnny Kerr was very much in the same mold. Then aged 26 and a native of Painesville, Ohio, he had been in radio for six years. He got a job when he was only 19 by writing to *five hundred* radio stations, sending off the letters in batches of fifty a month. Several of them offered him work, and he began his broadcasting career at Station WPIC in Ashtabula, only thirty miles from his home. Later he worked in Phoenix, Arizona, and Sharon, Pennsylvania.

He was the one rescued from peeling potatoes as a lowly private at an Army camp to take over *Duffle Bag* (then called *Barracks Bag*). He turned it into AFN's most popular program. In a poll of U.S. Army troops on their favorite radio shows, it came out top, ahead of all the glittering programs from the United States. Kerr said he ate, drank, and slept *Duffle Bag* and thought of little else. "I get a tremendous thrill out of it," he told a journalist writing about AFN.

His postbag numbered requests and fan mail of over 200 a week. Women wrote in to tell him how much they liked his laugh and his catch phrases such as "No kiddin', I *mean* it." Many of the letters were from British listeners, but sadly for them none of their requests were played, on the orders of the station commander. "We don't want to invade the BBC's field by responding to English listeners," he said. "We owe them too much as it is."

Duffle Bag eventually ran for two hours a day, and interestingly Kerr said he preferred whenever possible to use not phonograph discs but transcriptions of music from recorded radio shows. He thought the quality was better: they had a fuller tone than ordinary records. Added to which the shows regularly featured numbers which were not on disc at all, or were on records which had not crossed the Atlantic.

Another popular figure was Dick (Saddlebags) Crawford. He read the news but also presented *Miss Parade*, a weekly program of pin-up favorites, and he later featured in a medley of Western music called *AEF Ranch House* as the genial Corporal Saddlebags. (That was before, like most of his fellow announcers, he was promoted to sergeant.) He was noted for his wisecracks and atrocious puns. He had worked at several radio stations in his native California before joining the U.S. Second Armored Division, from where he was seconded to AFN.

Dick Dudley, from Nashville, Tennessee, had been working in radio since he was 15—his father was connected with show business and screen advertising. Dick later worked with NBC, where he was one of the announcers for the Jack Benny show, among other programs.[16]

Listeners also have fond memories of Ralph "Muffit" Moffat, said by the veteran British DJ Pete Murray to have been one of his inspirations. "He was the first to have the style that was copied by many disc jockeys," Pete is quoted as saying. Another presenter recalled with affection is Johnny MacNamara (signature tune: Bing Crosby's **MacNamara's Band**). He was outside the mold of those AFN regulars with a broadcast background. Before joining up, he had been recreational supervisor for the Board of Education and Parks Department in his native New York City, where he also organized and led community singing in the city's parks.

A later addition to the AFN staff was Keith Jameson, who had been presidential announcer for the Blue Network in Washington, DC. He recalled that his most unnerving moment on the air came during a nationwide broadcast when he was introducing a speech by President Roosevelt from an Armistice Day ceremony. The arrangements were altered at the very last moment, and he was left to ad lib for something like ten minutes. He was to display similar coolness under enemy fire, as will be recounted later.[17]

Another member of the AFN staff was Broderick Crawford, the film actor, later to become an Oscar winner but then a humble sergeant in the army. He is recalled as a lover of Scotch whisky, and on one famous occasion downed a great deal of it while waiting in a pub in London's Leicester Square for Marlene Dietrich, who was to appear in an AFN program. She was waiting in a different pub, and legend has it that by the time the two met up neither was in a fit state to broadcast.[18]

Army red tape sometimes got in the way of experienced broadcasters joining AFN. That was the lot of Corporal Verner Paulsen. He had worked in radio for eight years before being called up, so he was assigned to AFN shortly after he reached the United Kingdom. But there was no accommodation for him in London, and he was sent to an army camp some distance away—and promptly forgotten. Fed up with fatigue duty and desperate to broadcast, he scoured the camp for talent and wrote four half-hour programs which he called "Rhapsody in Khaki." They were forwarded to AFN but without his name on them, and he heard no more. Finally, someone remembered the "lost" corporal and he was called to the broadcasting studios in London. There he was presented with his own program idea and told to "knock it into shape." It was a long while before anyone would believe he had dreamed it up in the first place![19]

Surprisingly, perhaps, there were very few women's voices heard on AFN, apart from star performers. Johnny Kerr had a WAC (Women's Army Corps) known as Freddie with him in the studio, and there was quite a lot of banter between the two of them. More formally, she was Private First Class Freddie Cox, and judging from her photograph she was a lively if perhaps slightly scatty young woman. That would make her the perfect foil for Johnny Kerr, whose punning introductions were legendary: "Once upon a time there were three bears, Momma Bear, Poppa Bear and Camembert. You know, all three of 'em listened to THE DUFFLE BAG!"[20]

It was a talented team, all the more remarkable since being but lowly sergeants and corporals they were the lowest-paid radio announcers in the business. But they got great fun out of what they were doing and communicated that pleasure to a multitude of listeners.

Their British audience remembers with pleasure the free and easy style of AFN, a style that is commonplace now but in those days was a revelation to an audience brought up on the more formal ways of the BBC. "Their cheery patter and the terrific big band music always had me glued to the wireless," a listener writes. One of his favorites was a request show called *Smash Hits*, where the presenter supposedly smashed a 78-rpm disc (named by listeners as the one they most disliked) over someone's head. "You heard the sound of smashing shellac all right but whether it was ever over a human head was open to doubt." Another recalls how George Monaghan took particular pleasure in keeping his listeners abreast of his regular promotion, culminating in his excited "Hey, fellas, I made sergeant."

Another abiding memory of many listeners was one particular number, **I'll Walk Alone**, sung by teenager Lily Ann Carol. As one of them recalls: "It was one of the most requested items. I used to listen in whenever I could just to hear this song, which was included in EVERY DAY's broadcasts."[21] Another big hit she had with Louis Prima was **Bell Bottom Trousers** but after the war she seems to have sunk without trace.

I'll Walk Alone is more popularly associated with Dinah Shore, regarded by many as *the* top American woman singer of the war years and frequently heard on AFN. But she had plenty of competition: Frances Langford, regular vocalist on the Bob Hope Show; Helen Forrest, known as the Voice of the Big Bands because she sang in succession with Artie Shaw, Benny Goodman, and Harry James; and Ginny Simms, singer with the Kay Kyser Band, with whom she was often heard on the radio and in movies. Then there was Doris Day, another dance-band vocalist (with Les Brown and His Orchestra) until she was catapulted into solo stardom after recording **Sentimental Journey,** which sold a million copies and was in the charts for six months. Another stylish vocalist was Bea Wain, who appeared regularly on the AFRS version of *Your Hit Parade.*

And what about the Yanks themselves? A wartime Wren who regularly visited a U.S. naval base saw for herself what AFN meant to the Americans. "They were so very homesick and AFN was their link with home. It was terribly important to them."[22]

It was even more important when battle was joined. During the hectic operations off the Normandy beaches that followed the D-Day landings, one sailor engaged in unloading supplies took a hurried break for a cup of coffee. The radio was on, AFN broadcasting a favorite program. "We all listened," he says. "For a moment the business of carrying on the war seemed remote. I imagined I was home safely listening to my bedroom radio."[23]

The AFN studios were favored with a constant stream of Hollywood visitors. Fred Astaire dropped in one day and tap-danced the letters A-F-N in Morse code, which was used for a while as a station ident. Bing Crosby was another regular visitor, not knowing then that his son Gary would later be a member of the AFN staff. Bing is said to have sat at the piano one day and composed a number called **Sinatra, Sinatra, Clear from Rangoon to Sumatra**. The title is apparently all that's now remembered of his impromptu composition.[24]

Although AFN did not carry any advertising, it had plenty of "commercials" of a different kind: the public-service announcements directed at its service listeners. One U.S. civilian visiting Britain was surprised to hear this coming out of a radio, set to a tune taken from a frequently heard American commercial jingle:

> Those MPs have enough to do
> Without their looking after you
> So my friends if you're fighting mad
> Wait for the Nazis—they need it bad.[25]

AFN was full of similar exhortations and good advice to the troops. It had a special section dealing with them: conserving jerricans, buying war bonds, sending V mail,[26] maintaining cleanliness, even taking precautions against trenchfoot. It irritated some listeners, including a British soldier who wrote to *Yank* magazine about the obviousness of much of the advice given, usually starting with the phrase: "Time to remind you soldier to. . . . " "Soon," he wrote, "they'll be telling them it's time to clean their teeth. If the Yanks could learn one thing from the BBC let it be the blissful effect of radio entertainment minus obnoxious commercialism and plugs."[27]

An amusing side-effect to this habit of public-service announcements is referred to in a memo from a BBC executive. He noted that an AFN announcer had suggested that American soldiers who were tired of London or other big cities should try taking some of their leave in Cornwall or Scotland. This was at a time when all travel on the over-crowded railways was severely discouraged—hence the famous wartime slogan: "IS YOUR JOURNEY REALLY NECESSARY?" Every town was expected to organize "Holidays at Home" so that people would not feel the need to travel. As the BBC man remarked, urging American soldiers to swan around Britain looking for holiday resorts "makes a poor contri-bution to our holidays at home campaign." It was another example of how most Americans, though well-meaning, did not find it easy to grasp the privations and problems of wartime Britain.[28]

Music was clearly what listeners wanted most from AFN. In the mid-dle of 1944, the station did a survey of the most popular songs of the past year. The results reflect the understandable preoccupation of men far from home and their loved ones. Number 1 was **Long Ago and Far Away**, with **I'll Be Seeing You** as runner-up. The others in AFN's Top Ten were: (3) **I Love You**; (4) **I'll Get By**; (5) **Amor**; (6) **I'll Walk Alone**; (7) **It Had to Be You**; (8) **San Fernando Valley**; (9) **Besame Mucho**; (10) **Trolley Song**.[29]

Another big hit of the time was **Paper Doll**, possibly the only song used as an instrument of private vengeance. One day during the war, a U.S. frigate, with pennants flying, steamed down a certain river mouth in Northern Ireland past a mansion used as sleeping quarters by the WRNS. Its PA system was blaring out **Paper Doll,** a number often heard on AFN, the words a plaintive lament about the fickleness of woman. Whether the flighty Wren at whom it was directed was there to hear it is not recorded, but doubtless she learned about it before long.[30]

Johnny Kerr had some interesting things to say about comparative ratings and also about the Crosby–Sinatra rivalry. He says he asked listeners to say whom they preferred: Sinatra or Dick Haymes. The answer was—Bing Crosby! "I got three times as many votes for Bingo-lito as for either of the others," he said. He didn't think Sinatra, who was the feature vocalist on the weekly *Your Hit Parade*, was all that popular with the average GI. "Most of the boys would never have heard of Sinatra if it hadn't been for his appearance on Hit Parade. You can't get records of him over here yet."[31]

From the number of requests he got for *Duffle Bag*, Kerr rated Crosby as the top male vocalist, followed by Sinatra and, perhaps surprisingly, Bob Eberly (vocalist with Jimmy Dorsey and brother of Ray Eberle who sang with Glenn Miller's band). Dinah Shore was the favorite fe-male singer, and after her came Lena Horne, Ginny Simms, and Frances

Langford. The top three dance bands were, in order, Harry James, Kay Kyser, and Fred Waring.

Of course, AFN was not all big bands and comedy. There was news, which does not seem to have appealed to most British listeners. In this field, unlike the record shows, they much preferred the no-nonsense style of the BBC and the authoritative voice of the familiar news readers.

One listener recalls he enjoyed *Information Please*, the witty and polished quiz show presented by Clifton Fadiman, which in America ran throughout the war and drew twelve million listeners a week. Starting off with a modest prize of $5 for any listener who beat the panel, it was eventually offering them a complete set of the *Encyclopaedia Britannica*. AFN ran its own version of *Information Please*. Called *Combined Operation*, it featured three American and three British servicemen asking each other questions about their respective countries. In one show, the Americans were asked to name Britain's winter sport and four teams that played it. An American private had the reply off pat: "The British national winter pastime is sitting in front of an open fire in a vain attempt to get warm. And the four teams playing it will be any four American soldiers in the British Isles." But lighthearted though it was, it helped the two sides to become familiar with each other's prides and prejudices, as one broadcaster put it.

Another Anglo-American program on AFN was *GI Tommy*, in which a British soldier back from one of the fighting fronts was given the air to talk about his experiences. Other shows were aimed at cementing good relations. *Weekend Leave* gave advice about where to go in England for short breaks (perhaps this was the program the BBC official had objected to), while *Invitation* was the opportunity for mayors or other prominent citizens in a range of towns to extol the attractions and give interesting information about their localities. There was also *Learn on Your Leave*, which was intended to encourage GIs to take specially arranged short courses at seats of learning throughout the country. *Visiting Hour* involved a series of outside broadcasts with the help of the BBC, visiting U.S. troops in hospitals throughout the country, a program in which the Glenn Miller band later took part.

Mention should also be made of another AFN program whose name indicates the station's predilection for punning. Aimed at the Women's Army Corps (WAC), it bore the excruciating title of *WACS Museum*.

AFN was able on occasion to help its British hosts in practical ways. A child suffering from a rare disease needed bananas as part of her diet. During the war, to save valuable shipping space for war materials, no bananas were imported into Britain. But the Americans came to the rescue and somehow produced enough bananas to keep the child going.[32]

AFN carried a great deal of sport, broadcasting live commentaries on major league baseball, American college football, boxing, and ice hockey with a frequency few radio stations can now approach—or afford. That aspect of its output is still remembered with pleasure by British listeners whose first introduction to America's national pastime came through AFN.

"The commentaries came direct from America on short wave, often indistinct and fading," one listener recalls. "Every now and then an authoritative voice would announce: We pause now for station identification, a phrase that was so American and emphasized that I was listening to a far distant station the other side of the Atlantic." Not everyone, though, was enthusiastic about the station's sport coverage. "I think I liked almost all AFN programmes," was one comment, "except for what seemed to be the interminable commentaries on baseball."[33]

As Christmas 1943 approached, U.S. Ambassador John G. Winant wrote to the BBC's director-general to express his appreciation of the "great generosity" the corporation had shown over the setting up of AFN. "I have been told by the Army, and know from many sources," he wrote, "what a tremendous factor the Network has been in improving the morale of our troops, especially in isolated units. . . . The BBC has made a real contribution to our war effort and mutual relations for which it deserves great credit."[34]

AFN itself reported the approval of the troops themselves. "Since it first went on the air . . . the network has received letters from hundreds of men and women of the American Armed Forces stationed in the European Theater of Operations who have expressed their appreciation of its activities." And it went on to say that commanding officers in the field had written to put on record "their conviction of the importance of the American Forces Network as a medium of maintaining morale, and of insuring an efficient and personal chain of communications between the High Command and the men under its leadership."[35]

Captain John Hayes, the operational head of AFN, could feel well pleased with what his small team had achieved in such a short time. He had something else to be pleased about, too. He found himself on the receiving end of rapid advancement, being quickly promoted to major and then, before long, lieutenant colonel.

Within a year, the new network had become an established part of the broadcasting scene. American journalists in Britain to write "color'" stories on the war were invited to visit AFN and express their admiration. They did so in glowing terms. "The greatest thing in the air since the Flying Fortress," one wrote. He was apparently quoting the men of the Eighth Air Force, who had transformed East Anglia into a giant air base.

The same writer described AFN as "a composite of incredulities." It was an all-American network that could not be heard in America; its listening figures were a military secret; and, while all of its broadcasts originated in London, it could not be heard on radio sets in the London area. And "although it has no paid commercials . . . it definitely and proudly plugs America's finest product: the well-informed, well-entertained, ready-to-fight American serviceman."[36] After comments like that, the folks back home could be in no doubt that the boys over in England were being looked after in true American style.

NOTES

1. DeLay says nine transmitters were operational on opening day, but the Gurney–Hayes progress report "This Is AFN" (BBCWAC, R34/907) puts the number at seven. Since this is the official, contemporary figure, I have chosen to accept it. A full list of transmitters is given in Appendix I. It can be be seen from this that it is not known for certain which ones were operational when the service opened.

2. Reynolds, *Rich Relations*, pp. 107 et seq.; Gardner, *Over Here*, pp. 64 et seq.

3. BBCWAC, R53/8.

4. Ibid.

5. BBCWAC, R34/907 (Hayes–Gurney memo).

6. Private letters to the author.

7. BBCWAC, R53/8.

8. *History of AFRTS*, p. 40.

9. Private letters to the author.

10. Interview with the author.

11. Private letter to the author.

12. Ibid.

13. Radio Luxembourg was probably the most popular of a number of Continental commercial stations. It had begun broadcasting in 1932 on longwave at a power of 200 kilowatts (far more than was needed for a small country like Luxembourg), with the deliberate aim of beaming commercial programs over a wide area, in defiance of the International Broadcasting Union. In Britain, it was seen as a particular threat not only by the BBC, fearful for its monopoly, but by the newspapers as well, worried about losing advertising. They refused to publish its program schedules, so it started its own weekly program magazine, a lively, well-illustrated publication, *Radio Pictorial*. It had big listening figures, largely on Sundays when the BBC programs were regarded by many listeners as being too staid and serious. The BBC, supported by the government, made all manner of efforts to keep Radio Luxembourg off the air, but without success. It took the war to do that. Ironically, after all its opposition to the commercial station, when war was imminent, the BBC changed its tune and supplied Radio Luxembourg with special recordings of broadcasts by Prime Minister Neville Chamberlain and assumed a much more helpful attitude. See Briggs, *History*, Vol. II, *The Golden Age of Wireless* (1965), pp. 361–369, and *When the Ovaltineys Sang*, a monograph on Radio Luxembourg by Ron Montague (privately printed, 1990).

14. Private letters to the author.

15. Cecil Madden's personal scrapbook, now in the BBC Written Archives. It consists of several volumes and is an interesting picture of the career and times of one of the BBC's leading producers of the period.

16. The BBC program magazine *Radio Times* carried a series of biographical articles by Margaret Forster about the AFN announcers when they became widely known to

British listeners through the Allied Expeditionary Forces Programme (see chapters 8 and 9). The article on Johnny Kerr appeared on 1 December 1944, George Monaghan on 5 January 1945, Dick Dudley on 26 January, Saddlebags Crawford on 9 March, and Keith Jameson on 6 May.

17. Ibid.

18. Christman, *Brass Button Broadcasters,* p. 41.

19. *Saturday Evening Post.*

20. BBC radio program "Oranges and Lemons," broadcast 7 June 1984 to mark the 40th anniversary of the AEFP [hereafter Oranges and Lemons broadcast].

21. Private letters to the author.

22. Audrey Johnson, author of *Do March in Step Girls.*

23. *History of AFRTS,* p. 60; Christman, *Brass Button Broadcasters,* p. 31.

24. Christman, *Brass Button Broadcasters,* p. 41.

25. *Saturday Evening Post.*

26. With millions of Americans serving overseas, the strain on postal services was immense. So too was the pressure on shipping space. It is said that on average each member of the armed forces received a dozen letters a week from home and sent three back in reply. The government recognized the morale value of this huge volume of correspondence. General Doolittle, in command of the U.S. Eighth Air Force, summed it up perfectly when he told Glenn Miller he was the greatest morale builder in the ETO—"next to a letter from home." So V mail (Victory mail) was introduced. Letters were written on a special form, then microfilmed to reduce them in size. A ton of letters transferred to microfilm weighed no more than 25 pounds, a valuable saving of shipping space, which could then be used for vital war materials. There were disadvantages. The V mail had to be kept short, and the reduction in size meant it was not always easy to read. But at least servicemen and women could keep in touch with home, and the V mail was moved faster than ordinary letters going by sea. It was the British who had pioneered the use of microfilm for wartime mail. Their "airgraph" service was introduced in 1941, and by the end of the war 350 million forces letters had been sent by this method.

27. Letter to *Yank* magazine, 19 December 1943. Unlike *Stars and Stripes,* which was a daily newspaper, *Yank* was a weekly magazine for the forces. It was started in April 1942 and was based in New York but produced a dozen different editions in the various theaters of war. It was a lively, literate, well-illustrated publication and was particularly noted for its often outspoken "Mail Call" feature which allowed servicemen and women to sound off about all manner of subjects, like the one quoted here. It ceased publication with the end of the war.

28. BBCWAC, R34/907/1 (DPP memo, 24 July 1943).

29. Christman, *Brass Button Broadcasters,* p. 52.

30. Audrey Johnson.

31. *Saturday Evening Post,* the source of much of the program information in the preceding pages.

32. Ibid.

33. Private letters to the author.

34. BBCWAC, R34/907 (J. G. Winant letter to BBC DG, 17 December 1943). It should be noted that at this time, the BBC had two joint director-generals, one of whom was Robert W. Foot. It was he who was principally involved with all the negotiations over AFN and to whom Winant's letter was addressed. He was succeeded as sole director-general in March 1944 by William Haley, who had previously

been the joint managing director of the *Manchester Guardian* and the *Manchester Evening News*.

35. BBCWAC, R34/907 (Hayes–Gurney memo).

36. *Saturday Evening Post*. A straightforward account of AFN's activities is to be found in Edward M. Kirby and Jack W. Davis, *Star Spangled Radio* (Ziff-Davis, 1948), pp. 58–60.

FIVE

BBC and AFN

Commercials, surprisingly perhaps, proved a problem in the early days of the relationship between the BBC and AFN. As has been noted, these were supposed to be removed from programs before AFN got them from the AFRS. But clearly this was not always the case. The BBC felt obliged to make representations about "advertising references" in several programs. And the embarrassed head of AFN was said to be particularly unhappy about the fact that the network he controlled was advertising Coca Cola, a firm with which the American Army had a huge contract. He did not need the gentle reminder from the BBC that that sort of thing might lead to repercussions back in America. As a corporation official noted, "the Americans could not have shown themselves more ready to meet us" and guaranteed to eliminate all such references in future.[1]

Later in the war, Coca Cola was to provide another example of the BBC's obsessive concern over advertising in any form. When the Andrews Sisters had a big hit with **Rum and Coca Cola**, the corporation insisted that any broadcasting version of the song should use the words "Rum and Limonada." The BBC was much exercised at all times about the lyrics of popular songs, so much so that in July 1942 it set up what became known as the Slush Committee. This referred not to slush as in bribe money, but slush as in silly sentiment. The corporation's executives considered that in a time of war there was too much "overdone" sentimentality in both the lyrics of songs and the way they were sung. The committee's brief was to vet both, and as a result a number of songs—not to mention some performers—were effectively blacklisted. It was a remarkable form of censorship and indicates the extent to which the BBC swallowed its principles in agreeing, only a year later, to the setting up of AFN, whose attitude to popular music was so much more relaxed. However, at its first meeting the committee had accepted it could exercise no control over U.S. programs broadcast by the corporation, so once again a special exception was made for the Americans.[2]

On the program side of the relationship, things seemed to be going reasonably well. The Americans were able to offer the BBC the choice of a range of broadcasts and arranged for the corporation's program planners to listen to extracts from them as a preliminary to a more detailed "audition." One noted that Captain Hayes "was very helpful and allowed me to hear snippets of some 20 different programs." Apart from comedy shows, the great majority were "of the dance music type and there are much fewer light music programs than we expected to find"—another indication of the differing tastes of the two broadcasting organizations in the musical field, and presumably of their audiences.

Some of the programs that were offered still contained advertising, which, of course, had to be removed. The same official commented that a producer would have to decide whether or not he could cut out all the commercials easily, and by how much this would reduce the program length (normally by four or five minutes, a big gap to fill). But the BBC man added: "I know we shall have as much co-operation as we want from the Americans, who went to a great deal of trouble on my behalf."

Apart from commercials, there was another complication. The Americans offered the BBC the use of the latest hit records from across the Atlantic, and that posed difficulties over performing rights. The same BBC official commented: "I expect we shall get into trouble, just as the Americans do, over the use of one or two of the numbers which have not yet been released in this country." But, he added, that was a problem they were already familiar with from the musical numbers in such programs as *Mail Call*, which the BBC was broadcasting regularly.[3] In fact, AFN had virtual carte blanche over using copyright material, and if anyone ever expressed any doubts, the answer always was: "If they don't like it, tell 'em to sue Uncle Sam."

The corporation was certainly doing well out of its liaison with AFN. In November and December of 1943, its domestic services carried 112 American entertainment programs, as well as a considerable number of documentaries and talks.[4] Among British listeners, there was a keen interest in documentary programs about America and its people. That was an interest the BBC believed it should encourage, according to one departmental head. But he had reservations about other aspects of the broadcasting "lend–lease":

The value and desirability of our [continuing to broadcast American] entertainment programmes is more arguable. They command enthusiastic listeners (with enthusiasm varying in inverse proportion to age), they supplement
BBC resources in the field in which at present we are weakest, and they are
free and therefore supplement a programme allowance which has not kept
pace with increasing programme costs. On the other hand, they whet an
appetite which we shall not be able to satisfy after the war.[5]

He was right about that. Almost as soon as the war ended, the programs—like lend-lease itself—ceased. As a BBC memo lamenting this
pointed out, "The programs were broadcast during the war by arrangement with the US government for the benefit of US soldiers in Britain."
The corporation's use of them was a wartime bonus, but only a temporary one.[6]

The BBC was very much aware of the number of English listeners
AFN was attracting. Many recall they had no problem receiving the
station. "It was as loud and clear as the BBC all day long," one Midlands
listener remembers, "though our house was certainly a good way from
the nearest American base."[7] One of the BBC's senior officials living in
Sussex noted that he heard AFN down there "quite well," though again
he was some distance from the nearest transmitter. He recommended
that "we should take every step to check up on the number of civilian
listeners." But it should be done discreetly so that gratuitous attention
was not drawn to the rival network. If it was found that the number of
English listeners was considerable "we should ask the Americans to
reduce power or take whatever steps may be appropriate."[8]

In the event, it was something the BBC had to put up with. Ultimately,
the British listening audience outnumbered the American, which is surprising, perhaps, considering the limited power of the transmitters and
the fact that there were none in the London area. It was estimated that as
many as five million Britons were tuning in regularly to AFN, far more
than the total number of U.S. servicemen who passed through Britain
during the entire war.[9]

Interestingly, the BBC had established that AFN's British audience
included many teenagers, the listeners of the future, and that too was a
matter of concern. But despite the BBC's understandable misgivings, the
British audience for AFN was never enough to make serious inroads into
the corporation's listening figures. However, those who had expressed
reservations about the ammunition AFN would give the commercial
radio lobby were proved right. The advocates of commercial broadcasting lost no opportunity to point out that AFN's programs were much
more popular than those of the supposedly "highbrow" BBC.[10]

So the corporation was right not to ignore the newcomer in its midst,
whatever its audience figures. The same official who said the whole idea

of AFN was so alien to the tradition and practices of broadcasting in Britain emphasized that "we must continue to be watchful." And so the BBC was.[11]

It was certainly watchful about how AFN was carrying out its promises over using BBC material. It monitored it carefully and noted that the amount used was a good deal lower than had been expected. Apart from news programs, AFN was using about eleven hours of BBC material a week, including *ITMA* (*It's That Man Again*, which was Britain's most popular wartime comedy show), the BBC Northern Orchestra, Sunday Serenade, and RAF camp concerts, as well as various talks on current affairs.[12] *ITMA* was a fast, wisecracking program of the kind that should have appealed to the Americans, but apparently they were not greatly enamored of it. The AFN presenter George Monaghan said he did like it, but Johnny Kerr found it too fast, a reflection perhaps of the very English nature of its humor. Many of the topical allusions probably meant little to the Americans, though seemingly the reverse did not apply. The British audience was treated to a diet of Bob Hope, Jack Benny, Fred Allen, and others and apparently had no difficulty in coping with their wisecracks. Again, it was a reflection of the different approach to humor of the two English-speaking nations, though it has to be said the American artists were more familiar to Britons through Hollywood films.

In an attempt to increase the number of BBC programs heard on AFN, one of the corporation's senior men had a meeting with the OWI's Guy della Cioppa, who was sympathetic but not encouraging. "He saw great difficulties in increasing the BBC representation in the American Forces Network. The Americans mainly want to hear the big variety shows to which they are accustomed in the States, and [AFN] aims at putting them on as far as possible on the day and at the time at which they are broadcast at home." The BBC executive noted that the Americans were "not in sympathy with our Forces '*Background Hour*' policy. They frankly believe that their forces want to hear, and will arrange to hear, the big shows and they have plenty of them to give." Rather than informed current affairs programs, the U.S. servicemen were interested in fifteen or thirty minutes featuring the top dance bands, Tommy Dorsey, Harry James, and the like.[13] This squares very much with the listening preferences of the British forces in the Middle East, referred to earlier. There, it will be recalled, the universal complaint from the troops was that "when you tune into the BBC you get nothing but talk, talk, talk. The troops want music—light music and dance music." So in this regard at any rate, the American and the British fighting men were clearly at one.[14]

Nevertheless, the BBC continued to press the notion of "quality broadcasting." In September 1943, the director-general called a meeting to discuss with the Americans "the policy of the American Forces Network in the widest sense." He thought that "over and above providing dance music and light entertainment," AFN could play a part in furthering Anglo-American relations. The main American representative, Wallace Carroll, of the Office of War Information, said the U.S. Army had been having discussions with the British army educational body ABCA (Army Bureau of Current Affairs) and hoped that as a result there would be broadcasts on AFN which would contribute towards "a more serious element" in the output. And he agreed with the director-general that "circumspect infiltration of occasional concerts of serious music . . . feature programs and talks, e.g. *War Commentary*, would be a wise policy." He promised to raise the matter with the American military, and from a study of the AFN schedules it seems that some effort was made to meet the BBC's point.[15]

It was soon established that AFN was devoting about 25 percent of its air time to BBC programs, rather than the 50 percent hoped for. However, the corporation had to accept that this could be described as "substantial" and so complied with the letter of the agreement. In any case, as a BBC official noted, "I am not at all sure it would be in the best interests of broadcasting in this country to ask the Americans to take more material from the BBC." And he went on: "Is it not better that the Network manager schedules a judicious small selection of BBC programs which he knows will appeal to his audience, than that he should be forced to observe some weekly quota and thereby take BBC material which will not be popular and can therefore do us and the cause of Anglo-American relations no good?" It was a realistic and sensible point of view and was the one that prevailed, though the BBC continued to monitor AFN output. It was also recommended that "the BBC should, from time to time, unofficially keep alive in the minds of those running the Network their concern that there should be reasonable representation of BBC output."[16]

In engineering terms, AFN had a lot to thank the BBC for. All its live play-by-play broadcasts of baseball and American football came via the BBC's powerful shortwave receivers. AFN started a series of weekly outside broadcasts from U.S. bases throughout the country, which needed domestic engineering effort. The Americans tended to be casual about carrying out the correct but at times irksome technical and booking procedures without which outside broadcasts do not happen. This sometimes resulted in problems, testified to by a number of mildly exasperated memos from the BBC, though generally the tone was amicable enough.[17] AFN relied on the corporation's engineering staff in all sorts of other ways. For instance, when it wanted to stay on the air after midnight, by which time the BBC domestic services had closed down, because the signals went through the main control room at Broadcasting House there had to be BBC engineers on duty to make it possible.

AFN had continued to agitate for a transmitter in the London area but finally gave up. Had it persisted, it might have got its way. A BBC memo, after another such request, admitted that "if we are pressed, I think we should probably in the end give way."[18]

It was in the news field that most problems arose. This is where the Americans' breezy self-confidence came unstuck at times.

By this stage of the war, the BBC provided what was probably the best news service in the world. It was widely heard and respected all over Europe. General Eisenhower is said to have had a very high opinion of its trustworthiness. Even the Nazis grudgingly admitted that, privately at any rate. It was straightforward, accurate, and—given the constraints of war—remarkably objective. If the British suffered a defeat (as they did frequently until late 1942), the BBC made no effort to dress it up, unlike the blatant propaganda of the Axis radio controlled by Dr. Goebbels.[19]

The BBC had become expert at spotting misleading stories planted in neutral countries; it knew which sources were reliable, what were unfounded rumors, which had some basis in fact. It had a large experienced staff and unrivaled sources. On occasion, even Churchill himself, with all the information at his disposal, would ring the newsroom to see if they had anything new. AFN was not in the same league, nor did it profess to be.

Censorship was also another problem. In the United States the government had decided this should be voluntary for broadcasting organizations, despite the opposition of some military leaders. After one particular breach, involving an unwitting reference to atomic research, they even demanded a military censor at every broadcasting station. But apart from such isolated incidents, the system worked well, and there were no major problems. In Britain, close to the battlefront and a network of enemy listening posts, some form of censorship was essential if security was not to be breached accidentally. For the BBC it was routine, but it was something the Americans had to get used to.[20]

Clearly AFN recognized all this and was happy to carry the BBC 6 p.m and 9 p.m news bulletins each day. But the troops naturally expected news in the American style and with American voices. And they wanted news from back home.

Home news from America was no concern of the BBC, but world news was different. The director-general made it known that he "attached great importance to ensuring that the Americans do not follow a different standard of news value to our own."[21]

In Britain at that time, programs were interrupted only for news of the greatest importance, but it was feared the Americans might follow a different pattern. The BBC controller of news worried that important news might get slipped in at all sorts of odd times, which could create rumors and cause confusion. "It is also on the cards," he wrote, "that if big news comes in they will add it to their ostensible sports or home news programs. If, for instance, it became known at 6:50 p.m. that Rome had fallen, Hitler had chucked himself off the pier at Hamburg, etc., then I don't mind betting it would be in the US 7 p.m. sports bulletin."[22]

The matter was discussed at some length, though the view was expressed that, seeing how limited an audience the new network was expected to have, rather than risk looking churlish it might be better simply see how things worked out.

But Controller News came to the conclusion that "we should ask the Americans to agree never to break programs for news items unless we are going to do so. After all, they are playing on our ground and using out bats and wickets."[23] To which a more senior (and realistic) BBC executive replied: "The Americans are playing on our ground but not surely using our bats and wickets. I wish they were and have said so several times but baseball it is, and not cricket. Still, I think they would agree not to break programs unless we are breaking also." And he offered to arrange a meeting between the head of news and Guy della Cioppa, assistant head of the OWI in Britain and "a pleasant, forthright person to deal with."[24]

In the event, the Americans agreed to consult a senior BBC newsman over major news breaks and to have regular daily discussions between the AFN editor and the BBC home news duty editor. These discussions helped, but still there were problems. These are best illustrated by quoting from the correspondence within the BBC about AFN's news coverage, a correspondence which reflects the very different attitudes to news of the British and the Americans.

I went down to see the new American news set up at Carlos Place last night. . . . I find that the so-called news headlines which they put out at 10 o'clock are all produced by one man who uses as his news source Reuters and the Exchange Telegraph, the London evening papers and the American paper Stars and Stripes. They seem to realise down there the shortcomings inherent in such a limited staff and more particularly such poor sources of news. They appear to have no guidance, very poor liaison even with their own headquarters and no facilities for research, library or map work. . . . I discussed with them specifically the treatment of the Russian story on Tuesday night and convinced them that it was unfortunate that we should say one thing in our 9 o'clock bulletin and that they should say another an hour later.

This was a reference to two markedly differing reports by the BBC and AFN of what was happening on the Russian front. The BBC senior duty editor noted that what was going on in the AFN newsroom was not "a very satisfactory" state of affairs, and he had offered to let the Americans have advance copies of the BBC news bulletins. This would give them a basis to work on and "an idea of what we considered to be the facts of each of the main war stories." He says the Americans seemed very pleased that the BBC was prepared to help in this way.[25]

I spent two or three hours last night with the people who are running the American Forces Network . . . I am more than ever convinced that they really do want to play ball with us but the machinery of collaboration is still creaking a little. I discovered, for instance, that on Sunday night in their 10 o'clock broadcast they made use of the Stockholm message which had appeared in most of the Sunday papers reporting that Axis headquarters had moved from Sicily to the mainland, and that there had been no consultation with Balkwill [a senior BBC journalist] on this point or indeed on any other point about that particular bulletin. The Stockholm message in question did not do any particular harm in this instance but Nussbaum [Major Nussbaum, responsible for AFN policy] agrees with me that this is a possible source of danger because Stockholm is so notorious as a seed for Axis plants.[26]

There were continuing problems about censorship. The censor responsible for the American news output was supposed to check the content of bulletins with the BBC man to make sure that nothing slipped through, since AFN regularly used different stories. But, as was noted, it was not possible for every sentence to be adequately discussed over the phone. Copies of the American scripts went to the BBC—but apparently only after transmission—so that factual errors and, more particularly, policy mistakes could be spotted and pointed out so there was no repetition. However, the chief censor himself intervened at one point to say that in his experience AFN had up to now always heeded advice on security matters given by the BBC.[27]

It was beginning to emerge that the two organizations had different views about what was newsworthy and what was not, as this somewhat irate memo indicates:

About 9:40 this evening I was telephoned by Lieutenant Woodey who looks after the news service for the American Forces. Among the items he asked about was a message from Istanbul about mobilisation in Bulgaria, and one from Stockholm about the possibility of the German Fleet taking part in the war. I told him that we should not use them in any circumstances and said it would be better for him not to. I explained that the Istanbul message was from a source well known as unreliable and probably nothing more than an unfounded and dangerous rumour. I made it clear that the Stockholm message was pure speculation from a source not to be trusted. Despite this both the items were used. With Mr Harrison I listened to the whole of the bulletin and we found it generally most dangerously crude and inaccurate. I do not know what the position of Lieut. Woodey is, but he seemed very unfamiliar with the war fronts and I had to put him right on points in the Russian and

Far East stories. He told me that with Sicily he was using the communique stuff (and gave me a resume) but it was written up in so optimistic and luscious a style that it might have come straight from one of the world agencies.[28]

This scathing blast resulted in a follow-up memo from Evans's superior.

The American censor came through half an hour after the time originally agreed with us. . . . [The Newsroom staff on duty were] particularly annoyed with their treatment of the Russian war, which was altogether over-optimistic and in at least one instance inaccurate in fact. They referred, for instance, to the Germans being cut off *west* of a river they called the Yper—presumably meaning *east* of the Dneiper—to which one of the wilder Reuter messages had referred. The same over-optimism and reports ahead of events characterised their treatment of Sicily.[29]

He went on to say that some closer check must be kept on the Americans' 10 p.m. news, though he accepted that they could hardly be expected to read out their stories word for word to ensure their accuracy. His comments about AFN's attitude to news reflects the BBC's very different approach. "Get it on the air first by all means, but above all else get it *right*" had always been the corporation's maxim, and it clearly irked their experienced news team to have the newcomers breezing in and taking what they regarded as a slaphappy attitude to what, for the BBC, was something like a sacred trust.

Of course, it was early days: after all, AFN had only been on the air for a few weeks, and it was bound to take them time to settle down. But how you start off can often determine the pattern for the future, and the BBC was concerned to get it right from the word go.

Once the dust had settled on the cases quoted, the assistant controller of news, J. C. S. Macgregor, wrote a carefully worded letter to Major Nussbaum at AFN. He referred to the American news team not having "seen eye to eye with our people on a couple of points . . . where it looked as though our advice had been ignored." Clearly anxious to pour oil on troubled waters, he doubted if a detailed postmortem would be worthwhile but suggested a number of practical points to avoid problems in the future. And he ended on an optimistic note: "It would surely help both parties if each could get to know the other and understand more completely one another's requirements."[30]

However, it was not all one-sided. On one occasion, a senior member of the BBC's Overseas Service spent some time listening to AFN's news bulletins and noted several items which had not been used on the BBC's nine o'clock evening news but which he considered newsworthy enough to have been included. So clearly the Americans did not always get it wrong by any means.[31]

Despite all the efforts to make things run smoothly, the problems continued, as indicated by a memo from two experienced members of the BBC newsroom staff who were later to hold senior posts in the corporation:

On some occasions, the Americans don't bother to ring at all. When their censor comes through he usually gabbles through the copy at a pace which makes it almost impossible either to understand him fully or to interject any comment. In any case, he appears to have little news experience and is not in a position to understand a point of policy even if we do point it out to him. He certainly seems to have no news sense. On some occasions, one has had to waste as much as a quarter of an hour reading over to him items from our news of particular American interest which the American sub-editors appear to have missed altogether. The other man, whom we take to be in some sort of editorial position, usually comes through very late with some bald announcement as "We've nothing here which wasn't in your nine o'clock." One can either take this at its face value and save time, or question the accuracy of the remark and make him read out the American version of our nine o'clock news. We hope it bears no relation to our version.[32]

Clearly the news staff were all for washing their hands of the Americans. But those in charge did not agree. The Assistant Controller News wrote: "I am very reluctant to drop the system of consultation altogether. ... I still think we could not afford to let the Americans run happily on their own." Then he adds significantly: "One of the interesting points about the whole business is the almost complete lack of evidence that listeners in this country are specially thrilled by these programs or tempted in large numbers to listen to them. Thus the danger which we feared at the beginning is perhaps less terrifying now, but it still exists."[33]

His own staff were less than convinced. The two newsmen already quoted probably summed up the attitude of most of their colleagues in the newsroom:

We both feel that the present arrangement with the American news people does no good to either side and might even cause irritation on theirs if they feel we are cramping their style or interfering with their bulletins. However hard we try we shall never make them present news in an objective and accurate way and we do not think we should be saddled with the responsibility of having anything to do with their services.[34]

In the end, the BBC seems to have come to the conclusion that AFN was writing a different style of news for a very different audience, with different expectations, and it was pointless to attempt to change them. It was the clearest indication that AFN regarded itself as an independent broadcasting organization that would do things in its own way.

Whatever professional disagreement there may have been, relations on a personal level were perfectly cordial. And when AFN came to celebrate its first birthday, there was a friendly exchange of letters between Major (as he now was) Hayes and the BBC's director-general. "May I thank you and your staff for your gracious co-operation during the past year," wrote the head of AFN. To which the BBC's chief replied: "We feel that very happy relations have been established between the BBC and the AFN."[35] A year later, the occasion of AFN's second birthday was marked with a special program, and among those taking part was the BBC's deputy director-general, Sir Noel Ashbridge, who clearly appreciated being asked to participate.

The Americans were always ready with the warm-hearted gesture that makes friends. After transmitting a BBC program to celebrate the corporation's 21st anniversary, the announcer added: "The American Forces Network is happy to add its voice to the thousands of friends of the BBC who congratulate it today on its anniversary. To the BBC, without whose continual co-operation and helpful assistance the American Forces Network could not operate, we say: HAPPY BIRTHDAY!" A copy of that closing announcement resides in the BBC Archives together with the note scribbled on it by one of the corporation's senior executives: "Quite a pleasant little gesture on the part of our friends at Carlos Place."[36]

NOTES

1. BBCWAC, R34/907/1 (DPP memo, 24 July 1943).

2. So that music publishers and bandleaders should be in no doubt, the BBC sent them a list of what would be banned: "Any form of anaemic or debilitated vocal performance by male singers. Any insincere or over sentimental style of performance by women singers. Numbers which are slushy in sentiment or contain innuendo or other matter considered to be offensive from the point of view of good taste, and of religious or allied susceptibilities. Numbers, with or without lyrics, which are based on tunes borrowed from standard classical works." An account of the working of the "Slush Committee" by Colin Morgan (based largely on material in the BBC Archives) was published in 20 parts in the magazine *In Tune* between 1989 and 1991, later issued as a complete publication. It is interesting to note that popular songs were still being vetted well after the war, a fact also referred to by Briggs, *History*, Vol. IV (1979), p. 58.

3. BBCWAC, R34/907/1 (Program Organiser R. MacDermot memo, 24 July 1943).

4. BBCWAC, E/109.

5. Ibid. (Wellington memo to DG, 20 July 1944).

6. Ibid.

7. Private letter to author.

8. BBCWAC, R34/907 (DPP memo, 24 July 1943).

9. *History of AFRTS*, p. 50; Christman, *Brass Button Broadcasters*, p. 56.

10. Briggs, *History*, Vol. III, p. 647, quoting *Broadcasting: Radio & Television since 1900*.

11. BBCWAC, R34/907/1 (DPP memo 24 July 1943).

12. Ibid. (10 August 1943).

13. Ibid.

14. BBCWAC, R34/373/2 (BBC Cairo representative's memo, "The BBC and the Middle East Forces," undated but ca. May 1942). From the ensuing correspondence, the report was clearly taken seriously by the BBC hierarchy and brought about a major rethink.

15. BBCWAC, R53/8 (Minutes of DG's meeting, 13 September 1943).

16. BBCWAC, R34/907/1 (DPP memo, 10 August 1943).

17. BBCWAC, E/109.

18. BBCWAC, R53/8 (DDG memo, 4 February 1944).

19. One of the BBC's senior newsmen summed up the corporation's attitude just before the outbreak of war: "It seems to me that the only way to strengthen the morale of the people . . . is to tell them the truth and nothing but the truth, even if the truth is horrible" (BBCWAC: RT Clark memo, 28 April 1938, quoted by Briggs, *History*, Vol. II, p. 656). Briggs also refers to the BBC having a reputation as "the most honest purveyor of news in the world" (p. 153).

20. Erik Barnouw, *The Golden Web* (OUP, New York 1968), pp. 156–157; Kirby and Davis, *Star Spangled Radio*, pp. 5–15 (a detailed account of how the system of radio censorship operated). For censorship in the United Kingdom see W. J. West (ed.), *Orwell: The War Broadcasts* (Duckworth/BBC 1985), pp. 279–283; and Gorham, *Broadcasting*, pp. 182–184.

21. DG's views quoted in BBCWAC, R34/907/1 (Controller News A. P. Ryan memo, 26 June 1943).

22. BBCWAC, R34/909/1 (Controller News memo, 17 June 1943).

23. Ibid. (Controller News memo, 21 June 1943).

24. Ibid. (DPP memo, 25 June 1943).

25. Ibid. (A. H. Wigan memo, 8 July 1943).

26. Ibid. (J. C. S. Macgregor memo, 20 July 1943).

27. Ibid. (R. H. Eckersley memo, 13 August 1943).

28. Ibid. (B. Evans memo, 10 August 1943).

29. Ibid. (A. H. Wigan memo, 11 August 1943).

30. Ibid. (Macgregor to Nussbaum, 24 August 1943).

31. Quoted in ibid. (R. MacDermot memo, 19 July 1943).

32. Ibid. (Balkwill–Taylor memo, 14 November 1943).

33. Ibid. (Macgregor memo, 17 November 1943).

34. Ibid. (Balkwill–Taylor memo).

35. Ibid. (Hayes to DG, 4 July 1944; DG to Hayes, 6 July 1944). Hayes had succeeded Col. Gurney as head of AFN in the spring of 1944. There is no record of when he relinquished the post.

36. BBCWAC, R34/907, undated.

SIX

Forces Broadcasting

The American Forces Network was by no means the first forces broadcasting service. Within a month of the start of the Spanish Civil War, the Republicans began broadcasting regular programs for their forces. The date was 14 September 1936, and the nightly transmissions were entitled *"Altavox del frente"* [the frontline loudspeaker] and subtitled, somewhat forbiddingly, *"Informacion y propaganda para el pueblo en armas"* [information and propaganda for the people in arms]. The programs consisted mostly of talks and patriotic music in a variety of Spanish languages. Later, transmissions in their own languages were started for the foreign volunteers fighting on the side of the Republicans.

It was the Communist Party in Madrid that recognized the troops might be interested in more than propaganda talks and began broadcasts with an element of popular music in them. The Russian contribution was limited to the kind of broadcasts that Radio Moscow had been putting out regularly for the Red Army since the early 1930s.

The ultimately victorious Nationalists, who at first did not have the same access to broadcasting stations as the Republicans, began forces transmissions later in the war. From the autumn of 1938, they ran a popular-request program for wounded soldiers, and some stations played Arabic music for Moroccans fighting with the Nationalist Army.[1]

The Germans, who intervened in the war to assist the Nationalist forces of General Franco, began broadcasts in 1938 for their own troops fighting with the Condor Legion, though these broadcasts were, in the main, relays of programs from Germany rather than a specially set-up forces broadcasting service. What the Germans did do was to provide technical help so that Franco could counter the monopoly the Republicans then had of powerful broadcast transmitters. The Germans brought in a mobile transmitting and studio unit mounted on four big trucks, whose large tubular sections gave rise to the wildest rumors—they were part of a super cannon to bombard Madrid, or even a ray gun! When it began broadcasting, it was the most powerful medium-wave transmitter in Spain, and its signals were so strong it was heard all over Western Europe.

By the time World War II began, only six months after the official end of the conflict in Spain, the Germans had a number of similar units ready for military broadcasting. Unlike the British, who broadcast to their forces from their studio complex in London, the Germans faced a different problem. They had rapidly conquered vast areas of Europe and North Africa, and their armies were spread over thousands of miles, so the powerful mobile units were ideal for military broadcasting.[2] It was one of these located near occupied Belgrade which broadcast the sultry voice of Lale Andersen singing **Lilli Marlene** to the Afrika Korps and ultimately to the British Eighth Army. The Germans were very much alive to the value of female singers and presenters: Axis Sally is one obvious example. Apart from her, the forces station in the Russian city of Kursk had a woman announcer nicknamed Gusti, who became a great favorite with the German armies invading the Soviet Union.[3]

The Russians, too, made full use of radio. They had morale-boosting broadcasts from the front for the civilians at home and were at pains to reassure the troops that the civilian population was coping, even to the extent of giving wartime-production figures, all interspersed with what is described as good music.[4]

In Britain, the BBC had, as already noted, created a special Forces Programme in January 1940 originally intended for the troops then serving with the British Expeditionary Force in France, before that country fell to the Germans. During the period of the "phony war" the men had more time on their hands than their commanders thought good for them. Radio was seen as a way of ensuring "the contentment and morale of the troops." To some extent, the BBC was spurred into action by a commercial station, Radio International, broadcasting from the Normandy town of Fecamp, with British financial backing from a firm which had its offices, rather cheekily, only a few doors from the BBC headquarters in Portland Place, London. It even distributed a magazine, *Happy Listening*, free to all the troops. With the exertion of British pressure, the French government eventually closed the station down, leaving the field clear for the new Forces Programme.[5]

   Although the Forces Programme was designed with the British Army in mind, it was intended to cater for listeners as a whole, with whom it proved a great success. Later in the war, British forces abroad were catered for by the BBC's General Overseas Service, which had a range of popular programs. But the troops felt the need for a radio link with the people back home, and so eventually it was decided to absorb the Forces Programme into the General Overseas Service. The aim was for the forces, wherever they were serving in the world, to share the same radio programs as their loved ones in Britain. In other words, the motives behind the change were very much the same as the ones that led the Americans to set up AFN.

   The new service, which began in February 1944, was known as the General Forces Programme. Ironically, it was not an unqualified success. Those members of the forces who wanted to hear the kind of programs and voices they had heard on the BBC's Home Service were disappointed. On the other hand, according to one source, for some home listeners the kind of material suitable for listening to in service canteens was not to their taste, and they switched to the corporation's other (less populist) domestic broadcasting service. By the war's end, the home listening figures were General Forces Programme 40 percent, Home Service 60 percent. With the old Forces Programme, the figures had been almost exactly the reverse.[6]

   The new forces program was run by the BBC as part of its national broadcasting setup, unlike AFN, which was an arm of the military establishment. So too, of course, was the biggest, the most professional, and the most successful of all forces broadcasting organizations: the Armed Forces Radio Service (AFRS).

   The AFRS had its origins in the period immediately before the war when three separate events pointed the way in which forces broadcasting would develop. One of the exhibits at the San Francisco International Exposition in 1939 was a powerful shortwave transmitter developed by the General Electric Company. Using the call sign KGEI, it began transmitting across the Pacific, beaming broadcasts to the Philippines in particular, aimed at the U.S. military stationed there. The programs were widely heard by Americans all over Asia and served to balance Japanese broadcasts emanating from Radio Tokyo. When the Japanese invaded the Philippines, KGEI became the main source of news and information for the American forces under the command of General MacArthur. The general also set up a small station on Bataan using a 1,000-watt transmitter, which relayed KGEI but mainly concentrated on countering propaganda and misleading information put out by the Japanese.

   Meanwhile, there had been broadcasting developments in the Panama Canal Zone. A series of American military radio stations were set up to link the isolated antiaircraft and other units in remote jungle areas. There were difficulties getting the troops to monitor the radio regularly, so a bright young sergeant hit on the idea of playing popular music over the air. His theory was that the servicemen might be persuaded to keep their sets on all the time if it was their favorite tunes they were likely to hear. The commanding general, surprisingly perhaps, approved the idea, and early in 1940 Station PCAC, run by the local military, went on the air. Before long, it was broadcasting news as well as music. The enterprising sergeant in charge of public relations then contacted radio stars in Hollywood and asked for their help. Jack Benny was the first to send a transcription of his program, on an autographed disc, and soon other network shows followed suit. In September 1941, NBC paid tribute to the miniature forces radio station with a nationwide broadcast, featuring many of the stars who had chipped in to help. The broadcast was followed by the dispatch of a huge crate containing, literally, a ton of recordings of network programs.

Because of increasing tensions with Japan, the War Department had decided early in 1941 to station troops in Alaska, an area which then had very few radio stations. Two soldiers, bored with the lack of local entertainment, decided to set up their own broadcasting outfit. Using makeshift equipment, they played borrowed records and persuaded fellow servicemen to play live music and organize impromptu entertainment. Unhappily, the FCC learned about the unauthorized station and closed it down in what seems a heavy-handed exercise of officialdom. However, by then the idea had caught on.

A former radio worker, now an officer with an army unit on Kodiak island, decided to set up a radio station for the local troops, but now he went about it in a more organized way. A first experimental broadcast in October 1941 consisted of a live band, singers, and a comedy sketch. This attracted the attention of civilian workers who were constructing military installations on the island. They raised money to buy a low-powered transmitter and other equipment and before long had constructed a studio, a control room, and an auditorium. It was a good example of military–civilian cooperation, symbolizing (as was pointed out at the time) the nation's unified war effort.

KODK, as the new station was called, began broadcasting on 1 January 1942, for fifteen hours a day, an ambitious schedule for such a small outfit. Its main output was recorded music and news broadcasts, but it also served as a useful outlet for army information. And this time, those running it had taken the precaution of obtaining an operating license from the FCC.

Like the station in Panama, KODK suffered from a lack of network material, but one day Joe E. Brown, the film and radio comedian, paid a visit during a tour of U.S. bases. As a result, when he got back to

Hollywood, he made sure his friends in the entertainment business sent transcriptions of their radio programs to the station.

Before long, another military radio station was set up in Alaska, again with support from the local civilian population. Station KRAY in Sitka began with a flourish: a 90-minute live variety show, with several bands plus soloists and a dramatic sketch. The station operated from a three-studio complex with an auditorium seating 100 people. It was soon followed by several other military stations elsewhere in Alaska.[7]

What all these separate and mostly uncoordinated developments indicated was that there was a clear need for entertaining the troops. Radio was the easiest method and helped servicemen in isolated units to keep in touch with home and all that was familiar. When soldiers are bored and feel deprived, their morale suffers, and the army chief of staff, General Marshall, set great store by morale—so much so that in March 1941 he created a Morale Branch, under his direct supervision.

The man chosen to head it, after the original appointee fell ill, was a civilian, Frederick Osborn, who achieved the considerable distinction of being promoted instantly to the rank of Brigadier General. He was a friend of President Roosevelt and chairman of the Rockefeller Foundation. Before his sudden military promotion, he had headed a high-powered Washington body, the Joint Army–Navy Committee on Welfare and Recreation. This committee was responsible for the establishment of the United Service Organizations (USO), so called because it embraced such diverse organizations as the YMCA, the YWCA, the National Catholic Community Service, the National Jewish Welfare Board, and the Salvation Army. Its task, performed with notable success, was to provide off-duty services and comforts to members of the armed forces (and, on occasion, to civilian workers in war plants). The 2,500 USO clubs in the United States and overseas, and the USO camp shows, proved enormously popular with America's servicemen and women.[8]

The new brigadier general established a Special Service Division, and it was decided that one of its jobs should be to inform American servicemen and women why they were fighting. It was General Marshall himself who chose the noted Hollywood film director Frank Capra to undertake this particular role. Capra, who had just been drafted into the Army Signal Corps, had directed such notable films as the Academy-Award-winning *It Happened One Night*, *Mr. Deeds Goes to Town*, and *Lost Horizon*. In the army, he was to produce a series of documentary films under the title *Why We Fight*, explaining the war and its causes to the men and women in uniform. It came to be regarded as one of the most outstanding film documentaries ever made.

At the same time, the army was planning an even more ambitious radio setup, and to run this it had its eyes on a man called Tom Lewis. He was well known and respected in Hollywood, with a reputation as a person who got things done. He was married to the movie star Loretta Young and was vice-president in charge of radio production at Young and Rubicam, one of the country's biggest advertising agencies, based in Hollywood. Within a short time Lewis found he had exchanged his desk at the advertising agency for a commission in the U.S. Army.

His brief was a daunting one. He was told that the army wanted a worldwide radio service that would be bigger than all the commercial radio companies put together. The aim was to give the military listeners the news from home wherever they were plus every kind of entertainment, from top comedy shows and the best in popular music to the greatest possible range of sporting events. "We want them to know that we care" was to be the maxim by which he worked.

Lewis set to work at once to plan how to go about his new job. He pinpointed the places overseas where, in the rapidly expanding war, the armed forces were most likely to be fighting. Given the distances and the number of time zones involved, he realized the new service would have to be on the air twenty-four hours a day. He estimated how much material he would require: studios, radio equipment, transmitters, receivers by the thousand. He worked out what programming would need to be specially created from scratch, what could be adapted from network broadcasts. His first task was to find premises, and eventually he moved into the old 20th Century Fox lot in Hollywood, which Frank Capra had also selected for his offices. Lewis then began recruiting staff and quickly gathered around him some of the leading names in the radio business, executives as well as writers. Many were former colleagues of his who had been called up; others volunteered. Among them were some of the top comedy writers, responsible for producing the scripts for stars such as Jack Benny and Bob Hope.

Lewis's new empire was unofficially given the title of the Armed Forces Radio Service (though technically it was, and remained for some time, the Radio Section of the Morale Services Division of the War Department).[9] It came into being on 26 May 1942, but unfortunately it had not yet been allotted a budget. So to get things going, Lewis made temporary use of a fund set aside for "the welfare of the enlisted man"— but he had to guarantee, using his own personal bank account, the $50,000 he took out!

Soon after taking over, Lewis made a trip to Alaska so that he could see at first hand the way the small military stations there were operating. It gave him a much clearer understanding of the audience he would be catering for and the kind of programs they would expect. As a result, these became something of a model for future AFRS stations.

Money was still proving a problem, but by now Lewis had established relations with the organization that was shortly to become the Office of War Information. That did have a budget, and it guaranteed that it would finance the setting up of the American Forces Network in Britain and make all the necessary arrangements to keep it going until the AFRS became fully operational.

Lewis drew up a memorandum on program policy. He decided first of all that AFRS would use recording discs for the bulk of its broadcasts (other than live commentaries on sporting events) rather than shortwave transmissions, which were liable to be affected by atmospheric conditions. The output would come from two main sources: commercial network broadcasts and such programs as AFRS produced itself. Lewis already had his eye on the highly successful *Command Performance*, which, as previously noted, was the brainchild of the Radio Division of the Public Relations Bureau of the War Department. By now, the responsibility for it had been absorbed by the OWI, which had no inclination to let it go.

A long battle ensued which was by no means solely about *Command Performance*. The OWI had taken over several other broadcast services for the armed forces and, just as importantly, had control of the transmitters and studios to do it. It took well over a year of sometimes heated negotiations before Lewis got his way. In the end, the OWI agreed to relinquish control of all radio shows for the troops and also make its shortwave facilities available to the AFRS. By then, relations between the two organizations were so strained that on Lewis's orders military guards stood by to exclude OWI personnel when his people were using their studios!

It should be emphasized that Lewis was not merely empire building. There was a genuine difference of principle between the two. The OWI was in the business of propaganda. The head of AFRS saw his job as bringing the voice of home to the men overseas. His aim, he said later, was to establish a 24-hour worldwide broadcasting service "free of propaganda and totally operated by soldiers for the welfare of soldiers."[10]

Nevertheless, two branches of the U.S. government involved in a world war had spent months wrangling about who should control what. Lewis admitted he did not find the military mind easy to cope with. Whatever the men at the very top, like General Marshall, felt about the importance of morale, there were many lower down in the army leadership—and elsewhere in government in Washington—who needed convincing that radio was so important in the military scheme of things. They controlled vital resources Lewis needed, such as the vinylite used in the manufacture of the program recordings that would soon be going out in considerable volume to the growing network of AFRS broadcasting stations.

In deciding to record its programs on such a scale, AFRS was breaking new ground. Before the war, most network radio programs were broadcast live. Amazingly, to cope with the time differences between the East and West Coasts it was customary to perform the same show twice within a few hours. It was a tenet of faith among many network broadcasting executives that audiences wanted live shows: AFRS proved them wrong.

The broadcasters themselves appreciated the change. AFRS shows were often allowed to run for forty-five or fifty minutes, then the best thirty minutes were chosen for broadcast. Entertainers were not fighting against the clock and did not have to rush through their shows, so they gave more relaxed and polished performances. As a result, after the war many of them demanded the same freedom from the constraints of time, and ultimately the networks gave way, especially after Bing Crosby switched from NBC, which banned recordings, to ABC, which had no objection to them.

Recordings, or transcriptions, were used by AFRS for several reasons. The sound quality was far superior to shortwave broadcasting, which was subject to fading and interference. It gave stations scheduling flexibility since they could transmit programs at whatever time they wished. And unlike live transmissions, there was a measure of security control over the material broadcast. The recordings had to be shipped out to the units that broadcast them, which required a well-organized distribution system. It also took time; however, since there was no pressing urgency about comedy or music, the need for quality was considered more important.

Lewis and AFRS set to work on a major recording program. And in order to help the transcription industry on the West Coast expand at a rapid rate, AFRS was able to bring political pressure to bear to give transcription companies top priority in obtaining materials and staff as well as the building permits when necessary.

The process of transferring and editing half-hour programs from a pair of original master discs on to new sixteen-inch masters from which the final copies were pressed was an art in itself. It needed a great deal of precision: one mistake, one playing needle dropped onto the disc in the wrong place, and the whole process had to be started all over again. Editing apart, there were other problems. As the master disc was cut, the waste material had to be siphoned off. One engineer recalls experimenting with a big industrial vacuum cleaner in a soundproof closet connected to smaller hoses close to the cutting-head. At first, the suction was so strong it lifted the disc off the lathe! Care also needed to be taken with the waste, which contained nitrocellulose—an ingredient of TNT—and was highly volatile. At one stage, it had been siphoned into a water-filled container, which passing personnel were apparently occasionally tempted to use as an ashtray if the lid had been left off. It was not a habit that lasted long. . . . But the engineers soon mastered the problems and techniques involved, and AFRS became very much a pioneer in disc editing and the assembly of recorded programs on any sort of scale. In doing so, it made a real contribution to the development of the broadcasting industry.[11]

One of the main purposes of the editing was to remove commercials from network programs. The decision to do so, originally taken by the OWI, aroused some controversy. It was pointed out by their officers that the men liked the commercials because it made them feel at home. However, it was felt that it would be wrong for the U.S. government "to speak to the world with the voice of commercialism." Then again, the advertisements would tend to make military personnel want things they couldn't get. The point was emphasized when men on Bataan, desperately short of food, were treated to a description of the "rich, creamy goodness" of some brand of ice cream. And it was borne in mind that when AFRS began broadcasting in Britain through AFN, the use of commercials was bound to cause problems with the BBC, as has already been seen.[12]

Although the bulk of the AFRS output was on disk, it also ran a thriving shortwave section broadcasting over 100 hours of programs a week. Apart from play-by-play sport commentaries and the usual network shows, these included six hours of its own programming. Other than news, it set great store by a daily fifteen-minute program called *Hometown Highlights,* which relayed stories and interviews about happenings in smalltown America and was apparently greatly appreciated by men far from home. AFRS paid close attention to what its listeners wanted. Changes were made as a result of suggestions they put forward. Interestingly, they were not keen on westerns, much preferring mystery dramas—especially if they introduced a flavor of horror. News was obviously a key part of the output. The aim there was to give the forces the same sort of news and information service as they could expect back in the United States, free from any suggestion of government manipulation. "The average GI could hear another GI giving out the same news heard by his family at home. He could depend upon its veracity," Lewis said later. "That . . . was not only morally correct, it was good American common sense."[13]

The service personnel stationed in the United States were not neglected, even though they were able to listen to the normal commercial broadcasting stations. There was enough AFRS programming of relevance to them, apart from military information broadcasts, to justify feeding them the entire output (in most cases by landline, a technique that Lewis had noticed being used successfully on his trip to Alaska).

While Lewis aimed to have all military broadcasting units under a single unified command, there was one that came into being without even knowing about AFRS. When the Allies invaded North Africa in November 1942, a small unit was deputed to broadcast instructions in

French to the civilian population, with the aim of averting unnecessary bloodshed. It was under the command of Lieutenant Andre Baruch, in peacetime a popular radio announcer (he presented *Your Hit Parade*, among other shows), who had worked with Lewis before the war and was the husband of the singer Bea Wain. After the invasion, he persuaded General Patton, the army commander, to let him set up a broadcast station in Casablanca for the American forces in the area. One of its notable successes was a locally written drama featuring Humphrey Bogart and Frederic March, who happened to be on a USO tour in North Africa and who knew Baruch from his days in the entertainment industry back home. In time, the impromptu broadcasting unit developed into the American Expeditionary Station (AES), which was eventually drawn into the AFRS and broadcast widely throughout the Mediterranean for the rest of the war. By January of 1944, eight stations were operating, from Casablanca to Naples. From there, a two-vehicle "radio station on wheels" slogged all the way up the leg of Italy with the U.S. forces, carrying its own 90-foot aerials, with a power unit and mobile studio, until finally it was able to establish a firm base in Rome. Within a year, there were eight separate stations in Italy alone, a "remarkable growth" story.[14] An indication of the power of some of the transmitters is that AES Rome was heard clearly as far away as Stockholm.

It was, by all accounts, an enterprising outfit, and unlike AFN it made good radio use of the women serving overseas. *Barracks Bag*, the AES counterpart of *Duffle Bag*, was presented from Rome by Anita Love of the American Red Cross. Corporal Frances Rudman ("your buddy Ruddy") compared the Florence station's record-request show, and a similar program broadcast on Sundays from Leghorn that had a WAC from Texas, Margie Smith, at the microphone. Local talent was much in evidence too. AES had its own weekly *Mediterranean Hit Parade*, and one of the top numbers was a tune unknown in the United States called **Somewhere on Via Roma**, written by Pfc. John Forte, a musician from Philadelphia. It proved so popular that it was recorded by the AFRS Orchestra and broadcast on shortwave around the world.[15]

The AES, differing as it did from AFN, was an example of the variety to be found right across the Armed Forces Radio Service. AFRS provided the basic material and let the stations get on with it, each differing according to the tastes and background of those in charge.

NOTES

1. Information provided by Alan Davies, author of a number of articles on broadcasting during the Spanish Civil War.

2. Alan Davies, "The Catastrophe Transmitters," in *Radio Bygones*, June/July 1998.

3. Information supplied by Gregor Prumb of Krefeld University.

4. Doreen Taylor, *A Microphone and a Frequency* (Heinemann 1983), p. 6.

5. Briggs, *History*, Vol. III, pp. 126–129 et seq.

6. Ibid.

7. *History of AFRTS*, pp. 6–9.

8. *Encyclopaedia of World War II*.

9. The precise if complex genesis of AFRS is set out fully in a note in the National Archive files (RG330, format Y, 61A): "The Armed Forces Radio and Television Service began operations as the Civilian Contact Section of the Morale Division which was established in the Army Adjutant General's Office, effective 22 July 1940 by Mobilization Regulation 1–10 (1939). The Morale Branch replaced the Morale Division on 8 March 1941: the latter division was abolished by War Department letter 353.8 (3 March 1941) M and the broadcasting functions of CCS were transferred to the new branch's Radio Section. Though the Morale Branch continued to form a part of the AGO, it functioned directly under the control and supervision of the Army's Chief of Staff in accordance with General Orders No 2 of 14 April 1941. Following a succession of reorganizations and redesignations of the Morale Branch and specifically its supersession by the Morale Services Division on 30 November 1943, the Radio Section was renamed the Armed Forces Radio Service by AG's letter 311.23 of 15 December 1943. Previously however with the appointment of Lt. Col. Thomas [Tom] H. A. Lewis as commanding officer of the Radio Section on 26 May 1942, the Radio Service had operated unofficially thereafter as the Armed Forces Radio Service."

10. *History of AFRTS*, pp. 14–17, 19–22.

11. Ibid., pp. 31–34; Barnouw, *Golden Web*, p. 194. The information on editing techniques and the "explosive" water containers was provided by Marty Halperin, a former AFRS engineer. For the technically minded, the transcription masters were single-sided 16-inch, metal-based discs (normally aluminum, but when aluminum ran short because of the demands of war production, glass was used). They were coated with cellulose nitrate and although commonly called acetates, were apparently more properly referred to as "lacquers." These were copied onto two further masters, each of 15 minutes' duration, and from these the final pressings were made; these were the discs that went to the broadcasting units in the field. They were 16-inch, double-sided, made of virtually unbreakable vinyl (or a variant thereof), and running at 33⅓ rpm.

12. *History of AFRTS*, p. 29.

13. Ibid. (the reference to shortwave broadcasting is on p. 58; to troops' preferences, p. 29, and to Lewis on news, p. 22).

14. Briggs, *History*, Vol. III, p. 648.

15. *Stars and Stripes* (Mediterranean edition), various issues between March and May 1945.

Colonel Tom Lewis, wartime head of AFRS.

V-disk label of one of Glenn Miller's best-remembered numbers.

PROGRAMME

Monday, October 23rd, at 7 p.m.
"STARS IN BATTLEDRESS." A Musical Novelty
DANCING TO HAL KENT'S BAND

Tuesday, October 24th
DANCING TO HAL KENT'S BAND

Thursday, October 26th

THE AMERICAN BAND OF THE A.E.F.

conducted by

MAJOR GLENN MILLER

Executive Officer Lt. Don W. Haynes
Programme Director W.O. Paul Dudley

Piano	S/Sgt. Mel Powell	
	Cpl. Jack Rosin	
Drums	T/Sgt. Ray McKinley	
Guitar	Cpl. Frank Ippolito	
Bass	Sgt. Carmen Mastren	
	S/Sgt. Trigger Alpert	
	Cpl. Joe Shulman	
Trumpets	M/Sgt. Zeke Zarchy	
	Sgt. Bob Nichols	
	Sgt. Whitey Thomas	
	Sgt. Bernie Privin	
	Cpl. Jack Steel	
Trombones	Sgt. Jimmy Priddy	
	Cpl. John Halliburton	
	P.F.C. Nat Peck	
	Cpl. Larry Hall	
Vocalist	Sgt. Johnnie Desmond	
Crew Chiefs	Sgt. Steve Steck	
	Cpl. Eugene Steck	
	Cpl. Arthur Malvin	
	Cpl. Murray Kane	
	Cpl. Lynn Allison	
Saxophones	S/Sgt. Hank Freeman	
	Sgt. Michael Hucko	
	Sgt. Vince Carbone	
	Sgt. Jack Ferrier	
	Cpl. Fred Guerra	
	Cpl. Mann Thaler	

Violins N/Sgt. George Ockner
S/Sgt. Harry Katzman
Cpl. Ernest Kardos
Cpl. Eugene Bergen
N/Sgt. Carl Swanson
Cpl. Milton Edelson
Sgt. Dave Herman
Cpl. Phil Coglizno
Cpl. Joseph Kowalewski
Sgt. Dave Schwartz
Cpl. Henry Brynan
Cpl. Earl Cornwell
P.F.C. Fred Ostrowsky
Cpl. Morris Bialkin
Cpl. Bob Ripley
Cpl. Stanley Harris
Sgt. Emanuel Wishnow
Cpl. Dave Sackson
Cpl. Nole Kaproff
Cpl. Richard Macolinski

French Horns Cpl. Addison Collins, Jnr.

Arrangers T/Sgt. Jerry Gray
M/Sgt. Norm Leyden
S/Sgt. Ralph Wilkinson
N/Sgt. Jimmy Jackson

GUEST ARTISTS

and

Production T/Sgt. George Voutsas and Sgt. Harry Hartwick
Stage Manager Sgt. Julius Zittelbat
Announcer Cpl. Paul Dubov
Assistant Executive Officers T/Sgt. Jack Sanderson and Cpl. Tom Cochran

Producer for the Queensberry All-Services Club: JOHN HARDING

Friday, October 27th
CARNIVAL NIGHT
DANCING TO TOMMY KEMP'S BAND

Saturday, October 28th

"THE CANADA SHOW"

THE NEW CANADIAN BAND OF THE A.E.F.

Conducted by Captain ROBERT FARNON (Canada's foremost Composer)

Trumpets	George Anderson	Drums	Cliff Knowlton
	Fred Davis	Soloists	Jeanne Dallas, C.W.A.C.
	Harry Freedman		Paul Carpenter
	Ron Neal	The	Margaret Hubbard, C.W.A.C.
Trombones	Floyd Roberts	"Canada"	Helen Farrell, C.W.A.C.
	Gary Hughes	Show"	Phyllis Gilliard, C.W.A.C.
	Bob Bland	Chorus	Evelyn Seaman, C.W.A.C.
Saxophones	J.Def. Wiechler		Ila Goudianing, C.W.A.C.
	Norm Barber		George Harrison
	George Naylor		Gerry Travers
	Ken He-lo		Jack McKeachie
Violins	Waldo Farnham		Albert Love
	Stan Kolt		Wally Goertz
	Joe Ezreti		Mac Pace
	Lou Herschenbaren		Gabe Lalonde
	Bob Latimer		Joy Portneus, C.W.A.C.
	George Yachmini	Writing Staff	Sherry Wills, C.W.A.C.
	Reuben Saxhur		Ben Valentine
	Roy Basse		Wilf Davidson
Violas	Jack Needham		Dick Misener
	Leo Danulyk		Dr. B. Holly
	Gil Markinson		Lieut. Douglass Montgomery
'Cellos	Tadeusz Hadiri'awn	Arrangers	Tony Braden
	Charles Dajok		Bob Farnon
Piano	Cliff McAtee	Administra-	S.Q.M.S. Quartley
Celeste	Jeanne Dallas, C.W.A.C.	tive Staff	J. Puff
Guitar	George Arthur		M. Gibson
Bags	Bowie Barans		

Announcer Lieut. CHARMIAN SANSOM, C.W.A.C.

GUEST ARTISTS

and

Sunday, October 29th. From 6 to 7 p.m.

"VARIETY BAND BOX"

JOHN BLORE AND HIS DANCE ORCHESTRA
PETER SINCLAIR—EDDIE HORAN—PAT LEONARD
MARILYN WILLIAMS—TED & BARBARA ANDREWS
THE VICTOR FELDMAN TRIO—VIOLET CARSON

M.C.: PAT LEONARD

DANCING TO HAL KENT'S BAND

A typical Queensberry Club musical program.

AFN's Keith Jameson doing an AEFP stint from a BBC studio.

HUBERT *by SGT. DICK WINGERT*

"This is the American Forces Network, broadcasting to YOU, The Fighting Men of the United Nations!"

V A L E N T I N E   G R E E T I N G S

from

THE OFFICERS AND STAFF OF THE AMERICAN FORCES NETWORK

Etousa

Typical of the humor that made AFN so popular.

1D.

THE STARS AND STRIPES

1D.

Daily Newspaper of U.S. Armed Forces

in the European Theater of Operations

Vol. 3   No. 207   New York, N.Y.—London, England   Saturday, July 3, 1943

Jap New Georgia Headquarters Struck

ETO Radio Network on Air Sunday

American-Type Programs Scheduled Daily for U.S. Forces

A "back home" radio program, designed to provide U.S. forces in the ETO with American-slanted broadcast, will get under way tomorrow at 5.45 PM. Shows recorded for the United States for troop broadcasts, Stars and Stripes news bulletins and special features will be presented.

Offered by the American Forces Network and administered by the Special Service Section, SOS, ETO, the program will operate with the cooperation of the British Broadcasting Corporation. The new service marks the first time Britain has granted broadcasting facilities on its home territory to an allied nation. There will be no interference with reception of BBC programs in areas covered by the American Forces Network.

An all-American radio staff, made up of soldiers who have had radio experience back in the States, will prepare part of the program. Two daily features will be "Sports News," gathered and presented by The Stars and Stripes, at 7 PM, and "Final Edition," the S and S round-up of world and sports events at 10 PM.

Top-Flight Radio Stars

Recorded shows of Bob Hope, Bing Crosby, Jack Benny, Dinah Shore, Fibber

Next Stop—Jap Territory?

New York Times Photo

These fresh U.S. troops disembarked recently at an undisclosed South Pacific port as reinforcements for Lt. Gen. Walter Krueger's Sixth Army, according to the caption on this picture just received in London. The Sixth Army, last reports show, was based in Australia as part of the Allied force commanded by Gen. Douglas MacArthur, who is directing the present island offensive in the South Seas.

Allied Air Attacks Crippling

U.S. Calls Advances Merely Preparatory To Major Offensive

These Outfits May Be In New Pacific Drive

Here are identification numbers of several Army and Air Force units and their commanders which already have been disclosed in previous Stars and Stripes news stories as based in the South and Southwest Pacific. Undoubtedly these organizations are included in the U.S. forces now taking part in the Solomons and New Guinea offensive.

25th Division—Maj. Gen. Joseph Collins, Guadalcanal.

32nd Division—Commander not given, New Guinea.

Sixth Army—Lt. Gen. Walter Krueger, Australia.

5th Air Force—Maj. Gen. Ennis C. Whitehead, Australia.

13th Air Force, Maj. Gen. Nathan F. Twining, Guadalcanal, South Pacific.

Foe's Munda Airport Menaced by Planes, Artillery, Troops

WASHINGTON, July 2.—American dive-bombers hammered today at what was believed to be the headquarters of Japanese forces on New Georgia Island, four miles from the big air field at Munda, as ground forces continued mopping-up operations on nearby Rendova Island and other scattered points of resistance.

Authoritative sources here, meanwhile, emphasized that the sudden American sweep northward through the Solomons was not a major offensive in itself, but rather a prelude to such an offensive.

Rejecting the much-criticized and "necessary" slow "island-to-island" policy, the United States forces have attempted to gain bases—particularly airfields—from which a real offensive can be launched, it was said.

Air Score: 123 to 25

The cost of the advance so far has been surprisingly small, according to figures reported by Adm. William F. Halsey, commander of South Pacific naval forces. His headquarters announced today that 123 Japanese planes were shot down over

Germans Shoot Greek Leaders

AFN is front-page news in *Stars and Stripes*. (By permission of the National Tribune Corporation)

The AFN uniform shoulder flash.

AFN's Hoechst Castle home in Frankfurt.

AFN birthday celebrations. The elderly civilian on the left of the loudspeaker is Sir Noel Ashbridge of the BBC. To the right is General Roy Barker and next to him is Colonel John Hayes, the head of AFN.

e AFN team that brought a welcome ray of sunshine.

atification logos and shoulder flashes.

Grosvenor Square, January 3, 1943.

80 Portland Place.

"Being but humble sergeants and corporals . . ." in front of AFN mike.

GI Jill with guest Bing Crosby.

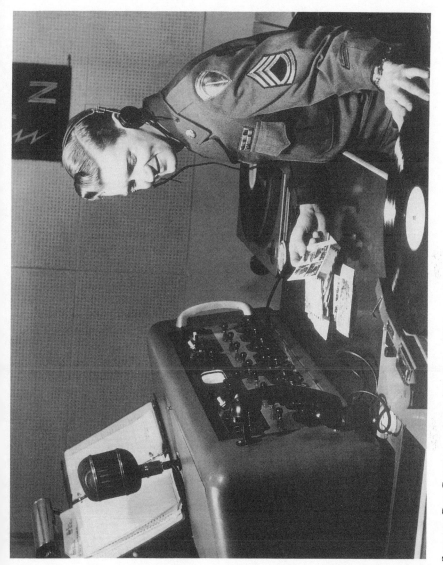

Sergeant Don Cosgrove spins a disk at the AFN console.

SEVEN

"The Greatest Radio Show in History"

As the war went on, the head of the Armed Forces Radio Service made it his policy to transfer to AFRS anyone from the radio industry found in the armed forces. Before long he had a highly professional, talented staff such as no commercial network could have afforded—and it was one that, without the financial pressures of the business world, could afford to take risks and had much more creative freedom. Given the writing and production expertise at his disposal, Colonel Lewis (as he now was) soon found the Hollywood stars lining up to volunteer their services. AFRS began turning out dozens of weekly programs featuring the big names in show business—actors, comedians, musicians, singers.

Although it was not AFRS's own creation, undoubtedly the jewel in the crown was *Command Performance*, a half-hour program of music and comedy featuring a dazzling array of talent. The original idea came from Glenn Wheaton, a Hollywood radio producer and scriptwriter. It is said that when it was suggested that the stars should be requested to appear, his response was: "Request, hell! Command them."[1] And so *Command Performance* it became. As producer he recruited Vic Knight, who gave up a thousand dollars a week producing the Fred Allen show to work for a nominal dollar a year, though when he was drafted into the army as a private his salary rose to a princely $21 a month.

The thought was that the forces should be able to "command" their favorite performers to appear on the program. And so they did, on a scale no commercial program could have matched. Apart from the stars, the program also broadcast special requests from servicemen missing the sounds of home: the noise of the traffic on Fifth Avenue, a slot machine hitting the jackpot, church bells ringing, fresh milk from a cow splashing into the milking pail, a baby crying. Perhaps the oddest request came from a sailor at Pearl Harbor: "Would Carole Landis step up to the microphone and just sigh—that's all." Miss Landis duly obliged, though what was so special about her sigh was never explained.[2]

The first program went out on 8 March 1942 and featured Eddie Cantor, Dinah Shore, Danny Kaye, Merle Oberon, and singer Bea Wain. Troops in Iceland had asked for something from the world of sport, so they were obliged with a re-run of the recently fought heavyweight championship bout in which Joe Louis knocked out Buddy Baer in the first round. And as a special touch of home, the Western Union boys sang a birthday telegram.

The first half-dozen programs were produced in New York, but it then moved to Hollywood, where so much of the talent of the entertainment world was based. A list of the stars who appeared on the show reads like a Hollywood *Who's Who*. The 1944 Christmas broadcast, for example, included Bob Hope as master of ceremonies, with Judy Garland, Dorothy Lamour, Danny Kaye, Spencer Tracy, Jack Benny, Fred Allen, Jimmy Durante, Dinah Shore, Frances Langford, Ginny Simms, and four of the top orchestras of the day. The *Los Angeles Daily News* called it "the greatest radio show in history," and it was estimated that if the show had been produced commercially the stars alone would have cost $150,000.[3]

In fact, the program had virtually no budget and paid no money to anyone. The radio networks provided their studios and staff for nothing. And the stars gave their services free. They considered *Command Performance* and the other shows AFRS produced part of their contribution to the war effort. At the beginning, concern had been expressed that performers could not be expected to provide an unlimited amount of free service, and arrangements would need to be made to cover the very heavy costs involved. But throughout the war, radio and film stars gave their time and talents unstintingly without any cost to the government.

Indeed, so eager were they to volunteer their services that some were in danger of being overused. So AFRS set up a special section made up of some of the leading talent agents in the broadcasting business, who were now in the forces. With their expert knowledge, they were able to liaise with the Hollywood Victory Committee (the industry's coordinating body dealing with entertainers' wartime activities) to make sure the load was spread evenly. This was essential, since apart from their normal radio and film commitments, stars appeared in an endless series of USO shows, Victory Bond rallies, and many other public engagements.

The most frequently used performer on *Command Performance* was Dinah Shore, with thirty-five appearances, followed by Bing Crosby (29), Bob Hope (26), Jimmy Durante (19), Frances Langford (18), and

Judy Garland (15), all of whom were specially requested by men in the services.[4]

Apart from the fact that it cost practically nothing, *Command Performance* was economical in other ways. Since the programs were not restricted to the usual half hour, there was often untransmitted material left over. On one occasion, when an even larger than usual star cast had been assembled, the recording ran to seventy-five minutes, which not only provided enough material for two whole programs but left enough over to make up a third when it was added to the earlier untransmitted broadcasts.

One problem the program makers had to overcome in dealing with network programs was the fact that at the end of shows the commercial sponsor was often mentioned several times in a short period of time, making it difficult to cut, so it was decided to record special openings and closings without any advertising references. Another difficulty was that cutting out commercials created gaps that had to be filled. To overcome this, a collection of musical cuts from programs that were allowed to overrun were assembled as a "fill-in" library when needed. AFN in Britain developed a similar technique to cover out-of-date topical references in transcriptions discs which had reached them late.

Before it took control of *Command Performance*, AFRS developed its own version of what was clearly a winning formula. The first such program entirely of AFRS's own making was *Mail Call*. This was designed to be "a letter written by the folks at home to a serviceman abroad." The early issues included a feature, "What's Going on at Home," followed-up by a brief sound-clip from a current film using the stars featured in the picture. But this made for unexciting listening, and before long the format was changed so that *Mail Call* more closely resembled *Command Performance*. The first program was recorded on 11 August 1942 and had as MC Loretta Young, the film star wife of the head of AFRS.

Like *Command Performance*, *Mail Call* had a distinctive introduction announced each week to a stirring bugle call: "*Mail Call* from the United States of America. Stand by Americans. Here's *Mail Call*, one big package of words and music and laughter delivered to you by the stars from whom you want to hear in answer to the requests you send to the Armed Forces Radio Service in Los Angeles USA."

The *Command Performance* opening became even more famously familiar: "*Command Performance* USA, the greatest entertainers in America, as requested by you the men and women of the United States Armed Forces throughout the world. *Command Performance* presented this week and every week until it's over—over there."[5]

The announcers intoning these words were just as well-known. The two best remembered are Ken Carpenter (145 appearances in all), whose announcing repertoire also included the Kraft Music Hall and the Edgar Bergen–Charlie McCarthy Show; and Harry von Zell, whose jovial tones were widely heard on a number of other radio shows, including Burns and Allen, Eddie Cantor, and Fred Allen. Another noted announcer with *Command Performance* and *Mail Call* was Don Wilson, who was familiar from his many appearances as comedy foil on the Jack Benny Show.[6]

One of the most innovative and successful of the AFRS programs was *Jubilee*, produced by Mann Holiner, who had specialized in black theatricals in peacetime and who had launched the careers of many noted black variety stars in a successful show of the same name. It first went on the air in October 1942 and featured such notable black performers as Lena Horne, Duke Ellington, Count Basie, and Eddie Anderson (famous as the gravelly-voiced Rochester on the Jack Benny show). The MC was the jovial Ernie "Bubbles" Whitman, and apart from "negro humor" there was a good deal of jazz and jive, which helped to make it popular with a wide range of listeners. Holiner came under pressure from General Benjamin Davis, then the only black general in the army, who wanted the program slanted even more so it would boost the morale of black troops. But Holiner was reluctant to do so, arguing that it would tend to emphasize the division between black and white in the armed forces. Eventually, the general was persuaded, and it became established AFRS policy that there would be no programs aimed specifically at any particular minority during the war. Later, when the low morale of black servicemen became a matter of concern, efforts were made to have black performers on *Command Performance* and, at the same time, whites on *Jubilee*, so that both shows were seen to be racially integrated, an important precedent for AFRS.[7]

GI Journal was a program that attracted a big audience. It was a half-hour "radio newspaper of the AEF, the paper that prints the poems and jokes sent in by you men overseas." These were nowhere near as dire as they might sound, apart from which there was a liberal spicing of music and comedy from top stars, assisted by "Private Sad Sack," a typical military buffoon army listeners delighted in. Each week, the program had a different celebrity as editor. When zany humorists like Groucho Marx or Kay Kyser occupied the editorial chair, comic mayhem was assured. Another AFRS program aimed at a particular audience was *Melody Roundup*, featuring many of the leading Country and Western singers and hosted initially by the cowboy crooner Roy Rogers. Other programs included *Personal Album*, given over to one particular performer (women vocalists to start with), and in a different vein *Yarns For Yanks*, a fifteen-minute telling of human-interest stories by a host of Hollywood stars. *Remember* featured the film actor Fred MacMurray, introducing a quarter-hour look back at events and the favorite music from a particular month in the recent past.[8]

Before long, AFRS had its own orchestra, conducted by Meridith Willson. He had been an orchestra leader on a number of radio programs in the early 1940s on the West Coast and had been given the rank of major after volunteering soon after AFRS came into being. It was he who set up the Armed Forces Radio Orchestra, a large, concert-style orchestra whose famous members included Les Paul, the noted guitar player. The orchestra, and its various sub-units, played everything from light music to jazz, and it appeared on many AFRS-produced programs. A particular favorite was *At Ease*, fifteen minutes of uninterrupted music.[9]

Meridith Willson apart, it is said the bandleader who made more AFRS broadcasts than anyone else was the "King of Swing" himself, Benny Goodman. He had his own weekly program, was a guest on other artists' shows, and also regularly played on *AFRS Magic Carpet*.

Probably the most popular performer on AFRS, and certainly the one who made the biggest impact on the troops' morale, was a young woman who was known as GI Jill. She presented a fifteen-minute daily program with the title *GI Jive*. It was a simple formula—a collection of record requests, some cheerful banter from GI Jill, and occasional interviews with celebrities such as Bing Crosby, Frank Sinatra, and Dinah Shore. It was the personality of Jill that made the program. She had a distinctive, charmingly reedy voice, and she was, to quote one listener, "warm, affectionate, intimate. Perfect for homesick servicemen far from home." To the GI she *was* the girl back home, and she had a nice homely touch. She would tell them she was just back from downtown San Francisco, where she'd been buying the records they were about to hear. In fact, many of the discs she played had not been released commercially, but the troops were not to know that. They wrote to her by the thousand, and to those who asked she sent a signed photograph of herself. She accounted for a quarter of all the letters AFRS received, and she answered most of them herself.

What was never revealed to the thousands of homesick servicemen who sighed longingly at the sound of her voice was her real name, Martha Wilkerson. Nor the fact that the 25-year-old presenter was married, with a young family. Her husband was Mort Werner, a senior broadcasting and advertising executive who for a time produced her program himself.

The effect she had on her listeners is summed up in this letter from a sergeant in the Pacific: "Your cheerful voice does wonders to our morale. Tokyo Rose is also on the air. It's as if two women of enemy countries were battling for men's minds. I'm glad you're winning, Jill." She was sometimes referred to as America's answer to Tokyo Rose and Axis Sally, but unlike those two ladies there was never any hint of propaganda in any of her programs.

Her sign-off became famous, related as it was to the fact that her program was heard all over the world in many different time zones: "Good morning to some of you, good afternoon to some more of you, and to the rest of you: Goodnight."[10]

GI Jill's program emphasized the importance of music to the servicemen abroad. Certainly it was a craving the AFRS programming laid great stress on. *Yank Bandstand* featured music from the service bands of the Army, Navy, Marines, and Coastguard. *One Night Stand* was a half-hour showpiece for the top orchestras, broadcast every single night. *Showtime*, presented by the ever popular Dinah Shore, "brings you the hit tunes from America's hit musical shows." And the thrice-weekly *Spotlight Bands* traveled to army camps, naval bases, and industrial plants all over the country, "taking Americans their favorite music played by their favorite bands, the nation's top bands playing the nation's top tunes." It started out as a Coca Cola–sponsored production in November 1941, but by early 1943 AFRS had started its own Spotlight Bands series along the same lines.

Also widely listened to was *Your Hit Parade.* This had been on the air since 1935, but when war began it provided another link with home. But the version the servicemen and women overseas heard was not the same as the one broadcast in the United States. It was a special repeat, with the same tunes in the same order but with one crucial difference: the performers were different. For example, the *Your Hit Parade* of 17 June 1944 broadcast to the home audience had Helen Forrest singing the No. 1 tune, **Long Ago and Far Away**, followed by **I'll Be Seeing You** at No. 2, sung by Bing Crosby, and **I'll Get By** at No. 3, with Dick Haymes as the vocalist. But the version put out by AFRS, although it featured the same three tunes in identical order, had Frank Sinatra singing the top tune, Bea Wain the second, while the third was sung by the Hit Paraders. Even more pointedly, in a later *Your Hit Parade*, the song that Bing Crosby made famous, **Swingin' on a Star,** was in sixth place and sung by Bing himself. But in the parallel AFRS show the artiste was Joan Edwards with the Hit Paraders.[11] Indeed, as already noted, it was Sinatra's appearances on *Your Hit Parade* that made his name with the GIs overseas, especially as new records were then in short supply because of a recording dispute. Thus he was able to reach a huge audience that otherwise would not have been available to him.

There was another odd twist to this juxtaposing of *Your Hit Parade.* In Britain, the musical magazine *Melody Maker* regularly published the U.S. hit parade. It, too, was identical to the American one, but it was always weeks late. Thus the list published on 15 January 1944 was actually the *Your Hit Parade* broadcast in America on 20 November 1943, seven weeks earlier. If it had arrived by mail, the delay would have been understandable since letters crossing the Atlantic in wartime were understandably slow to travel. But as the program could be heard in Britain on AFN, it seems strange that publication should have been so behindhand.[12]

One of the criteria for establishing the standings of tunes played on *Your Hit Parade* was the number of times a piece of music was requested on radio or played on a jukebox. However, the musicians got no recompense for these playings, despite pressing repeatedly for payment. Finally, its patience exhausted, the American Federation of Musicians told the four major record companies that from August 1942 they would refuse to take part in any more recordings unless royalties were forthcoming.[13] The supply of new music on record speedily dried up. But the troops in the field wanted to play records of current hits and the new singers they heard on radio programs. To meet that demand, the U.S. Army began the V-disc project. They reached agreement with the musicians' federation for recording orchestras and vocalists, provided the recordings were for U.S. servicemen only and were not used for commercial purposes.

So in the two years the musicians' dispute lasted, the V-discs filled the gap—at any rate, as far as the armed forces were concerned. It is generally accepted that the V referred to Victory, but there is a suggestion it was actually named after Captain (later Major) George Vincent, who ran the project. One account attributes this to his secretary, but another suggests that Vincent personally named the discs after himself!

Some recordings were taken from broadcasts or concert recitals, some from film soundtracks, many at specially arranged recording sessions which often produced unique combinations of artists since contractual obligations were not a factor. The performances were recorded on 12-inch discs, which were engineered to run for up to six and a half minutes, as against the three and a half minutes of the standard ten-inch 78s, so that gave the artists more time to develop their numbers. And because the records were made of unbreakable vinylite, instead of the usual fragile shellac (in short supply because the main source had vanished when the Japanese took over French Indochina), shipping presented none of the same problems.

Some 900 separate V-discs were produced, comprising over 2,500 musical numbers. And since the V-disc organization was the only one producing new releases of popular tunes during the musicians' dispute, they provided a unique musical record of the popular music of the war years. Although the V-disc organization was not part of AFRS, it was closely linked with it, and, of course, the discs were played regularly on its programs and shipped out to stations such as AFN. The whole project was another example of the way in which the army was prepared to spend money to keep the troops overseas happy, since the V-disc program called for a budget of a million dollars.[14]

AFRS was now expanding at a remarkable rate. By the end of 1943, it had more than 300 outlets operating all over the world, from small outfits serving remote areas of the Pacific to networks like AFN in Britain. The central Pacific was served by what came to be known, for obvious reasons, as the Jungle Network, while the widely scattered islands of the South West Pacific had their own Mosquito Network. The ever-present danger there, apart from the Japanese, was malaria, which was countered by a drug called Atabrine. It was easy to forget to take it regularly, and so, tongue in cheek, the network started the *Atabrine Cocktail Hour*, a program of recorded music which served as a gentle reminder. The Mosquito Network was heard by U.S. forces stationed in New Zealand, thanks to the cooperation of that country's broadcasting service, which provided technicians and a frequency, much like the BBC with AFN. And like that network, the programs were appreciated by civilian listeners. They wrote in saying not only how much they liked what they heard, but praising what it had done for N.Z.–U.S. understanding. "We feel we have learned to appreciate your American viewpoint, and perhaps you have done with regard to us," one listener wrote. So, like its counterpart in Britain, the Mosquito Network made a contribution to improving relations between the Allies.[15]

New Zealand was only one of many countries that cooperated in providing broadcasts for U.S. troops. Altogether, AFRS had agreements with some 140 overseas governments or broadcasting stations so that it could lease air-time to transmit its programs to American forces locally.[16]

All of these scattered networks received their supply of transcription discs mostly by air. Many were "radio stations in a suitcase" (or, to be precise, five suitcases), containing a 50-watt transmitter and all the essential equipment. The 300 outlets receiving the weekly transcription shipments in 1943 had grown to more than 800 by 1945,[17] with the package of recordings being passed on from one outfit to the next. The logistical problems are obvious, and even servicing AFN "just across the Atlantic" was not always straightforward. The "bomber run," as it was known, did not necessarily involve a direct flight across the ocean. Reinforcements for the Eighth Air Force in Britain often took the southern ferry route, especially in the winter, a circuitous journey across the Caribbean, then down to South America before heading towards England by way of French West Africa and French Morocco. Apart from the network of broadcasting stations, AFRS also ran 143 public-address systems overseas and in addition had a so-called Bedside Network in military hospitals throughout the United States.

To help make life easier for those organizing the broadcasts, AFRS provided them with a detailed suggested broadcasting schedule. The accompanying guidance notes give a good indication of the philosophy behind it. For example, the hours 0600 to 0800 and 1100 to 1300 are described as the times when service personnel are preoccupied with the preparations for going on duty. "Programming should then be lively, cheerful and invigorating. . . . Announcements should be short and alertly delivered. Musical selections should be brief, varied, largely popular and preferably melodic."[18] Although that particular example comes from a somewhat later period, it emphasizes the acceptance by those in charge of military broadcasting that "although civilians in uniform make up the audience, it is not a civilian audience," and it was no good simply repeating the domestic broadcasting formula.[19]

By May of 1944, AFRS was producing forty-two hours of broadcasting a week, comprising 106 shows, of which 60 were edited versions of commercial network programs. The journal *Daily Variety* estimated all this output would have cost ten million dollars a year at commercial radio rates. And it was all organized for the armed forces. The only show that was ever broadcast to listeners at home in the United States was a special Christmas Eve edition of *Command Performance* in 1942, which went out on the four major networks. Home listeners were even denied what is regarded as the high point of the AFRS comedy output, the *Dick Tracy Wedding Special*. This two-hour extravaganza had its beginnings with requests from the servicemen to transfer the comic-strip hero to the air. It had a remarkable cast: Bing Crosby (as Dick Tracy), Dinah Shore (his sweetheart Tess Trueheart), Frank Sinatra, Bob Hope, Judy Garland, Jimmy Durante, Frank Morgan, the Andrews Sisters and Jerry Colonna —a bevy of stars that commercial radio could only dream about.[20]

When one of the AFRS top brass paid a visit to the forces in the Pacific he drew up a list of their favorite programs. Predictably, *Command Performance* came out on top, followed by *GI Journal*, *Mail Call*, *Jubilee*, *Personal Album*, *GI Jill*, *Yank Swing Session*, *Downbeat*, and *Melody Round Up.* [21] Interestingly, at about the same time the AFN in Britain did its own listeners' survey (confined to the U.S. forces, naturally), with different results. Top of the poll, ahead of all the glittering Hollywood productions, was AFN's own *Duffle Bag*, a remarkable tribute to the presenter, Johnny Kerr, with an astonishing 72 percent of the audience saying they listened to him. After the News, the top listening was *Command Performance*, followed by *GI Jill*, *Guy Lombardo*, *Bing Crosby Music Hall*, *At Ease*, and *Mail Call.* [22]

The emphasis was inevitably on entertainment. But information and education was also part of the AFRS brief. The service's masters at the War Department considered this aspect of program output was being neglected and laid it down that an element of documentary material should be included. Although there were strong protests from Hollywood, in the event some of the programs insisted on proved popular with the service listeners.[23]

The programs continued to pour from the AFRS broadcasting "factory." In January 1943, the number of transcription discs produced totaled nearly 8,000. By the end of the year, the monthly output had increased to 37,720.[24] In the last year of the war, the total was over 100,000 a month, and, on 12 March 1945, disc number one million was formally handed over to the head of AFRS, Colonel Tom Lewis, in a brief ceremony. It contained the latest issue of GI Journal.

In a speech a little earlier, Colonel Lewis had emphasized the role AFRS had played in bringing "a little bit of home" to the millions of Americans serving overseas in the forces. "Victory through air power has come to mean not just wings of steel over Berlin and Tokyo," he said, "but wings of words over the world."[25]

Perhaps the best summation of the whole operation was that from one of the industry's senior executives, Pat Weaver, who later became president of NBC and was with AFRS during the war: "This was the zenith of American radio. AFRS may well stand as the highest expression of American radio broadcasting."[26]

NOTES

1. Harry Mackenzie, Command Performance USA (Greenwood Press, 1996).

2. Tune In magazine, March 1943; Kirby and Davis, Star Spangled Radio, pp. 42–51 (a good account of Command Performance's history, with a detailed and evocative list of the many "sounds of home" requests); Christman, Brass Button Broadcasters, p. 31.

3. History of AFRTS, p. 57.

4. Mackenzie, Command Performance USA.

5. Quotes taken from AFRS broadcasts 1943–45.

6. Ron Lackmann, Same Time, Same Station (Facts on File Inc., 1996).

7. History of AFRTS, pp. 27–28.

8. Ibid.

9. Chris Way, The Big Bands Go to War (Mainstream Publishing, 1991), p. 274.

10. History of AFRTS, pp. 57–58; article "Story of GI Jill" by Colin Morgan in Tune into Yesterday (newsletter), Issue 29; obituary notices; private letters to author.

11. Bruce C. Elrod, Your Hit Parade 1935–94, 4th ed. (Popular Culture Ink, 1994).

12. Melody Maker, 15 January 1944.

13. The long-serving president of the American Federation of Musicians, James Caesar Petrillo, was a noted union leader whose name became a byword for intransigence. He was no respecter of persons, and even the most distinguished conductor or musician was not allowed to appear on radio or records without joining the AFM.

14. Richard Sears, V Discs: A History and Discography (Greenwood Publishing, 1980); V Disc Catalogue (Deutscher Bibliotheksverband, Berlin, 1976); article, "The Story of the V Disc Record Label (1943–1949), by Chuck Miller in Goldmine magazine, February 1999. The V-Disc labels bore the wordy legend: "War Department. Music Section. Athletics & Recreation Branch, Special Service Division." They were also

marked "OUTSIDE START" to distinguish them from those 16-inch transcription discs that were played from the center outwards.

15. *History of AFRTS*, p. 23; Kirby and Davis, *Star Spangled Radio*, pp. 61–62 (atabrine), p. 65 (New Zealand); Barnouw, *Golden Web*, pp. 190–193 (AFRS expansion), p. 195 (atabrine).

16. *History of AFRTS*, pp. 61–62.

17. There is a marked discrepancy between Barnouw's totals of AFRS outlets (quoted here) and those in the official history. The latter gives them as 120 stations in December 1943 and 154 by March 1945 (*History of AFRTS*, p. 64). Barnouw's figures are 306 and 800 (Barnouw, *Golden Web*, pp. 190, 192). It seems clear that he is quoting all transmitters in use, both large and small (AFN, for example, was only one *station* but had over 60 transmitters, or outlets, operating). I have chosen to use Barnouw's figures since they give a better indication of the scale of the AFRS operation.

18. AFRS program guidance sheet, ca. 1955.

19. *History of AFRTS*, p. 27.

20. Ibid., p. 57.

21. Ibid., p. 64.

22. BBCWAC, E1/731/1 (U.S. Army listening survey, August 1945).

23. Barnouw, *Golden Web*, pp. 195–197.

24. Harry Mackenzie (with Lothar Polomski), *One Night Stand Series* (Greenwood Publishing, 1991).

25. *History of AFRTS*, p. 59.

26. Christman, *Brass Button Broadcasters*, p. 24.

EIGHT

AEFP Birth Pangs

Given the wealth of material supplied by the Armed Forces Radio Service, it was small wonder that the American Forces Network was able to provide the U.S. servicemen and women in Britain with the sort of radio they had been calling for. The AFRS programs, together with AFN's own output, added up to an unrivaled popular broadcasting service. AFN was also particularly fortunate in being able to call on a wealth of top-notch performers passing through London on their way to entertain U.S. forces at bases all over Britain.

Among them were Glenn Miller and his orchestra, whose arrival in the United Kingdom coincided with the start of Hitler's V-bomb attacks on London, the so-called flying bombs or doodlebugs. The Americans—unlike the British, who had endured five years of German bombs—were not used to high explosives falling on them, without warning, from out of the sky. They frankly admitted to being unnerved by the endless bombardment. The flying bombs were formidable weapons, 25 feet long and packed with high explosive. Just one which landed on a London shopping center killed or seriously injured nearly 200 people and destroyed scores of shops for hundreds of yards around. And altogether the Germans rained 6,000 of them on London and the south of England. Syl Binkin, the first man to put AFN on the air, recalls he was walking down Oxford Street one day when a V1 overhead cut out, indicating that it was about to fall to the ground and explode. He fell flat on his face and waited for the explosion, which he says was the loudest noise he had ever heard. He got to his feet and dusted himself down, feeling somewhat shaken, to see that the people around him had already resumed their shopping. "I take my hat off to the British," he said later. "If anyone ever criticizes what they did in the war I remind him of all they suffered and still came up smiling."[1]

The Americans had good cause, therefore, to feel uneasy. Quite apart from the danger of death or injury, Glenn Miller decided the constant rain of "doodlebugs" was not only upsetting the band's morale but interfering with their rehearsals. So he moved them out of London to Bedford, a town fifty miles to the north. The day after they left, the premises they had been using were blown to smithereens, with heavy casualties.[2]

AFN also considered the possibility of moving out of Central London, especially as the cramped Carlos Place studio was far from ideal, and began looking for a new home. It was the BBC again that came to the rescue; it suggested 80 Portland Place, conveniently close to the BBC's headquarters at Broadcasting House and altogether much roomier accommodation. The Americans must also have appreciated Portland Place, one of the widest and most handsome streets in London.

A team of BBC engineers began carrying out the work, wiring two studios on the first floor and a control room. There was room, too, for a suite of offices. One of the BBC men recalls that though it was a time of acute shortage, the wiring was done to prewar standards using materials he had not seen since the war started. "God knows how the BBC got hold of it," he says.[3]

"We worked flat out, coming in at all hours to get the studios ready." And all the time there was the constant threat posed by Hitler's secret weapon. But the ever-generous Americans kept up morale with a steady stream of Hershey chocolate bars and cigarettes, both hard to get in a London where everything was in short supply. He was impressed with how self-sufficient the Americans were. They not only had their own food, essential in rationed wartime England, but even imported all their office equipment, including typewriters and stationery.

The BBC engineers needed those Hershey bars to keep them going. They had also been wiring up two other sets of studios. One was a complex of news studios at SHAEF (Supreme Headquarters of the Allied Expeditionary Force) being made ready for D-Day. The other was the ABSIE studio in Wardour Street.

ABSIE (the American Broadcasting Station in Europe) was operated by the Office of War Information. It was directed partly at the people of occupied Europe to prepare them for the forthcoming invasion, but it also broadcast music programs aimed particularly at the German forces and scattered with what it was hoped would be morale-sapping messages. It was over ABSIE that Glenn Miller and his orchestra broadcast a number of programs, with Miller making the occasional announcement in halting German. And Sergeant Johnny Desmond even contrived to sing one big hit entirely in German. The tune would have been no problem to anybody, but many might not have recognized in **Lang ist es her und weit zurück** the familiar words of **Long Ago and Far Away**. Apart from the Miller band, Bing Crosby and Dinah Shore were among other leading performers who appeared on the ABSIE programs.[4]

All the time, the V1s were falling, soon to be followed by the even more deadly V2s. The AFN announcers were under strict orders to make no reference to them, even if the sound of the explosions was heard when the mike was open or when the blast knocked the tone arm off the record that was being played. For the first time, the BBC stopped broadcasting the familiar chimes of Big Ben live. Instead they used a recording, to avoid the risk that a V-bomb might explode as the chimes were being transmitted and so let the enemy know that they had the range right. This required a program engineer to start the recording disc of Big Ben at the precise second, but unhappily on one occasion all did not go smoothly. A repeating groove, or what the layman calls "a stuck needle,'" gave the game away and prompted a cable from a listener overseas asking if Big Ben had taken to drink![5]

Doodlebugs or not, broadcasting went on. Some of the servicemen listening tuned in to their favorite programs in unusual circumstances. A group of American airmen who had crashed in Belgium had to spend some time hidden away by the Resistance until they could be got back to England. They spent much of the time listening to Johnny Kerr's *Duffle Bag* and George Monaghan's *On the Record*. "It just about kept us going," they told Monaghan when they returned to the United Kingdom, much to his intense pleasure.[6]

Not all the AFN broadcasts heard further afield were straightforward entertainment. On one occasion, the station was asked by the military high command to broadcast the music-hall favorite **Lily of Laguna** at precisely 2.43 p.m. on a particular day. Another time, **Sur Le Pont d'Avignon** was played fourteen times in a single day. It is safe to assume that these were not for some homesick GI but for the Resistance across the Channel in occupied Europe.[7]

It was the summer of 1944 that saw the beginning of the end of the Nazi occupation of the continent. D-Day, on 6 June, was the greatest invasion in military history. And broadcasting was destined to play its part, on the direct orders of General Eisenhower. His decision to do so caused an even bigger Anglo-American set-to than the start of AFN. It soon developed into an almighty row, or, as one writer more tactfully put it, "intricate negotiations."[8]

Eisenhower, as the commander of a vast and disparate army made up of sensitive and often suspicious nations, regarded Allied unity as being of paramount importance. The concept of unity figures repeatedly in his volume of war memoirs. "Immediate and continuous loyalty to the concept of unity . . . is basic to victory," he wrote.[9] Anyone who rocked the boat did so at his own peril. He told one of his most senior commanders: "If you or anyone else criticizes the British, by God I will reduce you to your permanent rank and send you home."[10] And to prove he meant it, soon afterward he ordered a colonel back to the United States in disgrace for insulting a British colleague—not because he called him a blankety-blank but because he called him a *British* blankety-blank.[11]

As the plans for the invasion of Europe had developed, Eisenhower was exercised by a morale problem. How were the troops who would soon be advancing towards Germany to be kept informed and in touch, and also provided with some entertainment in their brief but precious moments of relaxation? AFN, supported by AFRS back in the States, believed that each of the Allies should provide a radio service suited to its particular needs. The BBC felt the same.

But the military commanders thought otherwise. What they proposed was to combine the separate British, American, and Canadian broadcasting services into one program that would serve everyone and make sure that all the men in the great army preparing to invade Europe got the same message from the same source—in other words, an Allied Expeditionary Forces Programme, or AEFP, as it soon came to be known. There is some suggestion that the original idea came from Eisenhower himself. Certainly, he indicated he would be taking a close personal interest in developments. Whoever was the author, the man who fleshed out the original notion and put it into effect was Major General Ray Barker, assistant chief of staff at SHAEF responsible for personnel (G1). He believed that if it was done properly the proposed new service would eliminate nationalistic rivalries and foster a genuine team spirit, aims dear to Eisenhower as supreme commander.

The first priority was to secure the help and cooperation of the BBC. In the last resort AFN could always be ordered to do what it was told, but the corporation had to be persuaded if the plan was to work. The first formal approach was made at a meeting at Broadcasting House on 30 March 1944. With General Barker were two British officers from SHAEF and Major John Hayes, head of AFN. After Barker had put forward his tentative proposal, there was a discussion about whether it was technically feasible. The main BBC representative, J. B. Clark, controller of overseas services, was at pains to emphasize that not only would expert engineering advice be needed, but that policy decisions would have to be taken at the highest level. He immediately sent the director-general a detailed account of the meeting in which he noted Barker's reference to Eisenhower's personal involvement: "General Barker took the opportunity of laying special emphasis on General Eisenhower's position as the Supreme Commander. . . . The programme they had in mind would be required for the Supreme Commander's forces and the Supreme Commander himself would be directly interested in its general policy and lay out."[12]

Significantly, there was also a warning sounded over AFN's position. "It was rather implied that the American Forces Network would go out of business if the new programme came into being." The alarm bells rang instantly with the man in charge of AFN. He immediately got in touch with Colonel Tom Lewis, the head of AFRS, who arranged to fly post-haste to Britain.

At this stage, the talks were "exploratory and non-committal." Indeed, General Barker wrote to one of his superiors, Lieutenant General Gale, that they could all be canceled "without embarrassment to any of the parties concerned should these proposals not be feasible." General Gale noted that while "we may not be able to get the BBC to go all the way with us ... the discussions so far are auspicious."[13] A series of meetings was held at Broadcasting House to discuss the details of what the Americans were proposing. Apart from the BBC, they involved representatives of SHAEF, the 21st Army Group, and AFN. The area to be covered by the broadcasts had to be kept secret because it closely coincided with the area chosen for the invasion. The date when the programs were likely to start was an even more closely guarded secret. The minutes of one of the meetings noted: "Starting date for new proposed Service: See attached strictly secret memo (one copy only, no carbons)." However, it was accepted that the reception area would be within a radius of 300 miles from London. The medium wave would be used as there would not be enough shortwave frequencies available, given the huge volume of military radio traffic the invasion would generate. Since the troops in the field understandably were discouraged from listening to broadcast programs on service receivers, it was accepted that arrangements would have to be made to provide the forces with the considerable number of sets that would be needed if they were to get the maximum benefit from the new service.

Aware of the threat hanging over his network, Major Hayes of AFN was at pains to emphasize the contribution he was only too willing to make. If "military developments on the continent lead ultimately to the abandonment of the American Forces Network in this country," he said, his staff would nevertheless supply a whole range of American broadcasts for the new service at whatever times might be required. General Barker, who had earlier expressed his "great satisfaction" with the quality of the BBC News which was transmitted by AFN, agreed that "English voices for continuity would be acceptable," an assurance that proved to be short-lived.

Who should run the proposed new service, and how, was the subject of much debate. General Barker suggested that SHAEF officers should be in charge, but that was not the BBC's view. If the BBC was to put the new program out, then the BBC "would have to assume responsibility for its direction." Another stumbling block was over whether General Eisenhower should have a veto over programs. While the BBC objected to a formal right of veto, it was emphasized that it would not broadcast anything that was in opposition to the expressed wishes of the Supreme Allied Commander. And it was accepted that he might wish to use the AEFP to convey "instructions" to his armies, though what form these might take was not spelled out. Under the heading "Miscellaneous programme points" were such items as the order of precedence of national anthems at close-down ("suggested this should be alternated to achieve balance"), the proportion of "serious material" in programs (General Barker was in favor of this), and religious broadcasting.[14]

It was this last which caused a near apoplectic explosion from the BBC's director of religious broadcasting, the Rev. J. W. Welch. The plan was that there should be alternate British and American broadcast services each Sunday. Dr. Welch listened to one of the American broadcasts, *Radio Chapel*. He wrote that it consisted of a boys' choir singing "an appalling record"; then came a hymn "with fruity American harmonies"; this was followed by "a pep talk on popular psychological lines"; and finally an "emotional" rendering of another hymn.

"I cannot accept any responsibility . . . for this appalling mush," he wrote. And he went on:

I flatly refuse, either as a BBC person or an Anglican parson, to have anything whatever to do with it. The trouble is that, disclaim as we may all responsibility at the microphone, this kind of stuff will go out in a BBC programme and my colleagues and I, and indeed the BBC, will be blamed for this travesty of religious broadcasting and for offering this sugary rubbish to men who are about to face death.

He was particularly incensed at the effect it might have on men going into battle:

It is quite possible that some men and women will receive their impression of the Christian religion, and come to a decision about it, by what they hear coming out of the loudspeaker when, inevitably and naturally, they turn in moments of danger and stress to the comfort of the message of religion, and it is a shocking thought that this projection of the Christian faith (though it is not worthy of that name) may be the only one they hear at such an important period of their lives.[15]

Nothing could illustrate better the gulf between British and American attitudes than that outburst, though it should be said that Dr. Welch accepted that *Radio Chapel* was probably not a fair representation of

American Christianity. But he considered that whatever the Americans broadcast should be dissociated as completely as possible from BBC religious broadcasting policy.

The exploratory talks went on for nearly three weeks, and finally the Americans came up with their firm proposals. When he saw them, the BBC man who had been conducting the negotiations, Norman Collins (later to play a prominent part in the setting up of commercial TV in Britain after the war), wrote a detailed assessment. He made several important points stressing the not always smooth relationship between the two countries. "I have been much impressed in the course of these discussions," he wrote, "by the extent to which, even though SHAEF is an integrated Allied Command, American influences predominate. There are, moreover, strong American Radio Network influences within SHAEF." (He was presumably referring to AFN.)

Collins regarded it as of the "utmost importance" that the British representative on a suggested military advisory body should be of sufficiently high rank not to be overruled by a higher-ranking officer representing the U.S. Special Service Division. And as to who should actually run the new service, he wrote: "SHAEF direction, as opposed to BBC direction, of the proposed service has been the main source of dissension in our discussions. The fact that General Barker made two visits to the BBC purely to re-raise this matter is an indication of the importance which SHAEF attaches to it: the principle of BBC direction, though now fully recognised, has, it should be realised, been agreed to only very reluctantly." So whatever General Eisenhower may have felt about Allied unity, to some Americans it meant the U.S. being in charge.[16]

It seems likely that one of those Americans was Colonel Ed Kirby, who, as head of broadcasting at SHAEF, was in an important and influential post. By that time he had conceived a strong dislike of the BBC hierarchy, which he described later as inflexible and stiff-necked, "brooking no opposition from any quarter." Unhappily, that antipathy colored his judgment and was to have unfortunate consequences.[17]

The formal American proposals were sent in a letter dated 28 April 1944 by Eisenhower's right-hand man, Lieutenant General W. Bedell Smith, his chief of staff. They were much as had been discussed: a medium-wave broadcasting service, operating between 6 a.m. and 11 p.m., with program material reflecting the relative military strengths of the American, British, and Canadian forces. AFN would be responsible for supplying the American content of the program. The new service would be run by the BBC with an advisory committee which would meet weekly to "review progress." The job of continuity announcing would be shared 50–50 between American and British voices, a significant revision of General Barker's original intention. The Supreme Commander would be given facilities to broadcast 'instructions' from time to time to his armies, and there would be a SHAEF officer appointed to act as liaison officer to keep the BBC informed of General Eisenhower's views about the new service. There was also another important proviso laid down about news broadcasts. Since these would be heard by all the forces, "it is vital to the success of the project that [they] in no way exaggerate or minimize the participation of one of the component parts thereof." And to make sure, SHAEF would issue regular communiqués, which would be the basis of the news broadcasts as far as they dealt with SHAEF operations.

It so happens that the original draft of the proposals is still in existence, and it is clear that the final version was watered down so as not to give gratuitous offense. In particular, the original stipulated that it was "the Supreme Commander's express desire that the Service should in every way be made as fully acceptable to listeners of the three major nationalities under his command as possible." That phrase was struck out completely. And another was considerably amended.

The Supreme Commander fully recognises the objective nature of BBC news broadcasts, but feels it necessary to place on record that as these broadcasts . . . will be heard by Americans and Canadians as well as by British Forces, it is fundamental to the success of the project that nothing should be done which might in any way exacerbate the feeling that any one of the component parts of the invasion forces is receiving greater notice than any other.[18]

This was replaced by the more tactful wording already noted. Clearly, there were those at SHAEF intent on making sure that the more aggressively pro-American elements were restrained from offending their British allies. The BBC hierarchy now sat down to consider the proposals. The more they saw of them, the less they liked them. AFN took the same view. The professional broadcasters could see what the military could not, or would not: that shared programming for audiences with very different likes and dislikes was a recipe for trouble.

Since the head of AFN was under the direct command of ETOUSA (European Theater of Operations, U.S. Army), it was decided that the man to fight the battle on his behalf was the head of AFRS in the United States, Colonel Tom Lewis. He flew to London and tackled General Barker head on. He has left a detailed account of their often acrimonious discussions in an unpublished autobiography.

He did not go empty-handed. He took with him his own counterproposals which he had discussed with Major John Hayes of AFN. The American Forces Network would use one of the powerful BBC transmitters on the Channel coast to broadcast to the U.S. forces, while the BBC would use another to beam its General Forces Programme to the British troops. Once the invaders were firmly established, AFN would man a series of mobile transmitters, which would accompany each of the advancing American armies.

General Barker was furious when this plan was put to him. He pointed out in strong language that it was "a complete reversal of the plan of operation I've told you I'm in favour of." Colonel Lewis stuck to his guns. His plan was one which he and others competent to judge believed to be correct. And he emphasized: "I cannot endorse a plan which my professional judgment tells me is a mistake." At this, General Barker blew up. "Only one thing wins wars, colonel: leadership. Not radio leadership, not Madison Avenue leadership, not Hollywood leadership. MILITARY leadership!"

The problem, as Lewis admitted, was that General Barker simply did not understand what the AFRS and its AFN offshoot were trying to do. The general believed he had created something new in a field that was new to him, and he was determined to stick to it. "I searched my soul for a way to help him understand what mischief his stubbornness could bring to pass," Colonel Lewis wrote later. But he failed. He returned to America "blocked and frustrated" and with a metaphorical bloodied nose. Now it was all up to the BBC.[19]

The ruling body of the BBC, the Board of Governors, met in conclave with the director-general, the executive head. After much heart-searching, they decided to reject the American plan. It was not an easy decision. All were leading members of the British Establishment, and they had no wish to bring down on their heads the wrath that was sure to follow. But they believed the plan was wrong, and honesty compelled them to say so.

The director-general set out their views in a long letter to General Bedell Smith. The essence of it was contained in one paragraph:

While making it clear that the BBC fully sympathises with the objects which we understand the Supreme Commander has in mind, it is our view that the proposed composite programme will not achieve the results desired. We have the conviction that, on the contrary, it would be difficult to control, would tend to stress differences, and would lead to dissatisfaction.

The letter then came up with a counter-proposal: the BBC would transmit its General Forces Programme to the British troops on the Continent (and would make sure Canadian interests were taken care of) while the American forces would continue to receive the present AFN program. It went on: "Both sections of the Allied Expeditionary Force would in this manner take with them to the continent the wireless programmes to which they have hitherto been accustomed."[20] It was exactly the same idea that Colonel Lewis had put to General Barker on behalf of AFRS and AFN. Whether they and the BBC had been liaising with each other is not known, though it has to be said that it was the plan any broadcaster worth his salt would have put forward anyway. Indeed, it was a logic with which it should have been difficult to argue. But they were up against General Eisenhower's determination to do all he could to avoid the dangers of inter-Allied rivalries and his total commitment to the idea of a single unifying command for the entire operation. They were also up against the military mind, which inevitably had a limited grasp of broadcasting requirements and was not prepared to compromise.

As soon as the BBC's letter reached SHAEF, General Barker was round to see the director-general. He had a powerful weapon still in his armory, and it was now time to use it. A brief penciled note in the BBC archives on the meeting indicates that the general was confident of the full support of the Supreme Commander: "Eisenhower considering whether he would take the matter higher." "Higher" in that context meant only one thing—the prime minister himself, Winston Churchill.[21]

And so, on the eve of the greatest invasion in history, the man in command of it, with all the multitude of problems and responsibilities it entailed pressing down on him, took time off to write a letter to the most powerful man in Britain about a forces broadcasting service. It was an indication of the importance he placed in the project. The letter General Eisenhower wrote, dated 11 May 1944, so completely encapsulates his arguments that it is worth quoting in full:

It has been my hope that for the impending operation we would be able to institute a radio broadcasting service which would present a program especially designed and produced for the Allied Expeditionary Force. Such a service would be of the greatest value as a factor in the maintenance of morale and would serve as a medium for disseminating "AEF" information to the forces from time to time as is now being done so successfully by the Armed Forces Radio Service in the Mediterranean theater. But of perhaps larger significance is the greater potentiality which such a service would have as a means of welding our troops into a closely knit fighting team, and of promoting a closer relationship between the British, American and Canadian Forces. I feel that this is an opportunity which we cannot afford to miss. With the above thought in mind we have been exploring the subject and have held a number of conferences with officials of the British Broadcasting Corporation, whose co-operation would be essential to the project. Following these conferences I submitted to the Director-General, B.B.C., a proposal for the establishment of a service along the lines indicated above and requested his collaboration. In reply the Director-General stated that he did not consider our proposal to be a practicable one nor did he believe that a combined service of this nature would accomplish the desired end.

As a counter proposal he offered to place at the disposal of the American Forces the necessary facilities for establishing its own broadcasting service. For the British–Canadian forces he proposes to provide the present General Forces Program, with appropriate adaptations. In addition, the Director-

General has offered to place the facilities of the BBC at my disposal for any announcements or statements which I may desire to make to the Forces, at any time.

The Director-General's reply was a disappointment to me and I must add that I am not at all in agreement with his conclusion that our proposed "AEF Radio Service" would be difficult to control and would not achieve the results desired. On the other hand, I feel that with the American Forces broadcasting their own programs a spirit of competition may be engendered which might have undesirable results. Furthermore, it would make more difficult the problem of co-ordinating news broadcasts and commentaries, since, quite obviously, it would be impractical to use British material of that nature on a purely American program, although this could be done on a "combined" program.

I feel there is so much merit in our proposal for a combined British–American–Canadian Radio Service for the AEF that should you take a like view of the matter, may I ask that you take whatever steps you consider expedient to enlist the support and co-operation of the BBC in its establishment.[22]

Sent a letter like that from the Supreme Commander of the Allied Expeditionary Force, Churchill was left with no choice. He forwarded Eisenhower's letter to the minister of information, Brendan Bracken, and made it clear that he was to exert whatever pressure was needed to get the BBC to toe the line.

Bracken apparently thought it worth while meeting General Barker himself to see if he could be persuaded to see the corporation's point of view. He is quoted as telling him he had never known the BBC governors so determined and so unanimous. How could such different tastes and interests as those of the Americans and the British be served by just one broadcasting service? And he is even said to have quoted as an example of that the very differing styles of humor of Bob Hope and the popular British comedian Tommy Trinder, whose cockney accent most Americans found difficult to understand. But General Barker was unmoved, and Bracken's persuasive words fell on stony ground.

The only source for this meeting is Colonel Kirby, who later wrote what can only be described as a highly dramatized account of it. He represented that the BBC's announcement of their opposition to Eisenhower's proposal came as a complete bombshell to the Americans, which, given the detailed negotiations of the preceding weeks, is clearly not the case. His attitude goes some way to confirming the views of those who believed that hostile American influences were at work at SHAEF.[23]

After the failure of his meeting with General Barker, Bracken arranged to see the BBC director-general, William Haley, on 22 May and spelled out to him the stark choice he was facing. If the BBC did not do the program, then the whole thing would be handed over to SHAEF to do themselves. That in turn meant that the corporation would be denied the extra transmitter facilities it wanted for its General Forces Programme once the troops were on the Continent. That was the end of the argument, and the BBC capitulated. That Bracken was unhappy about the whole business is clear from his reply to the prime minister, dated 25 May: "The request made by General Eisenhower in his letter to you of 11 May presents all sorts of difficulties for this Ministry and for the BBC. It is in fact a nightmare for me. But as General Eisenhower and Bedell Smith are most anxious that we should start this Allied forces programme I feel that we must fulfill their request. Our people and the Americans have begun work together today."

Churchill conveyed the glad news to Eisenhower in a brief note, dated 27 May: "My Dear Eisenhower, You should see what the Minister of Information says about your request in your letter of 11 May, and that we have deferred to your wishes, but not without misgivings. I hope that if difficulties arise, adjustments may be considered between your people and ours."

A greatly relieved Eisenhower replied on 30 May thanking Churchill for his timely intervention. After expressing his appreciation of the BBC's assistance, he went on: "We shall do our utmost to compose all difficulties of viewpoint in a manner which will meet the wishes of Mr. Brendan Bracken. My staff have been for some days at work with the BBC officials. Reports indicate all is going well and that thus far no real difficulties have been uncovered."

Thus the problem was only finally resolved after the involvement of the two most powerful men then in Britain. At least at the end of it the BBC could draw some consolation from all the wrangling: The BBC was to run the new program. It was to provide the world news for it. The advisory body was to be just that—advisory, with "no mandatory powers" to order the BBC to do anything. And all the costs were to be met by the U.S. and British governments. The BBC also appointed the man who was to run the new service. His first priority was to press on with all urgency organizing a completely new broadcasting service in the very brief time available.

NOTES

1. *Encyclopaedia of World War II*; Norman Longmate, *The Doodlebugs: The Story of the Flying Bombs* (Hutchinson 1981); Syl Binkin's recollections, in conversation with the author.

2. Way, *Big Bands*, pp. 169–170; Geoffrey Butcher, *Next to a Letter from Home* (Mainstream Publishing 1986), pp. 61–64; Oranges and Lemons broadcast.

3. In conversation with the author.

4. Way, *Big Bands*, p. 187; Butcher, *Letter from Home*, pp. 183–184 (Butcher gives an interesting detailed account of ABSIE and the Miller Band in his notes on The Lost Recordings: see List of Works Consulted 4. Audio/Visual); Briggs, *History*, Vol. III, p. 646; Kirby and Davis, *Star Spangled Radio*, pp. 123–131 (the most detailed account). There is also an amusing description on pp. 233–234 of how Bing Crosby was able to master a German-language introduction to his singing in just 15 minutes with the aid of a phonetic "crib sheet."

5. Trevor Hill, the former BBC engineer responsible, in a letter to the author.

6. Interview in *Radio Times*, 5 January 1945.

7. Christman, *Brass Button Broadcasters*, p. 52.

8. Briggs, *History*, Vol. III, p. 648.

9. *Crusade in Europe*, p. 175.

10. David Irving, *The War Between the Generals* (Allen Lane, 1981; Penguin Books, 1982), p. 9.

11. Article in *Transatlantic* magazine, December 1943.

12. BBCWAC, R34/184/1 (Controller of Overseas Services to DG, 30 March 1944, "Broadcasting to Allied Troops in Europe").

13. Public Record Office, London, SHAEF files (WO 219/6, Barker to Gale, 20 April 1944, Gale's handwritten annotation on Barker's letter).

14. BBCWAC, R34/184/1. The information in the preceding paragraphs comes from the minutes of a series of meetings held on 6, 10, and 14 April 1944.

15. Ibid. (Director of Religious Broadcasting memo, 18 April 1944, "New Invasion Forces Program: Religious Broadcasting").

16. Ibid. (General Overseas Service Director memo, 21 April 1944, "SHAEF Proposal").

17. Kirby and Davis, *Star Spangled Radio*, pp. 140–141.

18. BBCWAC, R34/184/1 (Letter from Lt. Gen. W. B. Smith to DG, 28 April 1944, and accompanying documents in the file).

19. *History of AFRTS*, pp. 41–42, quoting unpublished autobiography by Col. Tom Lewis.

20. BBCWAC, R34/184/1 (DG to Lt. Gen. Smith, 5 May 1944).

21. Ibid. (Handwritten undated note in the file).

22. Public Record Office, London, SHAEF Files, WO219/6 (General Eisenhower to Prime Minister, 11 May 1944). The same file contains all the correspondence quoted.

23. Kirby and Davis, *Star Spangled Radio*, pp. 137–144.

NINE

AEFP "Politics and Intrigue"

The person chosen to run the Allied Expeditionary Forces Programme was Maurice Gorham. He was the ideal man for the job. An experienced and able BBC executive, at the time of his appointment he had just completed a spell running the Corporation's North American Service.[1] He therefore had a lot of American contacts, among them Colonel Kirby, whom Gorham had known when Kirby ("a man with a talent for rapid-fire action") was radio public-relations officer for the War Department in Washington.[2] Gorham liked Americans and got along with them, but he was not a man who could easily be imposed on.

Although he did not know it, Gorham had just two weeks to get the new program started. The start date was D Day +1, but of course only the most senior military men knew when that would be. But Gorham was aware time was short. He was told of his appointment shortly after a social evening with Colonel Tom Lewis, who was pouring cold water on the whole idea and saying how much better AFRS and AFN could do it. Gorham was called in to see the BBC director-general, William Haley, on 23 May. Haley told him agreement had been reached over the AEFP, then talked about the difficulties of running it, how unpopular the job would be, and the opposition it would encounter. Then he said: "It's your job. Start now [it was just 6:40 p.m]. Come back in a day or two and tell me what you want."[3]

What Gorham wanted was almost everything. The engineers had assigned a transmitter for the new service: it was at Start Point on the cliffs of the Devon coast above the English Channel. It had been allotted a frequency, and SHAEF had agreed to release several former BBC staff now in the forces. And that was all Gorham had: no offices, no studios, simply a blank sheet.

The service was being started at a time when all the resources of the BBC were stretched to the utmost with the preparations for the coverage of the invasion and other special services for the military. It was, Gorham noted later, "very difficult to lay hands on an office, a studio, a recording channel, a programme engineer, or a telediphone (stenotype) operator who was not already assigned to a project intimately associated with the invasion."[4]

Remarkably, within a week the first "dry run" for the new service had been held. It was preceded by a period of intense activity. Somehow, offices were found for the new setup on the fourth floor of Broadcasting House, where Colonel Kirby was also provided with accommodation adjoining Maurice Gorham's office. The BBC headquarters building found itself full of armed American military police, the famous "snow-drops," from their white helmets, belts, and gaiters. As a BBC executive noted, there was one consolation from this unexplained invasion: "They brought with them some of the most beautiful girls, WACs acting as secretaries and the like."[5]

The whole operation was so secret that people in adjoining offices had no idea what it was all about. Nor to start with did the personnel recalled posthaste from the Forces. All they knew was they had been ordered back to "take up special duties." At least one assumed this meant some cloak-and-dagger operation and turned up at Broadcasting House "armed to the teeth," as Gorham noted, and accompanied by his driver carrying a bedroll. Several were most put out when they found that instead of the roles they had been allotted in the invasion, they were to embark on nothing more exciting than a new broadcasting enterprise.[6]

The first program-planning meeting was held on 25 May, and five days later came the first of a series of dry runs, or rehearsals. This involved a run-through of the complete program as if it were going on the air. The main aim, as Gorham wrote later, was "to get engineers and announcers into the tricky routine of switching and cueing, cutting into programs already running, and splitting feeds." That went on for a whole week and "served to disclose various operational snags which might have been disastrous if they had been discovered on D Day itself, when the BBC had many complex new operations on hand in addition to this one."[7] By now, all the program staff were assembled. They included Franklin Engelmann, an announcer who became a familiar BBC voice in the postwar years; Royston Morley, who produced the highly successful *Combat Diary*; and Cecil Madden, a top entertainment producer, who was responsible for *American Eagle in Britain,* a weekly program intended for the families back in America of U.S. servicemen in the United Kingdom. It was started before America joined the war when there were many U.S. volunteers with the British forces, especially the famous Eagle Squadron of the RAF (in fact, three squadrons made up entirely of Americans). The new service also had a lively team of women announcers, who helped to give the AEFP programs a special flavor. Another was the station ident, the tune of an old English nursery rhyme, **Oranges and Lemons,** whose jingling rhythm played on a novachord became a familiar sound to the forces, from Normandy all the way to the Rhine.

And for internal consumption only, the new service was allotted a color, as was the practice with all BBC channels, to avoid confusion over such things as scripts and studio locations. Ironically perhaps for a military service, the color for the AEFP was violet!

While the program preparations were going on, another political crisis erupted. Colonel Kirby presented Gorham with a letter from General Barker raising once more matters which had appeared to be settled. The main one was news. The Americans were unhappy about all the news being supplied by the BBC, though they paid tribute to its "splendid objectivity." They seemed to want the right to make any deletions or additions "which seem appropriate to the character of the program." And the letter added: "You will readily appreciate the position in which General Eisenhower . . . would find himself with relation to the American authorities and people, if he were to agree that the world news bulletins furnished US troops were prepared and controlled by the BBC." Since that was precisely what had been agreed after much discussion, it is difficult to see why the matter was being raised yet again.[8]

The Americans were also unhappy, more understandably, about the title of the new service: "The Allied Expeditionary Forces Programme of the BBC." Their suggestion was "The Allied Expeditionary Forces Radio Service." This was to be the source of a great deal of ill-feeling in the coming months, but for now the BBC was not prepared to yield. Nor was it going to let its news be "censored" by anybody—indeed, to attempt to do so would have caused a great deal of confusion and even more dissension.

General Barker met the BBC director-general to discuss his reservations, but beforehand he had lunch with Maurice Gorham. "I had heard General Barker described as a formidable character," Gorham wrote later, "and he was." He kept banging his fist on the table to emphasize his points and altogether displayed a good deal of aggression. However, Gorham says later he grew very fond of the general, who in turn became an admirer of the BBC.[9] At the meeting at Broadcasting House, the director-general, to quote Gorham, "gave a wonderful display of tough negotiations." The Americans emphasized that there was no question of SHAEF dictating news treatment to the BBC, and it all ended with the original agreement intact.

One of the points that had exercised the Americans, because of the need for strict censorship, was the question of ad-libbing. Colonel Kirby had agreed verbally that none was to be allowed, but, as the British pointed out, since ad-libbing formed a large element in the style of presentation favored by AFN, this needed to be confirmed and a close watch kept on it.[10]

AFN would be providing a good half of the program output, so they were naturally heavily involved in the program planning. Gorham's first meeting with them began at 10 a.m. and went on until after midnight. As it happened, Gorham knew John Hayes, the head of AFN, from earlier days, but even so things did not always go smoothly. "I felt that at all times I had to have my eyes very wide open in dealing with AFN," he wrote later. The great thing, from his point of view, was that they had every big band and comedy show that America produced. They had plenty of manpower, too, by now, though they never allocated anyone full-time to the AEFP, an indication of their continuing reservations about it. By contrast, the Canadians were most enthusiastic and were prepared to put a lot of effort and personnel into the new service, so much so that it proved difficult not to give them more than their fair share of the program.[11] Originally, it will be recalled, the plan was for the output to be in proportion to the numerical strength of the three countries' armed forces, but this was later changed to a simple 50–50 arrangement. The Canadians' share therefore was not defined, but in the event they did make a real contribution to the AEFP.

D Day arrived on 6 June 1944, as the Allied armies landed on the coast of Normandy. At 05.55 Double British Summer Time the next day, Wednesday, 7 June, the AEFP went on the air. It began with an announcement, read by Franklin Engelmann, setting out the aims of the new service:

Here is an announcement from Headquarters of the Supreme Commander, Allied Expeditionary Forces: We are initiating today a radio broadcasting service for the members of the Allied Expeditionary Force. We shall call this service "The AEF Program." It is to be a service especially prepared for you and we shall try to make it of a character suited to your needs. Its purpose is three-fold:

   To link you with your homes, by means of news broadcasts from the United Kingdom, Canada and the United States; to give you the latest news of our own and other war fronts and the world events; and finally, to afford you diversion and relaxation during those precious few moments of leisure from the main job now at hand.

For this latter purpose we shall bring you the best entertainment that can be summoned from our Allied Nations. The British Broadcasting Corporation has given generously of its resources and skilled personnel. The American Forces Network and the Canadian Broadcasting Corporation are working closely with the British Broadcasting Corporation in this project, making it a truly inter-allied effort.

We shall go forward together to Victory and on the forward road the AEF Program will be constantly within your reach, serving you, we hope, in a manner worthy of your needs.[12]

A prayer by an American army chaplain was followed by the world news headlines, the first of a series of news bulletins every hour on the hour—commonplace now, but then something quite new. They came from the BBC Overseas News department at 200 Oxford Street, because it was used to doing hourly broadcasts and considering listeners who were not a home audience. The station's signature tune was played for the first time, and then Franklin Engelmann introduced the AEFP's new daily program, *Rise and Shine,* a two-hour-long record show compered by Dick Dudley of AFN and Ac2 [aircraftman second class] Ronnie Waldman, the presenter of a popular BBC variety program, *Monday Night at Eight.* "As they themselves have risen and are about to shine," Engelmann told listeners, "let's hear what they have to say about it." They were the ideal Anglo-American combination, and their first words emphasized the two-nation approach: "Hi fellers" from Dick Dudley, and "Morning, blokes" from Waldman.[13] And so began a program that was to prove a great success with its military audience and with home listeners too, since a large area of southern England was able to hear the new station. It was actually "screened" to improve the reception across the Channel, but it does not seem to have stopped home listeners picking it up.

On that first day's broadcasting, a dozen programs came from AFN, including *Duffle Bag, On the Record, Mail Call, Bob Hope, GI Jive, Dinah Shore, Kate Smith,* and *Fred Waring.* Out of a total of seventeen hours' broadcasting, the Americans provided over seven hours, as well as a number of shared programs. Small wonder Gorham was grateful for the wealth of talent AFN put at his disposal.

The AEFP was transmitted on 285 meters (1050 kilocycles) to begin with, though this was later switched to 514 meters (583 kilocycles). As the Allied armies moved away from the Normandy coast and farther from the main transmitter, the program was rebroadcast on army field stations on wavelengths that gave better reception in certain areas. To prevent interference, these were strictly controlled by SHAEF on a carefully worked-out schedule. At one point the British First Army wanted to change the arrangements, but Lieutenant Colonel David Niven, as deputy director of SHAEF's Broadcasting Service, sent them a cable firmly ordering them to do as they were told.[14]

Niven's role with SHAEF was an interesting one. He had asked that no special publicity should be given to his appointment, much to the dismay of the BBC Publicity Department. They wanted to make capital of having a Hollywood film star working at Broadcasting House and demanded to know why they could not do so. They were told "Colonel Niven's personal reasons for desiring to avoid publicity are concerned with his army career and have no reference to Hollywood."[15] Niven had been in the army before he went to Hollywood, and when war broke out he immediately volunteered his services. He had taken part in several commando raids and was apparently most upset when SHAEF dragged him away from the chance of taking part in the D-Day landings for an office job. Maurice Gorham believed that Ed Kirby wanted Niven as his number two largely because he was a film star. Kirby apparently liked surrounding himself with celebrities.[16] The likelihood is, therefore, that Niven deliberately eschewed publicity for that reason. Cecil Madden, the BBC producer working with AEFP, recounts how Niven used to arrive punctually for planning meetings, immaculately uniformed and charmingly courteous. He would wait until his presence had been re-corded and then, after a decent interval, make his excuse and leave. "What he was actually supposed to be doing was a mystery we never solved."[17] However, Maurice Gorham's view was that Niven was as quick-witted and business-like as anybody he knew, and certainly his cables to units in the field show a thorough and authoritative grasp of the situation. This is confirmed by the fact that when Colonel Kirby returned to America in October, Niven was appointed as his successor. Oddly, although Niven wrote two volumes of autobiography, he never mentioned his time with the AEFP in either.

From the start, the AEFP was at pains to emphasize that it was an inter-Allied effort. Margaret Hubble of the BBC would hand over to Corporal George Monaghan of AFN, who in turn would be followed at the microphone by Lieutenant Charmian Samson of the Canadian Women's Army Corps. Gorham wrote later that "the listener gets a continuous impression of Anglo–American–Canadian co-operation; in fact, he never knows which nationality he is going to hear next."

The women announcers were a particular feature of the AEFP. The American Forces Network had none (one wonders why, considering that its Mediterranean counterpart, the AES, had several). In peacetime, the BBC had had none on any of its services (other than two television "hostesses"). But the war changed all that, and by the time the AEFP was in full swing there were twenty-six women introducing a range of programs across the BBC output. The interest of the listening public is indicated by an article devoted to them in *Radio Times*, the BBC weekly program journal. In terms that might perhaps be frowned on now by some for dwelling too much on their physical charms (but not unreasonably since the listeners never saw them), they were variously described: Charmian Samson, "petite, very trim with hair the colour of a wheatfield," but possessing "an enormous capacity for long hours and hard work"; Margaret Hubble, "slim with ash-blonde hair and an infectious laugh" and "a flair for keeping calm and collected whenever a situation becomes tricky"; and Joan Griffiths, "tall and graceful with a good steady straight-in-the-eye look" and "very competent at the turntables."[18] Also working with those three was Jean Metcalfe, presenter of a popular BBC program, *Forces Favorites* (later *Family Favorites*), linking the troops with their families back home through a collection of record requests. Mention should also be made of two other AEFP announcers, Betty McLoughlin and Jill Balcon, the daughter of noted British film producer, Sir Michael Balcon and, at the age of 19, the youngest of all the announcing team.

The news-reading duties were shared equally between British and American voices. Gorham commented wryly later: "This resulted in a standard of news reading probably more erratic than anything previously broadcast under the aegis of the BBC."[19] The news came from a variety of locations. Sometimes the AFN newsreader would be in the tiny continuity studio next to the wartime control room—the engineering nerve center of the BBC, far from German bombs and rockets, three floors below ground in Broadcasting House. The headlines and news bulletins still came from the BBC Overseas Service, which sometimes resulted in the use of such phrases as "the Home Country" or "at home," meaning Britain, which naturally jarred on American and Canadian ears. Gorham noted that this "sturdy British note [is] a little less than objective when it is addressed to a joint audience of the AEF . . . but I think we shall soon outgrow [it]." The Overseas News came from BBC premises at 200 Oxford Street, in what until the war began had been the Bargain Basement of the big London department store, Peter Robinson![20]

The American Forces Network, of course, continued to run its own separate service for the U.S. forces still based in Britain, of which there were many thousands at the air bases alone. Many of its programs were also broadcast simultaneously on the AEFP, which meant that British listeners who had been denied the pleasure of AFN, especially in the London area, were now able to receive it. This may possibly have influenced the BBC's thinking in what proved to be one of the most contentious aspects of the new program.

The corporation had insisted from the start that the AEFP must be referred to as "the Allied Expeditionary Forces Programme *of the BBC*."

The head of AFN, John Hayes, objected to this vigorously right from the start, and before long it was upsetting the Americans in a big way. The argument against the phrase was encapsulated in a strongly worded letter of protest from Colonel Kirby, as head of SHAEF broadcasting, to Maurice Gorham, dated 25 July 1944:

I again present the problem created by the title "This is the Allied Expeditionary Forces Programme of the BBC." As you know, I have consistently opposed the use of such designation on the following grounds:
   It is not a correct statement of fact. The AEF Program, originally unwanted by the BBC is not at all similar to the GFP [General Forces Program] or the Home Service, or the North American Service etc. The fact is that the AEFP was created at the insistence of SHAEF to provide an inter-allied radio service to men of the Allied Command, to draw upon program resources of the three countries involved, with the BBC being asked to provide transmission facilities and engineering personnel. It was only after reconsideration by the BBC that the BBC agreed to participate, and demanding that its operations be under the control of a BBC Director . . .[21]

The letter goes on to point out that SHAEF had put at the BBC's disposal British and American military personnel with broadcasting experience to make the program work. "If the BBC is unwilling to permit the service to be known as SHAEF Broadcasting Service, then it seems hardly consistent to call it the Program of the BBC." Furthermore, the letter says, "the designation 'of the BBC' delimits the scope and purpose of the program in the minds of soldier listeners. . . . This latter, especially from American elements in Normandy, is subjecting the service to undue criticism and resentment." The letter concludes: "To eliminate the objectionable features referred to and provide a designation that is more in line with the spirit and fact of the operation, it is proposed that the designation be as follows: This is the Allied Expeditionary Forces Programme transmitted through the facilities of the BBC."
   Kirby undoubtedly had a case, and in his protest he was supported by General Barker, the man who had been responsible for instigating the new service. Barker took the matter up with the BBC's director-general, but this time he came away empty-handed. The corporation's official attitude was straightforward enough: it had provided all the premises and all the technical support for the program at great inconvenience and very short notice, its own staff were running it, and the BBC was supplying half the output. Why, therefore, should it not take the credit? All the same, from the moment the BBC insisted on using the phrase, it must have been aware it would upset the Americans. The whole operation was supposed to be about Allied unity, but what the corporation was doing was the negation of Anglo-American cooperation. But it stub-

bornly refused to budge. It is said that General Eisenhower himself took the matter up with Winston Churchill, who apparently tried to persuade the BBC to give way, but without success. And on this occasion, unlike the decision to set up the AEFP, neither the prime minister nor the supreme commander was willing to press the matter further.[22]

The corporation's real motives remain obscure. It may simply have been an attempt to retrieve something of its wounded pride after having both AFN and the AEFP imposed on it. It may have been a gesture of independence, particularly as the Americans had been so insistent on wanting to run the AEFP themselves. There is another possibility. The corporation, aware of the large number of home listeners who would be tuning in and hearing AFN programs for the first time, may have felt it necessary to emphasize its own role. If so, the reverse happened. A good many Britons who had clearly been tuning in to the AEFP were convinced in years to come that they had been listening to AFN! In any case, whatever the BBC's motives, they could hardly have justified the resentment it aroused in Britain's American allies.

Nearly six months later, the intrusive phrase—as the Americans regarded it—was still giving rise to complaints. A report in December 1944 by a U.S. communications officer noted "innumerable comments in the field" about it. To troops who had come straight to France without ever having been stationed in England, the BBC was only a name. "It was, therefore, quite a jolt to them to have their own radio station suddenly become 'of the BBC.' Even though fifty per cent of the programs . . . are British, the general connotation gives the impression that it is a one hundred per cent British service." It was perhaps to create precisely that impression that the BBC persisted, but it hardly helped Anglo-American solidarity.[23]

It was certainly not the only political headache that Gorham, as head of the AEFP, had to cope with. At the weekly planning meetings, he wrote later, "every schedule change was hotly debated on nationalistic grounds and my time was spent in trying to keep the balance right, despite the much greater amount of material that the Americans had to offer." He said there was little finesse about the discussions and "everybody emerged rather battered." He told one of his colleagues: "If this isn't inter-allied co-operation I don't know what it is—unless it's murder."[24]

He was also having problems with Colonel Kirby. He had expected to be on good terms with someone he regarded as a "boon companion" from their days in Washington. But whatever their former relationship, "when we worked closely together [on the AEFP] we did not get on nearly so well." The supposed "boon companion" was even more forthright: Gorham was a "stickler for form" who was "the British counterpart of a Philadelphia lawyer." It was an indication of the way in which, because of political pressures, Anglo-American friendship did not always run smoothly even at the personal level.[25]

Thus the internal history of the AEFP was marked by politics and intrigue, as Gorham was to write afterward. But all that was at the political level. It needs to be emphasized that the rank and file of broadcasters were mostly unaware of the bickering at the top. All of them testify that the relationships between the three allies were warm and friendly. "It really was a pleasure to work with the Americans," one BBC announcer recalls, "and the Canadians too were lovely."[26] More important still, none of the high-level intrigue showed on the air. The tens of thousands of men and women in the armed services, as well as the civilians who happily tuned in to AEFP, were blissfully unaware of the political infighting that had accompanied its inception and that continued throughout its brief existence.

NOTES

1. At the time he became head of AEFP, Gorham had only recently taken up the post of Assistant Controller of the BBC's Overseas Services after a successful spell as Director of the North American Service.

2. Gorham's relationships with Kirby: Gorham, *Sound and Fury*, p. 140; "a man with a talent for rapid-fire action" (Barnouw's summing up of Kirby), Barnouw, *Golden Web*, p. 161. Barnouw noted (p. 161) that it was Kirby whose ideas and drive helped to create *Command Performance*. It was also Kirby, when he was at the War Department before becoming Head of SHAEF, who masterminded the successful *Army Hour* program—eyewitness accounts by the participants in military action, such as General Doolittle describing his air raid on Tokyo (Barnouw, *Golden Web*, pp. 162–163).

3. Gorham, *Sound and Fury*. This volume of autobiography by Maurice Gorham devotes a whole chapter to his time with the AEFP entitled "Oranges and Lemons." This is the source of the *Sound and Fury* quotations in this chapter unless otherwise stated.

4. BBCWAC, R34/184/1 (Gorham memo to North American Director, 13 June 1944, "Background Story on AEFP for NAD").

5. BBCWAC, S24/54/22 (Long memorandum on AEFP by Cecil Madden, entitled "Something for the Boys").

6. Gorham, *Sound and Fury*.

7. BBCWAC, R34/184/1 (Gorham memo).

8. Ibid. (Letter to DG from Maj. Gen. R. W. Barker, 25 May 1944).

9. Gorham, *Sound and Fury*.

10. BBCWAC R34/184/1 (Rendall memo, 28 May 1944).

11. Gorham, *Sound and Fury*.

12. AEFP Broadcast, 7 June 1944.

13. Ibid.

14. BBCWAC, R44/11 (Niven cable to British First Army).

15. Ibid.

16. Gorham, *Sound and Fury*.

17. Oranges and Lemons broadcast.

18. Article by Franklin Engelmann, *Radio Times*, September 1944. Later there were articles about Cecil Madden and Ronnie Waldman, as well as all the main AFN announcers (for details, see chapter 4). There was a special AEF edition of the *Radio Times*, distributed free to all the troops.

19. Gorham, *Broadcasting*.

20. BBCWAC, R34/184/1 (Gorham memo, 13 June 1944, "Progress of the AEFP"); (reference to 200 Oxford Street) Jill Balcon, former BBC wartime announcer, in conversation with the author.

21. BBCWAC, R34/184/1 (Letter from Col. E. M. Kirby, 25 July 1944, "AEFP of the BBC").

22. Cecil Madden's personal scrapbook. According to Madden, Eisenhower felt that the whole business was absurd. He was pacing up and down muttering, "Don't they know there's a war on," while Churchill spoke to William Haley, the BBC director-general. Eventually, the prime minister put the phone down and, turning to Ike, apologetically growled with typical Churchillian irony: "I'm sorry. I forgot the BBC is independent."

23. BBCWAC, R34/185 (Capt. Robt M. Light memo, 21 December 1944).

24. Gorham, *Sound and Fury* (Briggs attributes this remark to Major Max-Muller, but Gorham is quite clear about it).

25. Gorham's comments come from *Sound and Fury*, Kirby's from Kirby and Davis, *Star Spangled Radio*, p. 142.

26. Jill Balcon, wartime BBC announcer, in conversation with the author. Similar comments are made by Margaret Hubble and Trevor Hill, both former members of the BBC staff who worked with the AEFP during the war.

TEN

"The Best Entertainment Program Ever"

Music and light entertainment provided the great bulk of the AEFP output, but there was a leavening of serious programs too. Probably the most outstanding was *Combat Diary*, produced by Royston Morley. This was a daily fifteen-minute program of actuality reports by American, Canadian, and British correspondents in the field. A novel feature was one nationality reporting on another: an American describing the British rocket-firing Typhoons, or a BBC man with Patton's Third Army. From the correspondents' point of view, it meant that their reports were heard within a few hours by the men whose actions they had been reporting and with whom they were living and sharing hardship and danger (a Canadian correspondent, Captain Bud Lynch, lost his arm in Normandy). As Maurice Gorham said later, "This quick come-back made for accuracy and discouraged heroics."[1] Correspondents soon came to appreciate a few words of approval from the troops more than any amount of praise from their bosses in London or New York. As one writer noted, "Allied troops thirsted for war news and authentic descriptions, always however at tabloid length and easily heard under canteen or field listening conditions on indifferent receivers."[2] And it was a great boost to their morale to hear first-hand reports of actions in which they had taken part. There were many notable broadcasts, but perhaps one of the most memorable was the Canadian Stanley Maxted describing how urgently needed supplies for the hard-pressed British forces at Arnhem had been dropped in the wrong place and picked up by the Germans.

Another innovation was *Mark Up the Map*, which told the troops every day where the front line was. It meant that all the men in the armies fighting their way across northwest Europe were kept informed and up-to-date on just what was happening. It was precisely the kind of real communication with the troops that General Eisenhower had in mind when he pressed for the AEFP to be set up. It had three regular present-ers, British, Canadian, and American, the last named being the best known, the film star Broderick Crawford, serving with AFN.[3]

But for those "precious few moments of leisure" it was entertainment and music the forces most wanted. *Rise and Shine* was always a good start to the day, and the AFN favorites such as *Duffle Bag* and *On the Record* (soon re-titled *Strictly on the Record*) were as popular as ever, with the British and Canadian troops now as much as with the Americans. But it was the Queensberry All Services Club in London that became the center for a series of variety and music programs featuring the top bands and artists then performing in Britain. The club was in what had been the Casino Theatre (formerly the Prince Edward Theatre) in Soho and had been bought by the Marquis of Queensberry, Sir Simon Marks, and others to be turned into a place where the servicemen and women of all nations visiting London on leave could relax and be entertained. All the facilities were free, and since the theater could seat 3,000 people it was ideal for big shows. It was normally packed out, since a show was staged there almost every day. Masterminding all the productions there for the AEFP was the BBC's Cecil Madden. He was able to call on all the big Hollywood stars visiting Europe to entertain the troops—Bing Crosby, Marlene Dietrich, Dinah Shore, and many others.[4]

Bing Crosby shared a duet in one show with a young British singer, Anne Shelton, the girl who had recorded the best-selling English version of **Lilli Marlene**. She had the wit—and the temerity—to mimic Bing's famous deep-voiced "buh-buh-buh-buh," to the delight of the packed audience and to Crosby's amusement. Later, as Crosby was dining at a London restaurant, word got round and a crowd of several hundred gathered outside. He interrupted his meal, went out onto the balcony, and sang for them, unaccompanied and in the blackout. The star enter-tainers, in fact, were remarkably accommodating, especially for "the boys at the front." The story is told of Dinah Shore, who had given a lengthy performance for a large audience of GIs in Normandy. When it was over, she had no sooner changed into the military-style uniform she wore when traveling in the front line than two soldiers arrived, too late to see her show. They told her they had traveled a long way just to see her, so she changed back into her stage costume and sang a whole series of numbers just for them.[5]

The main Saturday show from the Queensberry Club was *AEF Special*. Sergeant Keith Jameson of AFN was the MC, and the theme of Allied unity was emphasized when the 7-foot Boston singer, Corporal Jack Powers, would sing an English song to a British band, supported by the girl bagpipers of the ATS (the British equivalent of the WACs) on a show with a Canadian producer. More Anglo-American emphasis came with *Atlantic Spotlight,* jointly produced by the BBC in London and NBC in New York. It was heard live in both countries and featured the top bands and singers from both sides of the Atlantic. Another big favorite was *Variety Bandbox,* an hour-long show that was one of the BBC's top variety programs, with the emphasis on comedy and new talent.

The Canadians made a substantial contribution to AEFP—more than their numbers demanded. The *Canada Show* was another acclaimed AEFP success, presented by Gerry Wilmot, a lively and always entertaining broadcaster as well as a capable war correspondent. His infectiously cheerful manner is typical of the program he compered. One of the few AEFP recordings surviving is an edition of the *Canada Show* in which two of the leading announcers from AFN, Keith Jameson and George Monaghan, engage in a piece of light-hearted badinage that epitomizes the broadcasting style of that era.

The music for the show was provided by the Canadian Band of the AEF, conducted by Captain Robert Farnon. It was one of three "house bands," the others being the British Band of the AEF, conducted by Regimental Sergeant Major George Melachrino, and the American Band of the AEF, conductor Captain (later Major) Glenn Miller. It was Colonel (as he had now become) John Hayes, head of AFN, who suggested the three orchestras should be given the generic title "of the AEF." He thought it would make it clear that the bands were there specially for the AEFP.[6] Indeed, neither the Canadian nor the American bands would have been in Britain at all had it not been for the new radio service.

Robert Farnon was (and still is) a composer of some note, and his talents as an arranger gave the Canadian band's performances a special flavor, especially on the *Canada Show,* which was their main showpiece. The fifty-strong band stayed on in London, braving the V-bombs, and found time for film work, notably *I Live in Grosvenor Square* (U.S. title, *A Yank in London*), starring American actor Dean Jagger and the English film star Anna Neagle. Another link with the film world was the band's number two and chief administrator Douglass Montgomery, then an army lieutenant and shortly to appear in one of the great wartime films *Way to the Stars.* Like the Miller orchestra, the band and its two principal vocalists, Joanne Dallas and Paul Carpenter, put in a lot of time touring military bases in the southeast of England. So, too, did units of the British Band of the AEF, which, apart from international stars like Marlene Dietrich and Bing Crosby, called on a bevy of guest singers. One of them was RAF Corporal Denny Dennis, a leading dance-band vocalist in Britain at the time, though almost blacklisted by the BBC's Slush Committee (see chapter 5). After the war, he joined Tommy Dorsey's orchestra, the first Englishman to appear with a big-name American band. The British AEF band escaped the remorseless V-bomb bombardment unscathed, but its leader, George Melachrino, did not. Tragically, his wife and son were killed by a V-bomb which destroyed their home. Some time later, Melachrino was appearing with the Miller orchestra at the Queensberry Club when a doodlebug passed right over the top of the theater but fortunately did not explode.[7]

Good though the Canadian and British bands were, it was Glenn Miller's band that eclipsed all others in popularity and fame. Just a few bars of one of its famous numbers today instantly brings back the memory and atmosphere of the war years for anyone who was there at the time. To the American forces for whom the band played at scores of concerts, it was particularly important. There is no doubt that the famous remark by General Doolittle, Commanding General of the Eighth Air Force, was the perfect tribute: "Next to a letter from home, Captain Miller, your organisation is the greatest morale-builder in the ETO."[8]

It was Colonel Kirby, the head of broadcasting at SHAEF, who was instrumental in bringing Miller and his band to Britain. On a visit to New York, he heard that Miller, who had volunteered for military service though he was nearing 40, was keen to take the band overseas to play for the troops in the field. He was just what the new AEFP needed. General Eisenhower sent an immediate cable to Washington asking for Miller and his orchestra to be despatched to Europe as a top priority to appear on what was expected to be "a potent instrument for the maintenance of troop morale."[9]

Miller himself was soon on his way by air, followed by the 60-odd members of the band and its entourage, making the hazardous journey across the Atlantic with 15,000 other troops on the liner *Queen Elizabeth*. It would be the first American band to perform in Britain since the mid-1930s, when U.S. orchestras were banned by the Ministry of Labour following a dispute with the American Federation of Musicians. It took a war to get the ban lifted.

So Glenn Miller came to Britain specifically to perform on the AEFP, a "terrific" boost to the whole setup, as Maurice Gorham acknowledged. Gorham also admitted that it was to bring him "plenty of trouble." In fact, of all the difficulties he encountered with the AEFP, Miller, he wrote later, proved to be "our worst crisis," even though he was such a great asset to the program.[10] They got off to a bad start because Miller had been led to believe that he was going to direct a program instead of simply supplying a band. Once that was sorted out, within a couple of weeks another dispute arose. Miller and his band had been playing on the BBC Home Service as well as on the AEFP. During very low passages on some musical numbers, listeners had complained that they thought the program had gone off the air. The BBC had the temerity to ask Miller, one of the great bandleaders of the era, if he would play at a more or less constant volume. He was furious. The contrasts in his music were for a definite purpose, he told them, and he had no intention of changing his style. "We did not come here to entertain civilians but to play for the fighting men of the allied forces," he said and walked out of the meeting.[11]

Miller had set himself a punishing schedule. He was not a man to spare himself or the band, and his aim was to entertain as many of the forces as he possibly could through live concerts. In all weathers, he toured constantly throughout the country, playing at air bases, army camps, hospitals, and clubs to audiences as large as 10,000 at a time. At one show the band met the queen (now the Queen Mother), who said the two young princesses were great fans and listened regularly to the band's broadcasts.[12] She was referring to the future Queen Elizabeth II and Princess Margaret. In between all this traveling, with only the briefest of respites, the band had to fit in its broadcasts. Miller wanted to record as many of these as he could in order to free him for live concerts. The BBC, on the other hand, were anxious to have the immediacy of live broadcasts in a program which was full of recordings. They had, in fact, obliged by recording a number of Miller's concerts, though nowhere near as many as he would have liked. And it was pointed out that Miller was here to broadcast on the AEFP, and the live concerts were secondary if there was any clash of priorities.

Frustrated, Miller fired off an ill-considered memorandum in which he used a number of unwise expressions, including a reference to the BBC's "lackadaisical and ineffective broadcast methods." This letter is quoted in full by Colonel Kirby in the account he wrote later, and it is not difficult to see his hand in the affair. Had he followed the policy line laid down by Eisenhower about Anglo-American relations, he would have been doing his best to calm Miller down, not stir him up. He also made much of a story that the Miller band was to be dropped from the BBC's domestic programs, a story apparently without the least foundation but which Kirby misrepresented by attributing to the corporation a particularly crass comment dreamed up by a journalist. By taking such a partisan approach, he did a disservice to the highly regarded but pressurized Glenn Miller.[13] The whole matter was smoothed over, and the BBC did all it could to meet Miller's requirements, but, as Gorham noted, by now he seemed to have decided everyone was against him.[14]

As part of the policy of inter-Allied integration, the BBC offered Miller the top British singers. But it soon discovered he did not particularly want them. As Franklin Engelmann later recalled: "He had a complete entertainment unit and a set of formats for all his shows. What he really wanted was to be given studios, technicians and air time and left to get on with it. In fact, he was pretty sarcastic about some of our attempts to be useful."[15]

In the event, the band did use a number of the leading British soloists more than once, and Miller was always charming to every one of them:

Vera Lynn, Anne Shelton, Dorothy Carless, Gloria Brent, and Paula Green among them.

The episodes involving Glenn Miller need to be seen in perspective. They were spread over several months at a time when everyone involved was under intense pressure, and the occasional misunderstanding or explosive outburst was only to be expected. It is interesting to speculate how different things might have been if AFN's original plan of keeping its D-Day programs completely separate from the BBC had been put into operation and Miller had worked for an American organization not a British one. The fact is that Glenn Miller was an extremely talented musician who understandably did not find what he regarded as the bureaucratic mind particularly congenial. He was to find it even less congenial later on when Colonel David Niven (who eventually took over as head of SHAEF broadcasting from Colonel Kirby) issued a firm directive about recordings and personal appearances in formal terms that could easily have caused offense.[16]

However, there were plenty of lighter moments. When the band moved out of London's "bomb alley" to Bedford, they found that it was also the wartime home of the celebrated BBC Symphony Orchestra. Its conductor, Sir Adrian Boult, often watched the Miller band rehearsing. "I found it fascinating," he said later. "Miller was a thorough craftsman. He knew just what he wanted from his band and how to get it and he didn't mind how hard he worked himself or them. The band included 20 string players, all from famous orchestras in the USA, some who had played with me in orchestral concerts." But he added: "I wished they could have been playing better stuff."[17]

At one show at the Queensberry Club, the mutes for the trumpets failed to arrive, so the band used empty tin cans instead. Another occasion gave rise to a favorite AEFP legend: Glenn Miller was unhappy about the sound balance of a number the band was rehearsing. It needed more microphones, he said: a lot more microphones. He suggested 24 would be about right, which represented one mike for every two players. The senior BBC engineer raised his eyebrows but agreed to do what Captain Miller wanted: it was his orchestra after all. When the recording was over, Miller turned to him and said: "There, you see what a difference it makes?" The engineer smiled and said nothing. What Miller did not know was that only eight of the mikes were energized. That story, which sounds apocryphal, is also told about Tommy Dorsey, so perhaps it has some foundation in fact.[18]

Though it was pre-eminent, the Miller band was only one of many heard on AEFP. Cecil Madden calculated that while it was on the air 149 orchestras took part in its broadcasts. One of the best was another American outfit, the U.S. Navy Band. Under the title Naval Reserve Band 501 and led by the celebrated clarinetist Artie Shaw, it had undertaken a long tour of the South Pacific in 1943. At the end of it, Chief Petty Officer Shaw was demobbed with a nervous breakdown after coming under repeated Japanese air attacks. The band came to Britain in 1944, with Sam Donahue now as its leader. In some respects it outshone the Miller band, as the British magazine *Melody Maker* reported in February 1945: "In spite of it not being heard to anything like the extent which the Glenn Miller band was . . . enthusiasts are unanimous in declaring that, considered purely as a swing combo, the Sam Donahue bunch is the more exciting of the two." That view was shared by others, and the orchestra has been described as "one of the most magnificent bands of all time."[19]

Where the Miller band scored particularly was that its size and wealth of talent enabled it to be split up into small sections, each of which was able to produce separate programs for the AEFP. Sergeant George Ockner and his string section contributed *Strings with Wings*, which Sir Adrian Boult guest conducted on one occasion at Miller's personal request. Sergeant Johnny Desmond had his own weekly program, *A Soldier and a Song*, which later became the vehicle for another singing GI, Corporal Jack Powers. The Swing Sextet was a small jazz group, led by pianist Staff Sergeant Mel Powell (who had played with the Benny Goodman band), which featured in another popular program, *Uptown Hall*. It had a notable signature tune, written by Powell, **My Guy's Come Back,** which became a hit in its own right. Perhaps the best remembered of all of the Miller band offshoots is *Swing Shift*, with the vocals from Johnny Desmond and the Crew Chiefs. It also featured a famous trio: Sergeant Ray McKinley on drums, Sergeant Peanuts Hucko, clarinet, and Mel Powell at the piano. McKinley was a Texan who, like so many of the band, had been a leading figure in the music world before being called up, having been a drummer with the Dorsey Brothers and later running his own orchestra. He was something of a contrast with the more reserved Glenn Miller. A BBC announcer who worked with him on AEFP says he was a most likable man, "very approachable with a nice sense of humour."[20] He was also a songwriter and he introduced *Swing Shift* with what became known as **Sergeant Mac's Git Along Song**. It was sung to an arrangement that Glenn Miller himself apparently composed in tandem with McKinley in no more than an hour or so. McKinley was responsible for the words and wrote fresh lyrics every time the program went on the air. Mention it to anyone who remembers the AEFP and AFN from the war years, and they will quote the first two lines without hesitation. It so conveys the flavor of the time that it is worth giving just one version of it in full:

> This is Sgt Ray McKinley saying how d'you do
> And all the boys of the band saying howdy too
> So light up a smoke and flip out an ear
> Here's a bluesy resume of what you're gonna hear.

> Because it's tradition to sort of start out strong
> We always pick a screamer for our opening song
> But then to equalise the pressure—there's so much strain—
> We slow down the next one in a quieter vein
> 'Course Sgt Johnny Desmond's gonna add his say
> About romance and heartaches and et set a ray
> Tonight we'll have a number by ye old tree oak
> Composed of drums, clarinet and a highee note
> Yup, some of it's old and some of it's new
> And some tunes are happy and some of 'em blue
> But whatever you prefer it's our intent
> That the next 30 minutes will see you sent.[21]

When the AEFP had been running barely two months, General Barker ventured to pronounce it a success. "It has been found that the listening habits and tastes of the three forces are so much alike that a program such as the present AEF Program is popular in all of them and fully meets their needs," he wrote. The man who had helped to instigate the new service was unlikely to be an objective commentator, and his judgment proved somewhat premature, especially in view of later critical comments from the men on the receiving end, most particularly the Americans. The general went on to say that "as long as active combat operations continue, an inter-Allied radio service promotes a community of spirit among the forces, since it emphasizes the singleness of effort of the three nations." There were practical reasons, too, for his optimism. "A single radio service effects a material economy in skilled manpower and technical equipment," he added, ignoring the fact that AFN was continuing to broadcast as if the AEFP did not exist.[22]

The man who was running the program, Maurice Gorham, wrote a somewhat more guarded assessment, concerned mainly with practical problems. He was especially concerned about audience reaction. "The whole of our present operation is being carried on in the dark owing to lack of reliable information on listening habits and tastes of the AEF overseas or indeed at home."[23] It was agreed at the first meeting of the AEF Advisory Committee that a full survey should be carried out of the troops' opinion of the new service. A detailed inquiry was made of the listening habits of British forces listeners, but the results were disappointingly lacking in specifics. What did emerge was a good deal of satisfaction with the programs, so clearly Gorham and his team were on the right lines.[24] The British troops, it has to be said, did rather well out of the AEFP, being offered a range of top American programs such as *Command Performance* and *Mail Call*, as well as Bing Crosby, Bob Hope, and a host of others, all familiar already to listeners to AFN. But the Americans were not so enamored, on the whole, of the British contribution to the program.

Something of their dissatisfaction percolated to the United States, and various congressmen and writers crossed the Atlantic to find out for themselves. Gorham wrote later that they had been told the troops were being fed un-American programs, but once they had heard at first hand what the AEFP was about they "were much impressed by the facts."[25] An article in the New York World Telegram praised the program as providing "the boys" with the best in radio fare, though understandably it was the American side of the output that was singled out for particular praise.[26]

If the transatlantic visitors had been around on Independence Day 1944, they would certainly have been impressed by what they heard. The AEFP broadcast a special three-way live show linking Normandy, Britain, and the United States. Such broadcasts are routine now, but in the middle of a world war half a century ago they were still looked on as something of a technical miracle. The SHAEF military transmitter in France was used for the link across the Channel, and the main U.S. Army signal station linking London with New York made sure that the transatlantic link worked smoothly. David Niven and Franklin Engelmann went over to France with an American army scriptwriter to organize the program, so that the voices of American, Canadian, and British troops in the field were heard not only in the front line but in their respective home countries as well.[27]

Given the very different approaches of AFN and the BBC, there were relatively few problems over program material. But there were the occasional culture clashes. The BBC was happy for the new program to have a relaxed style. But there were limits. On one occasion, George Monaghan of AFN was taken to task by the senior BBC announcer who oversaw all scripts, Franklin Engelmann. Dedicating the record **It Must Be Jelly 'Cos Jam Don't Shake Like That,** Monaghan mentioned in his script that it must refer to "a great big hulk of a woman." He was told that simply would not do: the British Tommy would find the phrase quite unacceptable. So the offending expression came out—another example of the differing attitudes of the two nations.[28]

The new-style news headlines gave rise to a peculiarly British problem. At certain times of the day, they were preceded by the chimes of Big Ben, which lasted a full minute. Since only three minutes was allotted to the news bulletin, the chimes were faded out to accommodate it. But as was pointed out, "a large body of opinion resents this. . . . The chimes have a special significance for the British listening public." And so the quick-fire approach of the New World clashed once more with the traditions of the Old, though the matter was settled, yet again, by sensible give-and-take on both sides.[29]

Within a short time, the AEFP had settled down into a regular schedule, which aimed to provide the right balance of programs to please all its forces' listeners. Record requests alternated with variety and comedy shows, sport with jazz and dance music. Talks and classical music were kept to a minimum as a matter of policy. The program makers were fully aware of the popular tastes of the great majority of their listeners and also of the conditions under which they heard the AEFP: crowded mess halls, noisy barrack rooms, PA systems blaring away. The letters that began to come in from the troops in the field showed how much they appreciated what the AEFP was doing.

But the rumblings from the Americans went on. Captain Robert Light, who was running AFN while John Hayes was involved with the AEFP, made a trip to the Continent and came back with a number of criticisms. First of all, there was not enough American sport news. British variety programs (particularly *ITMA*) were "fairly unpopular" among American troops, who, rather than listen to them, sometimes switched over to German radio stations playing popular music. But most of all, the "general opinion was that the news as a whole was slanted too much towards the British." When it was explained to them that 50 percent of the news was read by Americans, there was general surprise. "It still sounds like the same news we heard over the BBC back in England."[30]

The situation was not helped by Colonel Kirby, who was about to return to the United States at the end of his stint as head of broadcasting at SHAEF. He was asked to write a report on his tour of duty. He composed what he considered was a "frank and full" account but others called "provocative and controversial." As a result, just as he was about to fly back to America he was ordered to report at once to General Barker's headquarters. The general accused him of seriously jeopardizing the relationship between SHAEF and the BBC. He was ordered to recall all the copies of his "indiscreet" report at once and disavow the contents, under threat of disciplinary action. Only when he had made it clear in writing that the report had been written without the knowledge and consent of General Barker and did not represent the official views of SHAEF was he allowed to return home. He appears to think, with some reason, that he was lucky not to have been court-martialed. Kirby was clearly a man of considerable ability, who undoubtedly had American interests, as he saw them, very much at heart. But his prejudice against the BBC hierarchy (whose sometimes labyrinthine machinations are best countered by subtlety, not the bull-at-a-gate approach) achieved nothing other than his own undoing. It was an unhappy ending to an appointment that had only helped to sour Anglo-American relations.[31]

That Kirby was not alone in his view of the AEFP became very clear as the recriminations continued. Finally, the chief of Special and Information Services for the U.S. Forces in Europe sent Lieutenant Colonel True Boardman on a fact-finding mission. He visited the Seventh and Third U.S. Armies and reported in January of 1945. He acknowledged that the

AEFP provided radio of a high standard, and he was not criticizing that in any way. Furthermore, the combined operation after D Day had been essential. "It placed emphasis in every possible way on the fact that we came to the Continent as one force, one army, with absolute singleness of purpose." For that reason the "combined radio service was psychologically of great value." But by late 1944 the position had altered. By now the joint broadcasting operation, he believed, "provides a program service less than satisfactory to most American listeners. It works against, rather than for, friendly relations with our British allies."

He then went on to detail some of the criticisms made by the troops. They felt the AEFP was not what U.S. Army broadcasting ought to be— a strong and familiar tie with home. Some went so far as to regard it as "another Limey propaganda gag." Others referred to the supposedly inter-Allied service as "that BBC deal." Much of this feeling stemmed from that bugbear of the Americans, the continued use of the phrase "of the BBC." But there were other irritants: the GIs didn't want to know about British soccer reports; they disliked the British comedians, whom they neither appreciated nor understood; most thought British popular music was inferior to their own name bands. The AEFP was basically British in spirit, reminding U.S. listeners more of England than of home.

The news was another source of complaint. The GIs felt the BBC placed undue emphasis on British units at the expense of the Americans: British forces were always mentioned first. Also, they saw no reason why news coverage should be split evenly, since the United States had more troops in Europe than did Britain. Altogether, they did not believe the U.S. Army was getting the credit it should from the BBC. In this, they were supported by Colonel David Niven, who had been pressing for more American programs on the AEFP because by then the U.S. forces outnumbered the British. It may be this pressure that resulted in the headline in *Stars and Stripes* just before New Year's Eve 1944: "GI Gripes Win Continent AFN More of Own Shows."[32]

Boardman's conclusion was that the AEFP "actually mitigates against the very objectives which inspired its establishment. It engenders anti-British feelings on the part of American soldiers and deprives those same soldiers of radio as they prefer to hear it."

So, he considered that the original mission of the AEFP having been accomplished, "further continuance of the joint service is undesirable." He therefore recommended it should be discontinued forthwith. The British forces had the BBC's General Forces Programme to listen to. The Americans should be catered for by the American Forces Network, which was already operating transmitters on the Continent, even though it was not reaching all the Allied forces now occupying the whole of France and other parts of northwest Europe.[33]

It should be stressed that Boardman, who was part of the AFRS, was an interested party and so inclined to hear what he wanted to hear. But he believed that a more extensive scientific survey would still come up with the same answers. There is no record of any official reaction to his report or of any discussion of it. Maurice Gorham does not mention it in his autobiography, though it seems unlikely that he was unaware of it. Some time before, General Barker had recommended that the service should continue "during the period of active operations in North West Europe" and that "no effort be made to establish separate services on the continent during that period."[34] Whatever the military hierarchy may have thought of Boardman's views, in the event the AEFP continued until the war in Europe was over. To have accepted the recommendation to close it down prematurely would have been an admission that the whole costly exercise was wrong.

Yet what the complaints by the American troops amounted to was that they simply did not like listening to British radio programs. As in almost every aspect of the war, they were reluctant to put up with anything other than what they had always been used to. The British forces were happy enough to listen to American programs, though some of the humor must have baffled them as much as did British comedians the Americans. And British soldiers no doubt found reports on baseball and U.S. college football just as incomprehensible as the GIs did the soccer scores. But the Americans were seemingly unwilling to compromise and, as Boardman says, resented being made to do so. Thus the professional broadcasters' forecasts were proved right and the military wrong. Everyone but the military hierarchy would have been much happier if AFN and BBC had continued on their separate ways. It is perfectly understandable that the American troops should want their own familiar programs, but in the last resort the blame lay not with the BBC but with their own military leaders.

However, it would be unfair to suggest that the AEFP was a failure: far from it. Politically it may have been so, at least from the American viewpoint. It may not have achieved the kind of inter-Allied unity General Eisenhower had hoped for: rather the contrary in some respects. But as a broadcasting enterprise, it was a remarkable achievement. The three broadcasting organizations—American, British, and Canadian—had worked well together despite their differences of outlook and approach. They had produced a mixture of talented programs which, if they did not please everybody (what radio service ever has?), had given enormous pleasure to millions of servicemen and women and to civilians too. Maurice Gorham wrote that among the many letters of appreciation he had had from service listeners, "it was surprising how many of them appreciated the idea behind the service and thought better of their allies because of it, thus justifying SHAEF's original idea." He does not say so, but the context suggests that most of those letters came from British listeners. But even so, General Eisenhower clearly had something to be pleased about and some justification for his insistence on setting up the service. Gorham certainly believed that it had been a job worth doing, even though he was "accused of something by somebody at least once a week throughout the lifetime of the program." Given the wealth of talented material at its disposal, he considered it "the best entertainment program ever put on the air."[35]

NOTES

1. Gorham, *Sound and Fury*, pp. 146–147; *History of AFRTS*, p. 45 et seq.

2. BBCWAC, S24/54/22 (Cecil Madden, "Something for the Boys").

3. Kirby and Davis, *Star Spangled Radio*, p. 157.

4. Madden, "Something for the Boys"; Butcher, *Letter from Home*, p. 134.

5. Madden, "Something for the Boys"; Oranges and Lemons broadcast; Way, *Big Bands*, pp. 181–182.

6. BBCWAC, R34/185 (Gorham memo, 2 January 1944, quoting Hayes).

7. Way, *Big Bands* (Farnon, pp. 79–89, Melachrino, pp. 23, 26). The Denny Dennis reference comes from *I'll Sing You a Thousand Love Songs* by Mike Carey (printed for the Denny Dennis Society, 1992).

8. Way, *Big Bands*, p. 175; Butcher, *Letter from Home*, p. 115; *History of AFRTS*, p. 46.

9. Butcher, *Letter from Home*, p. 47.

10. Gorham, *Sound and Fury*, p. 151.

11. Way, *Big Bands*, p. 174; Butcher, *Letter from Home*, p. 92.

12. Way, *Big Bands*, p. 173. *Note*: The British Royal family played their part in the war. The King's brother, the Duke of Kent, who was in the RAF, was killed in an air crash. Buckingham Palace was bombed twice during the Blitz on London, the King and Queen having decided to stay in the capital and share the hardships of their people. And when she was 18 Princess Elizabeth (later to be Queen Elizabeth II) joined the women's army, the ATS, and trained as a driver. (Sources: *Whitaker's Almanack 1940–46*; *The Royal Family in Wartime* (Odhams Press 1945).

13. Kirby and Davis, *Star Spangled Radio*, pp. 151–153.

14. Gorham, *Sound and Fury*, p. 152.

15. BBC broadcast, 8 June 1953, "Close-up of Glenn Miller."

16. Butcher, *Letter from Home*, pp. 175–176.

17. BBC broadcast, "Close-up of Glenn Miller."

18. The source for this story is Cecil Madden. He recounted it in the Oranges and Lemons broadcast and is also quoted in Way, *Big Bands*, p. 175. Madden is not always the most reliable witness (he rarely let the details get in the way of a good story), but he worked closely with Miller and is hardly likely to have invented the episode.

19. Way, *Big Bands*, pp. 69–70, quoting *Melody Maker*, 17 February 1945; and George T. Simon, *The Big Bands* (Schirmer Books 1981), pp. 423, 475–476.

20. Margaret Hubble (now Horne), in conversation with the author.

21. AEFP *Swing Shift* broadcast 28 April 1945.

22. Public Record Office, London, SHAEF files, WO219/6 (Gen Barker's memo, 4 August 1944).

23. BBCWAC, R34/184/1 (Gorham memo, 13 June 1944).

24. Ibid. (Minutes of AEFP Advisory Committee held on 14 June 1944).

25. Gorham, *Sound and Fury*, p. 157.

26. *New York World Telegram* (BBCWAC, R44/11).

27. Gorham, *Sound and Fury*, p. 151; *History of AFRTS*, p. 45.

28. Oranges and Lemons broadcast.

29. Public Record Office, London SHAEF files (WO219/7).

30. BBCWAC, R34/185 (Capt. Robt Light memo, 21 December 1944).

31. Kirby and Davis, *Star Spangled Radio*, pp. 160–161.

32. Ibid., p. 162.

33. *History of AFRTS*, pp. 47–48, quoting report by Lt. Col. T. Boardman to Brig. Gen. O. N. Solbert, 22 January 1945.

34. Public Record Office, SHAEF Files (WO 219/6, Gen. Barker memo, 4 August 1944).

35. Gorham, *Sound and Fury*, p. 159.

ELEVEN

AFN on the Road to Berlin

All the time the AEFP was on the air, AFN was continuing to broadcast to the U.S. forces remaining in Britain. Six months after the invasion there were still over 650,000 of them, and even when the war in Europe ended there were more than 430,000. They were at air bases, service and supply units, and military hospitals, and they expected—and got—the all-American radio service that AFN provided.[1] Indeed, AFN was still opening new transmitters in the United Kingdom right up until April and May 1945. By the time the war ended, it had nearly seventy transmitters operating in Britain.[2]

AFN had been preparing for D Day for some time. Mobile broadcast vans were made ready to accompany the troops across the Channel, and the men who would operate them were fully trained and briefed. The plan was for AFN to have one mobile station with each of the U.S. armies in the field, using London as a network headquarters. The aim was achieved. Within a short while of the invasion, AFN began broadcasting from close to the rapidly moving Allied front line. Mobile stations, complete with personnel and records, were deployed to broadcast music and news to the troops in the battle areas and feed news reports back to the studio in London.

The mobile stations, including those the BBC also put in the field, broadcast as near to the front line as it was safe to get, often less than 30 miles from the fighting. It was not an easy life, sometimes sleeping in the open or, as the weather worsened, in freezing tents. Often the local populace, anxious to show their gratitude for being liberated, would offer accommodation and were only too glad to share the food the broadcasters brought with them since they had very little of their own. In Holland, the Dutch Resistance provided an unofficial armed escort for one of the British mobile stations since, so near the front line, they were vulnerable to enemy attack. Indeed, the AFN mobile unit with the U.S. First Army in Belgium was reported to have been "almost lost" in the Battle of the Bulge, the sudden German onslaught of December 1944.[3] The broadcasting service was vulnerable in other ways. A station calling itself Radio Arnhem, operating behind the German lines, would pick up the AEFP transmissions and relay them. Then it would slip in enemy propaganda usually intended to cause ill-feeling between the Americans and the British, praising General Montgomery to the detriment of General Patton or vice versa. The Radio Arnhem news was frequently mistaken for the AEFP and from time to time caused trouble between the allies, though usually short-lived.[4] One of its broadcasters was the American, Axis Sally, eventually to face trial for treason. Radio Arnhem was the German answer to broadcasts by the Psychological Warfare Division of SHAEF from Radio Luxembourg. The latter, calling itself "Twelve, Twelve," proved remarkably successful in spreading doubt and confusion in Germany by passing itself off as a German-language station.[5]

As long as the mobile stations transmitted the AEFP for much of the day, they were allowed to put out a couple of hours of their own local material whenever they were able to. This was regarded as complying with the letter of the directive from General Barker that "no effort be made to establish separate services on the continent" while military operations continued. Strictly speaking, AFN was not directly under his command, being part of ETOUSA, which was technically separate from SHAEF. But it needed SHAEF's authority to operate with the armies in the field. Not that military technicalities greatly troubled AFN, which had always been a law unto itself. John Hayes, as its commanding officer, was reluctant even to give the Armed Forces Radio Service credit where credit was due. It was the accepted practice for the BBC to announce after each AFRS program it broadcast: "This program was recorded in America and is heard by arrangement with the Armed Forces Radio Service." Hayes wrote asking the BBC to change that to "This program . . . is heard by arrangement with the American Forces Network of the Armed Forces Radio Service." And he supported his request by saying he had been sent a direction to that effect from the War Department in Washington—as indeed he had, but only because he had intended to take all the credit for AFN and not mention the AFRS at all![6]

AFN's independent attitude showed in other ways. As one writer has noted, some of its policies "seemed to be in direct opposition to the general good of troop broadcasting." It apparently made no great effort to help with command problems and played no part in organized military information or education broadcast campaigns. The aim of AFN "was predominantly morale and entertainment programming." It made full use of the star-studded programs AFRS sent it, but in other respects "it almost completely broke away from its AFRS attachments."[7] Hayes even emphasized the point with AFN's letterheading, which proclaimed on every sheet: "This is the American Forces Network."

Like all successful empire builders, Hayes was very publicity conscious and was particularly good at persuading journalists to write articles about AFN. Typical was a double-page illustrated spread in *Stars and Stripes*, lauding the organization and how it was bringing "the cream of US radio" to American troops. Perhaps it was this and AFN's sometimes high-handed attitude to the AFRS which prompted a vitriolic diatribe by Maurice Gorham. In a reference to Hayes' policy of getting newspapers to print articles "puffing" AFN's achievements, he wrote: "What I find most annoying is the friendliness and humility these birds show when they are asking for transmitters or concessions of any kind and the cock-a-hoop claims they are caught making as soon as they have got them." And he went on to produce a damning criticism of AFN and its announcing staff:

Although AFN in many ways has done a remarkable job here it is a very small town operation and we have found their announcers, when they worked for AEFP, not only illiterate but very unresourceful. We recently had to ask them to change one of their oldest hands because when a line failed he lost his head completely and made the most amateurish announcements I have ever heard. Of course, they can't read scripts and their strong point is ad-libbing commercial record programs which they do very well. The really remarkable thing about AFN is the AFRS supply of record shows which reflect the greatest credit on the Tom Lewis organisation [AFRS]. But what is done to them this end would often surprise the producers if they could hear it for themselves.[8]

Pretty savage stuff from a broadcasting ally. And condescending, too, from a man who worked for one of the biggest broadcasting organizations in the world, which had been in existence for twenty years compared with AFN's two. It was just as well it was for internal BBC consumption only and never reached any of his American counterparts.

Gorham certainly had his hands full with AFN and its allies. Before he returned home, Colonel Kirby had fired off another bombshell. This time he was orchestrating a campaign for the Americans to go it alone, cutting themselves off from the BBC altogether. The ostensible reason was that the reception of the AEFP on the Continent was unsatisfactory—a claim the BBC strongly disputed—and there were enough transmitters now available on the Continent to do the job properly. He claimed the scheme had the approval of General Barker, despite the general's directive that there was to be no separation. When the BBC resisted Kirby's proposal, he accused it of undertaking a campaign to discredit and undermine those involved. And further, he expressed the view that the BBC, having originally been reluctant to take on the AEFP, now wanted to retain it because it saw it as a "valuable property."[9]

The fact was, as Kirby should have known, that not only had his superior, General Barker, laid down that there was to be no separation, but the BBC had given a firm undertaking to General Eisenhower that it would continue the AEFP until he, as Supreme Commander, indicated the time had come to wind it up. Kirby's suggestion, of course, would have meant that AFN would take over all the broadcasting for the American forces, and Gorham understandably saw AFN's hand in all this. He was to write later: "ETOUSA [which controlled AFN] had not wanted the AEFP; they had wanted to give their troops AFN and all through its history ETOUSA thought that our program was all the better the more it sounded like AFN."[10] He must have been greatly relieved when Colonel Kirby finally departed, since he must have regarded him by now as a serious troublemaker, though no doubt the colonel believed he was acting in the best interests of the American troops.

On the Continent, Paris had been liberated. AFN's Sergeant Keith Jameson had a close shave when he was giving a commentary on the chaotic scenes that accompanied General de Gaulle's entry into the city. Suddenly firing broke out. "It went on all around us," he said later. "We were in the center of cross fire, with bullets flying everywhere. The top of our recording van was shot away in the hail of fire. Our assignment had been to give a 'color' broadcast but this was too darned colorful."[11] A woman who had taken refuge behind the recording van was hit by a stray bullet and killed.

Jameson was luckier than two others of his colleagues. Sergeant Jim McNally was killed in a German air attack when he was with the AFN mobile station with the Seventh Army. Not long after, Sergeant Pete Parrish, an AFN news correspondent, died while accompanying an airborne assault in France. Another AFN correspondent, G. K. Hodenfield (attached from *Stars and Stripes*), flew in a Lancaster bomber of the Royal Canadian Air Force on a raid over Berlin and saw the plane immediately ahead of him blow apart after receiving a direct hit. His account appeared on both AFN and Canadian broadcasting the next day.[12]

In October, turning a blind eye to SHAEF's policy of a single radio voice, Captain Bob Light went to Paris on Colonel Hayes's orders to put an AFN station on the air. He persuaded the French to give him a low-powered transmitter and also a studio, which became the operational center for AFN on the Continent. Soon it was broadcasting eighteen hours a day, and apart from the usual AFRS material there were record-request programs, with the station's own DJs playing the latest discs flown over from America and live shows featuring the stream of Hollywood stars who came to Europe to entertain the troops. Among them were Bob Hope, Marlene Dietrich, Paul Robeson, Ingrid Bergman, Betty Hutton, Jack Benny, and others whose first stop in Europe was AFN Paris. Many of them took part in a two-hour extravaganza to celebrate AFN's second birthday, a program which was broadcast by each of the four major American networks. Other regulars were Johnny Desmond and the Swing Shift unit from the Glenn Miller band. Small wonder that, like AFN in Britain, the station soon attracted a big audience among the civilian population.[13]

Elsewhere in France, AFN set up radio stations in cities liberated from the Germans by the advancing Allied armies: Dijon, Lyons, Nancy. And in the south of France, where a parallel invasion to the one in Normandy had taken place, AFN was soon broadcasting from Cannes, Nice, and Biarritz. It was hard going at times, but there were compensations. The station at Rheims, for instance, was set up in a chateau in the heart of the champagne country. Vintages that had been hidden from the Nazi occupiers for much of the war suddenly saw the light of day again, and legend has it that the AFN staff at that particular station proved to be an especially lively set of broadcasters![14]

With Paris liberated, the city became *the* center for American troops on leave, which was one reason why AFN had decided to set up a broadcasting center there. For much the same reason, it became the focus of attention for Glenn Miller, who wanted to see that the armies fighting at the front got the same sort of attention as those at the air bases in Britain. He therefore proposed moving the American Band of the AEF to the French capital. The military authorities supported him, provided it did not interfere with his AEFP broadcasting commitments. The BBC, however, was not keen. So soon after the liberation, the recording facilities in Paris were inadequate, and the landlines to London were not always reliable. But Miller came up with the idea of pre-recording enough shows in Britain to enable the band to spend six weeks in Paris. It would mean a very heavy recording schedule: thirty hours of recordings, amounting to over sixty programs (plus reserve programs) in addition to their current recording schedule of nearly four hours of live broadcasts a week—all this to be achieved in less than three weeks. The BBC agreed, though not without misgivings. So Miller's original idea of recording his shows so that he could perform live was finally realized. Ironically and tragically, getting his own way was shortly to lead to his death.[15]

The recordings were completed as the band got through something approaching four times its normal workload: six weeks in Paris, they felt, was surely worth it. The work done, Miller set off to fly to France—

and, as everyone knows, was never seen again. As the hours, then the days, went by with no sign of his missing plane, the broadcasts he had recorded went on the air. Even when it became clear that there was little chance of finding him alive, Miller's voice continued to be heard. The BBC was accused of hushing the matter up, but it was in a real dilemma since SHAEF refused to make any announcement at all, even to say he was missing. It was not until Christmas Eve, nine days after the plane vanished, that the military authorities finally announced Miller's disappearance. The shock and real grief at Miller's death has been extensively chronicled, and even after half a century we are no wiser about what happened to him, despite many bizarre theories.[16] After his death, his band continued broadcasting and was often heard on the AEFP via AFN Paris. By the time the war ended, it had completed over 500 broadcasts and had made more than 350 personal appearances, a remarkable achievement he would certainly have been proud of.[17]

As the Allied advance continued, a European broadcasting landmark was liberated. It was the Americans who recaptured Radio Luxembourg, the commercial station which had been a popular favorite in England before the war and had fallen into German hands in 1940. The retreating Germans had intended to blow the station up but had been diverted from their intentions by a wily engineer, who had told them it was easier, and just as effective, to shoot the transmitter valves to pieces. This they did, not knowing that he had hidden away a spare set of valves four years earlier. The station was on the air again in just twelve days, which was particularly welcome as it had an extensive collection of records, including Glenn Miller, the Dorsey brothers, and Benny Goodman.[18]

Among the equipment left behind by the Germans was a new kind of recording machine. It was called the Magnetophon and used a magnetized tape to record sound of far better quality than the wire recorders then in use, or even the discs commonly used by broadcasters. It is now familiar to everyone, but then it ranked as a real innovation. The BBC's Maurice Gorham was most impressed with it. A musician friend gave it as his opinion that the quality was as good as a live broadcast, and it was certainly very much easier to edit than discs. Gorham says there were Magnetophon machines there for the asking, and although he tried to persuade the BBC to install them it showed little interest, having just invested in a new and improved disc-recording system.[19] The Americans were not so slow to react to the new technology. When, a little later, they took over broadcasting stations in Germany, they quickly came to the conclusion that here was a superior sound-and-recording system worth exploiting. Within a short while, AFN started using it for broadcasts and became the first American station in the world to use audiotape on the air.[20]

Meanwhile, AFN's mobile stations were keeping up with the advancing armies. They were now using 1,000-watt transmitters, working with three of the four American armies; only General Patton refused to have one with his Third Army. AFN was with General Hodges' troops all the way into Germany, and the general personally reported the fall of Cologne on the air. When the Americans made the first historic linkup with their Russian allies, AFN was there to report it. The next day's entire program was dedicated to "Uncle Joe's Boys" ("Uncle Joe" Stalin, that is), with the emphasis on Russian tunes, such as **The Volga Boatmen** and **Dark Eyes**. AFN reckoned that well over three-quarters of the U.S. forces were within receiving distance of their transmitters most of the time.[21] And the station now had a new slogan: "This is AFN, the American Forces Network on the road to Berlin."

By this time, the end of the war in Europe was in sight. It came with the German surrender on 7 May 1945. Anticipating the event, AFN had asked General Eisenhower's headquarters for a message that could be broadcast on the following day, VE Day. Owing apparently to a misunderstanding, they were given a statement the general had made praising the workers of Britain for the wonderful job they had done keeping the factories going in the face of years of German bombing. It did not go out on the AFN. It is ironic that Eisenhower, who had set such store by encouraging forces broadcasting, was not heard on AFN congratulating the men who had helped achieve victory.[22]

With Germany defeated, AFN began preparing to set up a broadcasting network for the American troops who would make up part of the army of occupation in the ruins of the Third Reich. And before long, the British troops, too, would get their own broadcasting service at last, as the British Forces Network (BFN) was established in the part of Germany earmarked as the British occupation zone. They were waiting for the end of the Allied Expeditionary Forces Programme, which finally closed down on 28 July 1945, D Day +417. It had been in existence for some fourteen months.

In a farewell broadcast, General Eisenhower understandably emphasized that the AEFP had exemplified the spirit of teamwork that had permeated the entire Allied Expeditionary Force. "All of us had our sight trained on a definite goal and . . . we pulled together as a team." The shutdown was marked by a farewell party in London, which General Barker came over from Germany to attend. He told the BBC's director-general that it had been "a splendid institution throughout" and, at a formal ceremony soon afterward, presented him with a signed testimonial from General Eisenhower complimenting the corporation on the way it had run the program, "a most excellent radio service of news and entertainment." Colonel Niven was awarded the Legion of Merit, and the Bronze Star went to Captains Franklin Engelmann and Royston

Morley. AFN was not left out: Colonel Hayes received not only the Bronze Star but also the French Croix de Guerre. So after all the acrimony and misgivings at the start and the feuding during its lifetime, it ended with congratulations and medals all round.[23]

Interestingly, after all his attempts to play down the role of AFRS, when the time came Hayes was happy to pay a generous tribute to his "parent company." In a four-page news sheet published at the close of AFN's wartime operations, under the headline "No. 1 Reason for Success? We Say AFRS," Hayes listed all that AFRS had done for its European outlet. Of AFN's 140-hour-a-week schedule, 52 hours came from the Armed Forces Radio Service which also supplied all the latest musical hits on record every week as well as substantial quantities of hard-to-get equipment. The news sheet also noted that AFN's original staff of just 17 had grown to over 300, and their broadcasts had reached 85 percent of all the U.S. armed forces in the ETO.[24]

NOTES

1. Ruppenthal, quoted by Reynolds, *Rich Relations*.
2. BBCWAC, R53/80.
3. *History of AFRTS*, p. 50; *A Microphone and a Frequency*, pp. 35–36. DeLay, p. 417. It has not been possible to confirm the report that the AFN First Army unit was in real danger. It was based in Liège, a good 20 miles from the limits of the German advance, but being Christmas may have been out in the field with the troops.
4. Gorham, *Sound and Fury*, p. 159.
5. Briggs, *History*, Vol. III, p. 679; Barnouw, *Golden Web*, pp. 201–202.
6. BBCWAC, R34/909/2 (Major John Hayes memo, 25 August 1944).
7. DeLay, pp. 421–422.
8. BBCWAC, E1/731/1 (Gorham memo, 2 July 1945).
9. Kirby and Davis, *Star Spangled Radio*, pp. 158–160.
10. Gorham, *Sound and Fury*, p. 148.
11. *Radio Times*, 6 May 1945.
12. *History of AFRTS*, p. 50.
13. "This Is the American Forces Network" (news sheet produced by AFN, undated, ca. July–August 1945, a copy of which is in BBCWAC R34/909/2) [hereafter TITAFN].
14. Christman, *Brass Button Broadcasters*, p. 57.
15. Way, *Big Bands*, pp. 187–188; Butcher, *Letter from Home*, pp. 195–200; Gorham, *Sound and Fury*, p. 152.
16. Way, *Big Bands*, pp. 289–292; Butcher, *Letter from Home*, pp. 213–217.
17. Butcher, *Letter from Home*, p. 255.
18. The story about the Radio Luxembourg valves is quoted by Barnouw, *Golden Web*, giving as the source *Yank* magazine of 11 May 1945.
19. Gorham, *Sound and Fury*, pp. 155–156. Gorham is misinformed about the BBC's attitude to magnetic tape recordings. A senior corporation engineer had been present at a demonstration of the Magnetophon before the war but noted that its use was limited because the tape kept breaking. The Germans ironed out this and other

problems during the war, and a BBC engineer serving with SHAEF sent back a tape recording soon after the liberation of Radio Luxembourg. Once the war was over, the BBC laid its hands on seven Magnetophons, and magnetic tape was used for the first time in a program as early as 1946. Its value was obvious. The only problem was the shortage of Magnetophons and the lack of any similar British machine. But the BBC pressed ahead with the introduction of magnetic tape for recordings, and before long it was widely in use. See Pawley, *BBC Engineering 1922–1972*, pp. 387–390.

20. Christman, *Brass Button Broadcasters*, p. 68; Barnouw, *Golden Web*, p. 204.

21. TITAFN.

22. *History of AFRTS*, p. 52; Christman, *Brass Button Broadcasters*, p. 57.

23. Gorham, *Sound and Fury*, pp. 162, 167. Colonel Kirby was not left out either. He received the Legion of Merit and the Order of the British Empire. Syl Binkin, first man to put AFN on the air, got the British Empire Medal.

24. TITAFN. By this time, there were 28 medium-wave AFN transmitters still operational in Britain, AFN London (a powerful short-wave transmitter) as well as eight stations in France and six in Germany.

TWELVE

AFN Postwar

In Germany all was chaos. The population was utterly demoralized. Great areas of the main cities and towns were in ruins, public services had collapsed, the railways were extensively disrupted, food and all essentials were in short supply, starvation threatened. The first priority for the victorious Allies was to get the country back on its feet. AFN had a part to play by providing information and entertainment for the occupying forces. The aim was set out clearly in a headline in Colonel Hayes's news sheet: "To Bring Yank Radio to Yanks in Europe: That's AFN's Purpose."

Munich had been one of the first cities the Americans captured. The birth center of the Nazi movement had been the target of repeated Allied air raids, and much of the city had been destroyed. Searching for relatively undamaged buildings, Major Bob Light of AFN came across the residence of the former Nazi Gauleiter in what had once been the home of the nineteenth-century German artist Wilhelm von Kaulbach. He commandeered it for use as a studio, and it was to remain the center of AFN's operations in Munich for forty-seven years until its close-down in 1992. The station had a transmitting tower 850 feet high, said to be the tallest in Europe. The transmitter valves were over 6 feet tall and got so hot they had to be water-cooled—not surprisingly, since the station radiated signals with a power of 100,000 watts.

Bob Light managed to get the station on the air and opened it up with a famous faux pas which nearly earned him a court-martial. "Good morning," were his first words, "This is AFN Munich, the voice of the Seventh Army." What he did not know was that during the night General Patton's Third Army had taken over control of the area. The highly volatile Patton, who was intensely proud of his army's reputation, was shaving when he heard the announcement and was so startled he cut himself. He ordered the instant arrest of the offending broadcaster. Fortunately, Light was forewarned of the general's displeasure and made a rapid tactical withdrawal.[1]

That was on 8 June 1945 and the first AFN station in Germany to go on the air. Within three years Munich had a staff of thirty-five enlisted men, ten announcers, five music librarians, two musical groups, and five military musicians. It also gave work to forty German nationals, who were only too grateful to have a job at a time when their country was still struggling to come to grips with defeat. That applied to the other stations AFN established, where the employment provided for German staff literally saved them and their families from starvation in the bitter winter that followed.

In just over a month, on 15 July, AFN Frankfurt went on the air in premises soon judged too close for comfort to the headquarters of the military command in Germany. So in August it moved to the place that was to be its home for the next twenty-one years, the von Bruening castle in the suburb of Hoechst, a few miles from the city center. Part of it dated back to the fourteenth century, and it boasted a moat, a portcullis, a watchtower, and even a dungeon. Frankfurt was soon to become the headquarters of the whole AFN operation in Germany.

Later in July, AFN opened a station at Bremen, in northwest Germany, the British zone of occupation, to cater for the port of Bremerhaven which was the entry point for U.S. forces. The station switched to Bremerhaven itself in 1949 and is remembered for its late-night sign off. It always closed down at midnight with the words: "Good night—and good morning, American forces," followed by the **Star-Spangled Banner**.

The next station to begin operations was in the divided city of Berlin, an island in the middle of Communist East Germany. It started broadcasting on 4 August from an improvised studio in a hut on the back of a truck, using an aerial strung up between two trees. Sixty percent of the city was in ruins, and the supply of electricity was limited. Nevertheless, the AFN engineers managed to rig up a 30-foot-long electric sign proclaiming the presence of "AFN Berlin," which in a city virtually without street lights at night attracted large crowds of Berliners. The station made an equally attention-catching debut with a show that included a live performance by Jack Benny and Ingrid Bergman.

AFN Stuttgart was also on the air, broadcasting a feed from Munich. It, too, had an immensely powerful transmitter, and the joint station announced itself as "AFN Munich–Stuttgart, the twin voices of Southern Germany—100,000 watts each." Together the two stations blanketed Western Europe with their signal, which at times was even heard on the east coast of the United States. Stuttgart became a separate station in March 1948, with the top floor of the Graf Zeppelin hotel as its home. Another hotel, the Grand, was the location of AFN Nuremberg when it opened up in January 1950. The commanding general for the area threw the switch that put it on the air, unaware that it had been bought on the black market for two pounds of coffee.[2]

One of the first problems that the newly set-up stations had to cope with was the nonfraternization order imposed by the occupying Allies. This had been announced in September 1944 and prohibited all "mingling with the Germans upon terms of friendliness, familiarity or intimacy, individually or in groups, in official or unofficial dealings." There was to be no exception, not even for children. "If in a German town you bow to a pretty girl or pat a blond child, you bow to Hitler and his regime of blood." Exhortations such as these were given to the broadcasters with directions that they should be used regularly on the air. Typical was this sporting analogy: "We must not treat the Germans as we would our opponents in a football game after the final whistle. We do not want to play a return game next year or in twenty years." When words such as these had been used on the AEFP before the war ended, it could be argued they had some validity; however, in postwar Germany the policy was hard to enforce even though infringements resulted in disciplinary action. The prohibition did not last long, but it did give rise to one German joke when a barbed-wire fence was erected around the U.S. military HQ in Frankfurt—that the Americans were the only people who built concentration camps and put themselves in them![3]

AFN soon mounted another warning campaign which was very much a sign of the times. The message "VDMT" was repeated over the airwaves ten times a day for a week until finally it was spelled out: "Venereal Disease Means Trouble: for a moment of play you may have to pay." It was part of a drive to counter the sharp rise in the number of sexually transmitted diseases in a war-shattered Europe, where starving women were selling themselves for a square meal or a packet of cigarettes, then accepted as the main currency.[4]

By the close of 1945, AFN was well established in Germany. It was time, therefore, to wind up its U.K. operation. AFN's final broadcast from London, which had remained the administrative headquarters even though operations had been run from Paris for some time, was, appropriately, on the last day of the year. Judging from the few recorded fragments that survive of that very last broadcast, it was an emotional night. That is particularly evident in the final close-down: "AFN London now leaves the air after 53 months' faithful service," followed by the **Star-Spangled Banner**.

Before that, the BBC relented so far after its initial hostility as to broadcast a special tribute, *Farewell AFN*, on the Light Programme on 15

December. An indication of AFN's popularity with the British audience is that it went out on a Saturday night at peak listening time.[5]

AFN had proved popular with the French too, and when it was announced in the summer of 1946 that the Paris station was to close, there was a strong public reaction. A petition was presented to the U.S. ambassador asking for the station to be retained, and so it was kept on the air for diplomatic reasons.[6]

This was a period of transition. In Hollywood, it was by no means certain at first that the Armed Forces Radio Service would continue in existence. While its future was being considered, it began to curtail its scale of operations. The man who had run the whole setup since 1942, Colonel Tom Lewis, soon departed to return to civilian life. However, before long it became clear that the former ally, the Soviet Union, was an ally no longer. A strong American military presence would be needed in Europe and elsewhere for some time to come. So the AFRS would go on—but in peacetime it could no longer rely on the level of support it had from the stars. Bob Hope, whose broadcast appearances in the war had been legion, announced a drastic reduction in the number of shows he was prepared to do for the forces. The stars had performed free of charge, while the musicians and other performers had received only nominal payments. Now that the war was over, they asked for, and got, a review of the sums they were paid and the special arrangements about copyright and other music fees for broadcasts to the forces. Gradually, the amount of original programming by AFRS was reduced, from twenty hours a week to fourteen. By 1950, most of the AFRS output consisted of network shows with the commercials removed and disc-jockey programs. The era of AFRS as the center of creative programming was over.[7] But its output was still considerable. In 1951, it was broadcasting 400 hours of programs by shortwave and sending 40,000 transcription discs abroad every month.[8]

Because of the AFRS change of direction, AFN had to rely a great deal more on its own locally produced program output. In the past, it had resisted attempts to persuade it to help with command information. Now, with a new commander, its policy changed. It did itself a great deal of good, in the eyes of both the military leadership and the troops, by mounting a successful information campaign to clear up widespread misunderstandings about discharge dates. It also earned much credit with its detailed and authoritative daily reports on the Nuremberg trials of the major Nazi war criminals.[9]

Though AFN was no longer based in the United Kingdom, its powerful transmitters were heard in Britain loud and clear. There were few commercial stations on the air then in Europe, and interference with the signal was minimal. AFN retained the loyalty not only of its old audience but of new listeners, too. Many British servicemen had discovered

AFN, some through the AEFP, while fighting their way across Europe. Typical was the wireless operator in a tank who says he had tuned in whenever there was a lull in the fighting and had become hooked. Or the RAF mobile-radar operator who found himself in the American zone beyond the range of BBC transmissions so tuned instead to AFN.[10]

For a while, AFN had a bigger audience than it had ever had—among them, it is said, Engelbert Humperdinck and Georgie Fame, later to become notable pop stars in the 1960s. The mail that poured in from British listeners was double that from Americans and Germans combined. AFN is said to have received well over 150,000 requests and fan letters a year, many of them from England. And now they were no longer guests in BBC territory, they were able to respond to their many U.K. listeners.

It was a fact that did not go unnoticed by the BBC, especially when its attention was drawn to an unwelcome development that caused some soul-searching at Broadcasting House: sponsored broadcasting. AFN began putting out a daily musical program, *Personal Album*, "brought to you by the Theater Savings and Insurance Office. National Saving Life Insurance is the best bet for your future." It was British Government policy to discourage all sponsored broadcasting from Europe in English, a policy the BBC naturally fully endorsed. The AFN thin end of the wedge must be carefully watched, particularly "as it has without doubt a large audience in Britain." In fact, it seems possible that the BBC had got the wrong end of the wedge and that the scheme AFN was recommending was a U.S.-government savings scheme rather than a commercial one.[11]

Others in Britain had a different reason for being interested in AFN: the music industry. The network became the target of song pluggers in England who, well aware of the large number of British listeners, bombarded the disc jockeys with requests to play their latest hits. Specially singled out were top record-request programs such as *Bouncing in Bavaria* and *Midnight in Munich*. The latter was presented then by Ralph "Muffit" Moffat, who had a big following in Britain and is credited with making **Near You** by Francis Craig a huge hit. Moffat, who came from Milwaukee, paid a visit to Britain on one occasion, and, as an AFN broadcaster recalled, "the girls practically ate him alive." Later, he went to Radio Luxembourg, where he continued to be a great favorite.

Apart from Moffat, several other AFN notables made appearances at live shows in Britain, including George Monaghan, Jack Powers, and Dick Dudley, who also appeared in a BBC morning program with singer Dorothy Carless.

Another popular program was *Lunchin' in Munchen*—"with Stew." That was Stew Phillips, and the title is another example of the culinary puns for which AFN was noted. Then there was *Vocal Touch* (signature tune, **Out of My Dreams**, played by Andre Kostelanetz), presented by Mark White very much in the romantic mood. He always recited some poetry, and the last line of the poem would be the title of the music that followed. But as he wryly recalls, he unwittingly overdid it. One day an attractive young English girl turned up at the studio, having come all the way to Germany with her mother, hoping to marry him. She apparently believed all his dedications and romantic chat were intended for her! Unlikely—but an indication of the effect the AFN disc jockeys had on their often impressionable audience.[12]

An indication of the enduring nature of some of AFN's programs is afforded by a late-night bop show presented by "the Baron of Bounce." He used Benny Goodman's **Undercurrent Blues** as his theme tune, and as one listener recalls "he had a 'cool' voice, using a sort of hip, doom-laden delivery, vaguely like Vincent Price." The program, called *Hot House* (later *Cool Castle*), is credited with bringing a lot of the new jazz of Charlie Parker, Dizzy Gillespie, Stan Getz, and others to many listeners for the first time. The "Baron," otherwise Ken Dunnagan, says that after forty-five years he was still getting letters about the program and the character he created, and he confesses: "I have never been able to figure out his durability."[13]

AFN was fond of alliterative titles for its presenters. Don Cosgrove, of AFN Stuttgart, hosted a jazz program rejoicing in the title of "Dixieland Duke of Deutschland." Apart from jazz and swing music, AFN also catered for lovers of country and western. One program in particular that is recalled is *Stickbuddy Jamboree* presented by "your Texas buddy" (Red Jones), who signed off with the words: "Be good, be careful—and be back." Another very popular show was *Music in the Air*, whose presenter, Johnny Vrotsos, was with AFN for over twenty years, right from the wartime days in London. A "prince of a guy" is how one of his colleagues described him. That great favorite from the war years, *Duffle Bag,* was still going strong in the 1960s, as was George Monaghan's old program, which reverted to its former title, *Off the Record.*

AFN had a large audience among the Germans. Although there are no figures to indicate just how many, the British counterpart BFN estimated it had four to five million German listeners, so it is unlikely that the American network had any fewer.[14] It was claimed that it frequently had a higher rating than German radio stations, because younger listeners preferred the kind of music it played (shades of AFN's wartime days in Britain). AFN is credited with doing much to help foster good relations between the occupying American forces and a German population still trying to come to terms with their total defeat. Captain Bob Harlan, who was with the network for thirty-six years from 1949, says: "AFN was truly an ambassador of goodwill in furthering a good, solid US-German friendship. We gave them a picture of the world they were not getting through their own radio." He thought one of AFN's advantages was that it could be innovative in a way commercial stations could not, in particular putting on original drama with local writers and talent. Many Germans learned their English from listening to the station, and leading figures in the pop music field in Germany made their first acquaintance with modern American music through AFN. Such music had been regarded by the Nazis as "degenerate" and banned accordingly, so young Germans in particular could not get enough of it.

Music apart, the style of presenting mattered. As one German listener recalls: "We had been so used to the Nazi announcers barking out words as if they were all commands whereas AFN chatted to us as if we were close friends." A German newspaper summed it up thus: "It is the American sound which is heard on the shows that fascinates the listeners—the light, easy, often a little bit 'shirt-sleeve' way of the announcers who never are pompous or talking down to their listeners." A German radio executive suggested one other reason. In the immediate postwar years, there was a great deal of interest, especially among the younger generation, in the nation that had won the war. They wanted to know about America and all things American. And he, too, commented on the style of the broadcasters: "so relaxed compared with other, stiffer radio stations."[15]

There were occasions when AFN proved too relaxed. One of its staff, who shall be nameless, recalls being responsible for what he admits was probably the worst sport commentary in broadcasting history. He was covering a football game between American personnel from Bremerhaven and Stuttgart. It was raining heavily, and as the commentary box had no glass in the window it was difficult to see what was going on. The players were covered in mud, and in any case he discovered that the Bremerhaven team had switched jerseys, so he had no idea who they were. The officials proved so incompetent that the coaches stopped the game to check their knowledge of the rules. The scoreboard didn't work, the clock didn't work, and to cap it all he got the final score wrong.[16]

In the postwar years, AFN had its share of celebrities on its staff, among them Tony Bennett (who worked as a librarian), Gary Crosby (son of Bing), Rosemary Clooney's brother Nick (who became a TV executive in the United States), and the film actor George Kennedy. They were among the thousands of young Americans called up for military service as the Cold War showed no sign of ending.

It was in times of crisis that AFN was particularly appreciated. During the critical period of the Russian blockade of Berlin, AFN helped to keep the city's population abreast of the latest developments. When it went off the air for several minutes at one point, the switchboard was deluged with calls from worried Berliners concerned that the Americans were pulling out. AFN was a factor in reassuring the people of the city that the

United States was there to stay. It was valuable too in boosting the morale of U.S. troops there, while Allied pilots running the Berlin airlift asked for the station to stay on the air twenty-four hours. This was not only because they used its transmissions to help home in on Tempelhof Airport, but because the music helped relax them on their often dangerous missions, with a supply plane landing every three minutes day and night.[17]

Although the Russians apparently listened to AFN themselves, they were not so keen on others doing so. The station was picked up in Sweden, where it had a sizable audience (they sent AFN music requests), but then it was blotted out when the Russians began jamming it, perhaps regarding it in the same light as Voice of America.[18]

It was difficulties with the Russians that led to the setting up of RIAS (Rundfunk im Amerikanischen Sektor, or Radio in the American Sector). This was an American government radio station established because the Russians refused to agree to four-power control of Berlin Radio. RIAS came into being as the voice of the West in the divided city, at first using a captured German army transmitter. It was able to counter the Communist radio during Berlin's first postwar election and proved its worth during the blockade when, like AFN, it broadcast twenty-four hours a day, assuring the Germans the Western powers were not going to be driven out. When the Russians reduced the electricity supply, making it difficult for Berliners to use their own radio sets, RIAS set up a network of street loudspeakers so that its broadcasts could be heard all over West Berlin. Eventually it acquired a new transmitter which was so powerful that there were protests from distant Yugoslavia that it was interfering with broadcasts in that country.[19]

The Russian presence in Berlin posed one particular problem for U.S. troops stationed in or visiting the city, as emphasized by a regular warning on AFN: "When using public transport in Berlin do not fall asleep on the S-Bahn [subway]—you could end up in the eastern zone."

AFN's main transmitters were boosted by a network of relay stations, and as the political situation in Europe changed, an AFN presence was reestablished in France. In 1962 it had thirty transmitters in that country, two more than in Germany. Later, the U.S. Army set up AFN SHAPE (Supreme Headquarters, Allied Powers, Europe), serving NATO, with stations in Belgium and the Netherlands.

Ultimately AFN and the British Forces Network went their separate ways, but for a time something of the wartime camaraderie lingered. AFN was happy to let its British counterpart have regular copies of AFRS discs for broadcasting, and the two cooperated on a program called *Dancing Round the Baltic*, in which both Danish and Swedish radio also took part.[20] AFN also gave a helping hand to the neighboring Blue

Danube Network, an American forces broadcasting station in Austria which flourished for ten years until the Allied occupation ended. Like AFN in Germany, it had a big audience of civilian listeners and for much the same reasons: an opportunity to learn English and the kind of music they could not get from their own radio.[21]

AFN continued to have cordial relations with the BBC. A senior engineer from the corporation paid a visit to Frankfurt in the spring of 1948 to discuss technical help and advice for the Americans, who were having frequency problems and wished to avail themselves of the BBC's expertise. He also noted that AFN was obtaining audiotape for its recording machines "in various unorthodox ways" from European sources. He saw for himself some of the hundreds of letters from listeners all over Europe, the vast majority from the United Kingdom, and commented on the "considerable" volume of Russian listening. Most surprising, in view of AFN's reputation in the popular-music field, was the interest shown by the Americans in relaying the International Eisteddfod from Wales, the Edinburgh Festival, and the Three Choirs Festival from Gloucester, Hereford, and Worcester. They even asked for relays of regular programs featuring well-known British dance orchestras.[22]

Gradually, Europe returned to normal, and the airwaves became crowded once again. The U.K. audience dwindled as reception became more difficult. AFN was required to reduce the power of most of its transmitters and also change its frequencies, as part of a series of revisions of the general European broadcasting scene. Fashions changed, too. Gradually German announcers altered their style to fit that of the Americans, German dance bands played in the American manner, while AFN's music became different again and moved on. As one German listener put it: "This was not the music my friends and I had liked very much."[23]

Nevertheless, the German audience was still a big one. A U.S. Congressional report in 1962 stated that the "official policy of AFN forbids active encouragement of German listeners" (a statement that would have come as a surprise to many of them). Despite this, the report went on, of the 36,641 letters received by AFN stations in the third quarter of 1961, a third of them came from German listeners. The report quoted one German magazine as saying that the AFN network was "the most popular station with the young people in half of Europe" (that included not only Germany but France as well). And a leading German newspaper praised AFN as being "the only station which most readily complies with special requests from listeners. It responds much faster than German stations and with less redtape."[24]

AFN is still on the air today, with television as well as radio, but the number of stations has contracted as the need for U.S. troops on the

Continent has receded. AFN Munich closed in February 1992, Bremer-haven the following year, and, later, Berlin. AFRS is also still in existence, now as the Armed Forces Radio and Television Service. For both, their greatest hour came in World War II. AFN's stay in Britain lasted less than two and a half years, yet its impact has endured half a century. Listeners still remember it with affection and pleasure. One phrase sums up their feelings: "It was a ray of welcome sunshine in a gray wartime world."

NOTES

1. *History of AFRTS*, p. 53; Christman, *Brass Button Broadcasters*, p. 57; AFN broadcast to mark its 50th anniversary, 4 July 1993.

2. Mostly AFN broadcast, 4 July 1993, plus Christman, *Brass Button Broadcasters*, pp. 67–70, and *History of AFRTS*, p. 53.

3. BBCWAC, R34/184/1 (Col. John Hayes memo, 30 December 1944); *History of World War II* (Purnell, 1966), edited by Basil Lidell Hart, Vol. 8, pp. 3292–3299; *Encyclopaedia of World War II*.

4. TITAFN. It is surprising to note that according to official figures, the number of VD cases treated in Britain (mostly civilian but including some service personnel) was actually *lower* in every year of the war compared with the total for 1938. Possibly this was the result of the intense publicity campaign mounted by the government. (Source: *Fighting with Figures: A Statistical Digest of the Second World War*, Central Statistical Office, London, 1995.) By contrast, the number of VD cases among GIs was alarmingly high (at one time, double the rate in the United States) and regarded by the services as a serious health problem.

5. BBCWAC, R34/909/2 (Gorham memo, 26 November 1945), in which he makes it clear that although AFN was leaving the United Kingdom, some of its transmitters would continue to operate for some time; Way, *Big Bands*, p. 158. Like most of the AFN and AEFP broadcasts, no recording now exists, but the details of *Farewell AFN* are recorded in the BBC Archives. The announcer was Margaret Hubble, with AFN's Dick Dudley as compere. He also sang **When I Got in the Army** with his *Rise and Shine* opposite number from the AEFP, Ronnie Waldman, at the piano. Robert Farnon's Canadian Band provided the music, with Dorothy Carless and Jackie Hunter as vocalists. Brigadier Claude Thiel made a short valedictory speech, and the half-hour program ended with "Auld Lang Syne."

6. *History of AFRTS*, p. 51; Christman, *Brass Button Broadcasters*, p. 199.

7. *History of AFRTS*, p. 66 et seq.

8. *Radio and Television News* magazine, July 1951.

9. *History of AFRTS*, pp. 70–71, Christman, *Brass Button Broadcasters*, p. 69.

10. Private letters to the author.

11. BBCWAC, E1/731/1 (J. W. T. Eyton, European Liaison, memo, 26 May 1946).

12. Much of the information about AFN programs postwar comes from private letters to the author from listeners and from AFN broadcasts of the time.

13. Ken Dunnagan, in conversation with the author and from private letters to the author. Several recalled that "the Baron" started a Hot House Club whose colorful membership card, written in the hip style of the time, exhorted members to "dig the cool sounds at all times "and "if in doubt, bop."

14. *A Microphone and a Frequency*, p. 101.

15. AFN broadcast, 4 July 1993. The German newspaper quoted is the *Frankfurter Rundschau* of 25 October 1961. It listed the five top programs as being *Merely Music, Duffle Bag, Off the Record, Music in the Air*, and *Melody Go Round*.

16. Ibid.

17. *History of AFRTS*, p. 73.

18. (i) In the immediate post-war years, the Voice of America (VOA) was one of the U.S. Government's main weapons in the propaganda battle waged during the Cold War. Its immensely powerful transmitters beamed signals that could be heard all over Europe, when it was not being jammed by the Russians. It had begun life during World War II as an offshoot of OWl and at the war's end was broadcasting over 3,000 programs in 40 languages each week. Officially its aim was to present listeners overseas with a picture of the American way of life and the policies and aims of the U.S. government. To achieve the latter objective, in its efforts to counter Radio Moscow and other Communist radio stations it adopted what one commentator called an "aggressive hard-line approach." When the noted broadcaster, Ed Murrow, took over as director of the United States Information Agency, which by then was running VOA, he aimed to tone down the rhetoric and make the station more akin to the BBC's World Service. Over the years, VOA has broadened its programming to appeal to a wider audience and today continues to attract millions of listeners throughout the world with what has been described as a style both slick and colloquial—and not too obviously political. (For one listener's view of the contrast between AFN and VOA see Postscript, page 143.) (ii) The information about the jamming of AFN in Sweden comes from a private letter to the author.

19. Paper on "US Information Programs in Berlin," prepared for the Office of the U.S. High Commissioner for Germany in 1953.

20. Trevor Hill, former BFN broadcaster, in conversation with the author.

21. Christman, *Brass Button Broadcasters*, pp. 71–72.

22. BBCWAC, R52/2 (Memorandum [author identified only as MG], "The American Forces Network," 30 April 1948).

23. Guenter Lulay, producer of AFN Radio Souvenirs, an audiotape celebration of the American Forces Network in Germany.

24. Congressional Report on Overseas Military Information Programs: Thirteenth Report by the Committee on Government Operations (Union Calendar No. 646, House Report No. 1549), 30 March 1962.

Postscript:
Afterthoughts and Memories

Three questions need to be addressed about AFN's impact during its stay in Britain:

1. Did its presence and the associated Allied Expeditionary Forces Programme have a beneficial or negative effect on Anglo-American relations?
2. What effect did it have on the British listening public?
3. What effect did it have on the BBC's thinking?

First of all, it should be emphasized that the only evidence we have is largely anecdotal, and any conclusions drawn must therefore be tentative. There are not even reliable figures about the size of the nonmilitary audience for AFN.

Captain Bob Light has been quoted as stating that "by the end of its first year of operations an estimated five million Britons listened to AFN with regularity."[1] Maurice Gorham is on record as saying that AFN's civilian audience never passed the 10 percent mark, a figure based on BBC listener research.[2] Britain's wartime population was estimated at 50 million, so 10 percent of that would give the figure of 5 million quoted by Light. But 50 million was the total for the *whole* of the British Isles, including men, women and children, as well as all of Ireland. Excluding those under 15 and areas well beyond the range of the transmitters, the maximum potential audience (based on 10 percent of those able or likely to listen) comes out at around 3.5 million.[3] That is still a respectable total but no real threat to the BBC, which was getting four times that number most nights. Indeed, Gorham is quite definite about the "threat" from the American station: "The stories I read claiming that AFN had captured the British audience from the BBC made me laugh."[4]

Many of those who tuned in were young people—teenagers or somewhat older. This is clear from the letters the author has received from those who remember the program well. It was also the BBC's considered view at the time. As has been noted (see chapter 5), a senior corporation executive commented that American programs "command enthusiastic listeners with enthusiasm *varying in inverse proportion to age*" [emphasis added]. Maurice Gorham confirms that conclusion. The American Forces Network, he has written, was "the pre-ordained program for the bobby-soxers, with its American comedy, American swing and entire freedom from restrictions [on the playing of copyright music]" (Gorham, *Sound and Fury*, p. 171).

If that be the case, the listening figures can be viewed differently. The number of people in England and Wales aged between 15 and 25 during the war hovered around the 7 million mark. If most of the 3.5 million who listened to AFN were in this age group, then the listening figures jump from 10 percent to 50 percent, a very different story. Which simply goes to show that statistics can be made to prove almost anything—but it does indicate that among the most likely and impressionable audience, the proportion listening was not quite as insignificant as Gorham and others chose to believe.

Teenagers apart, the men and women in the services certainly listened a great deal either to AFN or to the AEFP (half of whose output came from AFN). Many of them liked what they heard and undoubtedly preferred it to the BBC. Typical is a comment from a corporal in Italy who wrote to the BBC: "The lads out here are particularly vehement in asking why British variety programmes are not of the same standard as those provided for their American comrades."[5] However, not all service people felt the same. A contrary view comes from a member of the women's services who worked closely with Americans. She says she and her colleagues hardly listened to AFN: "We liked dancing to American music but we didn't listen to it much on the wireless. We preferred our own familiar British programs, and we also liked light music and classical music, which we got on the BBC but not from the Americans."[6] That viewpoint is reflected in Gorham's comment that popular though the American programs may have been when the BBC broadcast them, a good British show was more popular still. The Jack Benny show on the General Forces Program was broadcast at the same time as the popular British comedian, Will Hay, on the Home Service, and the latter drew three times as many listeners.[7]

So what impact did AFN have on its British audience? Few doubt the long-lasting impression made by the wartime American "occupation" of Britain, and there is no reason to believe that the parallel broadcasting invasion was any different. The teenagers of today are the adults of tomorrow, and it seems safe to say that AFN whetted their appetites for the kind of music, in particular, which they could not get on the BBC. Nor did they get it after the war, or at any rate on the same scale, which is no doubt why AFN in Germany was receiving over 650 letters a month from British listeners.[8] For many, the American Forces Network had opened up the world of jazz and the big bands. It was this that made the most lasting impression, rather than the star-studded Hollywood shows such as *Command Performance*, popular though they were. The other great impression made on the British audience was that of the AFN announcers. As many listeners have testified, their friendly easy-going manner was a revelation after the more formal ways of the BBC. The corporation's awareness of this had been reflected in the more relaxed style adopted for the AEFP. To that extent, AFN had brought about a change in BBC attitudes, though partly that was because it was well aware that more than half the AEFP audience was American, as were many of the announcers. But was what was right for a forces audience in the war appropriate for peacetime?

The BBC does not seem to have given any special consideration to this aspect of the American presence. Immediately after the war, Maurice Gorham, who had run the AEFP, was made head of the new Light Programme, which undoubtedly reflected a more relaxed style though apparently not as a result of any definite policy decision. What did concern the BBC were two subjects that the presence of AFN had already spotlighted: its likely effect on commercial radio interests and the "Americanization" of BBC programs, something which, as we have seen, had caused much heart-searching during the war.

What was clear to everyone was that the sort of programs which had flourished under the AFRS and its offshoot AFN would simply not be affordable in peacetime. Had they been funded on a normal commercial basis, they would have cost millions. To attempt something similar in peacetime was out of the question. The argument had been well summed up by a senior BBC executive at a time when AFN was in its infancy:

The American Forces Network differs in several fundamental ways from any commercial American chain. In the first place, it skims the cream of the whole American radio entertainment business. No single chain could put out such a succession of streamlined, glittering shows, every evening of the week. The money and artists could not be found and besides the chains have certain obligations towards material of the serious talk, uplift, serious music kind. Besides the sponsored programs . . . there are the [AFRS] productions, for which every American artist, stirred by a patriotism that is not lessened by the law that limits their maximum incomes, gives his services free. This source will, of course, dry up when the war is over.[9]

The advertising agencies in Britain were apparently "lying in wait," with all their plans for commercial radio after the war prepared, but in the event they came to nothing. It will come as a surprise to many to know that the BBC itself seriously discussed the possibility of "carefully controlled" advertisements on some of its programs, though it eventually decided against it. If advertisers came in, as one senior man commented, "blurb would be king."[10]

The "Americanization" of programs was another issue. One BBC official wrote that "we don't want to end up just a pale copy of American radio, sans sponsoring." Another strongly believed that the BBC output should be "firmly British in character" and that there should be "an effective resistance to the Americanisation of our entertainment." The director-general expressed it thus: "We shall safeguard broadcasting from becoming a glorified juke box." These views were widely supported outside the BBC. An influential newspaper, the *Yorkshire Post*, had this to say: "It may be that British broadcasting would have gained in entertainment value if it had been developed on the American model with sponsored programmes, but we believe it would have suffered greatly as a public service."[11] So those who might have hoped that after the war the BBC would more closely reflect the kind of programs AFN had put on the air were to be disappointed.

As to the effects of all the disputes about AFN and the AEFP on Anglo-American unity, it has to be said that the proof of the pudding is in the eating. There were many differences and disagreements, but, like the alliance at large, it worked. If the Americans insisted on something that they saw as vital, they invariably got their way. But if the British really dug their heels in (as the BBC did over the phrase "the Allied Expeditionary Forces Programme of the BBC"), they were likely to win the day, especially if the point at issue was not of fundamental importance. The Americans recognized there were times when they had to make concessions, as they did over the refusal to let them run the AEFP, much as they wanted to do so. In this, they reflected the firmly anglophile attitude held by Eisenhower. Neither he nor Churchill intended to fall out seriously over the AEFP, despite their disagreements, and Ike's subordinates in the main took their cues from him. General Barker certainly did: Colonel Kirby did not, but in the last resort he was out-ranked and outmaneuvered.

At a different level, for all those GIs who objected to the "over-Englishness" of the AEFP, there were others who were happy with what came over the air. Those with prejudices had them confirmed. But there were many, particularly the thinking people on both sides, who felt that their views of their ally had been broadened and improved. If AFN may have given some British listeners a distorted view of the United States at times, it was nowhere near on the same scale that Hollywood was accused of doing.

It had been suggested that setting up AFN would be to encourage the American forces to live a separate existence from the people of the country where they were based. If so, there is no convincing evidence of it. Ask anyone who lived in Britain during the war if the GI hid his light under a bushel, and you are likely to be greeted with a rueful smile and the (usually) good-natured comment: "There were times when we saw too much of the Yanks!"

There was one other aspect of the AFRS–AFN–AEFP setup that impinged on ordinary Americans in the fighting services, as pinpointed in a perceptive article in the *New York World Telegram*. It pointed out that the GIs had been getting a diet of the best in American radio "without the curse of commercials." It went on: "Hearing only the best . . . it's not likely they'll accept some of our third-rate productions when they come home." And it forecast that some "first-rate, front-line invective" would be hurled at the radio "every time a commercial announcement intrudes its monstrous head."[12] Like the British listeners deprived of the pleasures of AFN, it was something the returning servicemen and women no doubt learned to live with.

All of which serves to emphasize that what British listeners had been hearing was a "sanitized" version of American broadcasting. Had they heard the original—commercials and all—they might have taken a very different view of transatlantic radio.

So much for what might loosely be termed the academic aspects of the American Forces Network saga. What of the personal side? The rest of this chapter is devoted to the recollections of those in Britain and elsewhere who have special memories of AFN and the wartime years.[13]

"The music was of another world" sums up the feelings of many of them. Another writes: "As a teenager during the war and a lover of big band music I spent hours tuned in to the record shows on AFN whose presenters I found so refreshingly different." Like so many who listened to AFN, he particularly remembers Johnny Kerr's *Duffle Bag* and George Monaghan's *On the Record*. "Their cheery patter and the terrific music they played always had me glued to the wireless."

It was a view widely held: "Messrs Kerr and Monaghan opened up a new world for me especially with the music of Stan Kenton," says one, and a wartime listener now nearly 70 writes: "I was a schoolboy during the war and me and my pals tuned in to AFN all the time, when the adults weren't listening to the wireless, that is. Every week we followed the Top Ten and argued a lot about our favorite tunes and also about who was the better singer, Crosby or Sinatra. Our school had been evacuated to a big house out in the country, but once a week we went to the old school in the town. . . . We usually went out for fish and chips at midday and the fish shop always had AFN on, *Duffle Bag* as I recall at that time of day."

One listener remembers that as a schoolboy he got up early on dark winter mornings to listen to a program called *Repeat Performance*, another chance to hear the previous night's top show. "When it ended I only just had time to run and catch the school bus." Ralph "Muffit" Moffat is fondly remembered—as, for example: "Moffat's style was so warm and I guess schmaltzy and made such an impression on a romantic teenager. The AFN DJs were so different from the austere BBC voices of that era. Quite often if they liked a tune they would play it twice in a row. It was the door to all kinds of new songs and music for me. It was AFN which gave me my interest in popular music and decided my eventual career in the entertainment industry."

Certain singers, now only names, made their mark. One of the most requested items was a record of **I'll Walk Alone** sung by Lily Ann Carol. "I used to listen in whenever I could just to hear this song, which was included in every day's broadcast, twice a day. It took me over 40 years to get a taped recording of Lily Ann Carol singing it. I play it regularly— it still does something for me (or to me!)." That young singer (she was apparently only 14) clearly made a big impact. "I can remember in my teens sitting around an old radio with mates listening to the big band sounds and the current crooners. Lily Ann Carol singing **I'll Walk Alone** was played so often that in the end the DJ of the time would simply say: 'And now we have LAC with IWA.'" Many wartime listeners testify to the fact that AFN gave them a fondness for a style of music that stayed with them for a lifetime. As one says: "One program was enough for me to be hooked on Glenn Miller's music for the next 50 years." Music could be deceiving at times for those not used to it. One listener recalls that as a boy he was listening to a Lionel Hampton number which featured a long earthy growl of a trumpet solo. Hearing it from the next room, his aunt called to him to get to the air-raid shelter quickly—another V bomb was clearly on the way!

Music was not everything, though, as this comment shows: "I became a regular listener to the comedy and musical shows. One of the reasons AFN was so popular during the war and in the years immediately afterwards was because the BBC were unable to match the all-star radio entertainment it provided." And another viewpoint: "Music yes but for me it was the easygoing style as contrasted with the BBC's stuffy presen-

tation that just chimed in with my very embryonic teenage rebellious-
ness."

For those who could not get AFN on their home radios, the Americans
were sometimes able to oblige. One woman writes: "I was a railway
booking office clerk when the Americans took over a huge army camp
locally. They fitted out one of our railway waiting rooms as a transport
office, and when I was on late shift they regularly brought their radio in
for me to the booking office and of course always tuned to AFN."

Another listener also recalls it was not only the studio announcers
who showed an individual touch. Each transmitter was manned by a
couple of soldiers, and at one base in Wiltshire they went on the air at
close-down to announce themselves as "AFN Shrivenham" and give a
brief roundup of base news.

There was a lot of sport on AFN, which did not find favor with much
of the British audience. One recalls: "I can honestly say that the only
programs I did not like on AFN were the (seemingly) interminable
baseball commentaries." But there were others who felt very differently:
"I listened to a lot of sport on AFN though here I ran into strong opposition from the grownups in the house. American football I found hard to
follow. It was mostly college football then and I was fascinated by the
names of the teams: Harvard, Yale, Purdue, Notre Dame, Duke. Where
exactly were they all, I wondered. But my favourite sport was baseball of
which I became totally enamoured. I had found many of the terms used
in the commentaries confusing at first so I wrote to the Office of War
Information at the American Embassy. Considering how busy they must
have been in the middle of a world war, they put themselves out to
answer a schoolboy's letter and provided me with a lot of useful information about America's national game which I have never forgotten."

Not everything about AFN pleased everybody: "About the only thing
about the programs that AFN broadcast that disappointed me was the
sickly sentimental way in which American radio celebrated Christmas.
Schoolboy though I was I found it quite nauseating."

A picture of life in the quiet East Anglian villages transformed by the
war emerges from the recollections of an RAF man. He remembers the
blackout and the dim lighting in the smoke-filled pub bar, packed with
servicemen, very few women. The pub rarely had spirits, just the local
mild and bitter beer, never any food or potato chips even, cigarettes
under the counter and sold only to the locals. Uninviting though it was,
"it just showed the need there was to get out of camp for a few hours
and socialise in a different atmosphere ... when AFN came along it
marked a turning point in our grim 'total war' mentality and made
things a bit easier."

It did not make things all that easier for his younger brother, still
at home on a farm which in those days had no electricity. He got into

trouble for listening to AFN in the small hours on the family's battery radio set, powered by an accumulator which needed recharging every week and which his father was saving so he could hear the news. Clearly, AFN met with widespread parental disapproval, judging from the number of those who were then youngsters who wrote saying they felt obliged to listen to it under the bedclothes!

The Anglo-American aspects of the station were not lost on some listeners. One comment reflects their viewpoint: "AFN was probably in my view the most powerful and effective means of winning friends for the United States from among the ranks of English-speaking listeners that was ever devised, even though that was not its purpose. In fact, the Americans were at their best just being themselves with no ulterior motive. The contrast with their later Voice of America, with its blatant propagandist content, could not have been greater. It must have undone all the good work done by AFN in winning friends and influencing people."

However, when all is said and done it was the music on AFN that mattered most. Here are four differing viewpoints on that aspects of its programming:

Much has been written about the music of the Second World War. It has endured, it's been said, not because it was especially good music—though some of it was—but because it is for ever associated with events which changed the lives of millions of people. Here is a personal selection of some of the characteristically American tunes I enjoyed hearing on AFN half a century ago: I remember a wealth of catchy tunes with very silly titles. The one everybody recalls is **Mairzy Doats and Dozy Doats,** which had nothing to do with a family called Doats and everything to do with the preference of mares and does for eating oats. Once you'd cottoned on to the way the English language was being abused it added up to sense of a kind. That was more than could be said of the **Hut Sut Song,** made up largely of incomprehensible and supposedly Swedish lyrics which fortunately were rendered into English. Then there was the **Flat Foot Floogie with the Floy Floy,** not to mention **Shoofly Pie and Apple Pan Dowdy,** both, we learned, real New England dishes. One song that was silly for different reasons bore the innocuous title **Ashby de la Zouch,** the name of a small town which we were informed was close to the sea, when everyone who lived in the English Midlands knew it was about as far from the sea as it was possible to get. Perhaps the irony was intentional.

Americans, we gathered, always seemed to be on the move by train. If it wasn't on the **Atcheson Topeka and the Santa Fe** it was the **Chattanooga Choo Choo**. Or they were heading for California and planning to settle down in the **San Fernando Valley**. We appreciated the star-bright nights **Deep in the Heart of Texas,** which matched perfectly with the lover of the great outdoors who pleaded **Don't Fence Me In**. Then there was the guy with a **Gal in Kalamazoo** which we in England were surprised to discover was a real place. But perhaps the most comprehensive survey of all was the number that managed to name every single American state, the now forgotten **Which of the Great 48 Do You Hail From?**

There were remarkably few jingoistic numbers. **Praise the Lord and Pass the Ammunition** was too American to catch on in Britain. Easily the most successful flag-waving number was **Comin' in on a Wing and a Prayer**. But the lyrics must have made the men of the Eighth Air Force want to throw up . Servicemen were naturally the subject of feminine admiration, especially sailors: **Bell Bottom Trousers**, with the accompanying navy suit, would have turned any girl's head then. And dancing was everyone's favorite pastime even if it might mean you were going to **Dance with the Dolly with the Hole in Her Stocking**. The notion of **Juke Box Saturday Night** filled us with envy especially as most of us had never even seen a juke box. **Drinking Rum and Coca Cola** sounded fine but we had doubts about patronising the restaurant where all you got was **One Meat Ball**. Grammar went by the board. **Is You Is Or Is You Ain't My Baby** rubbed shoulders with **It Must Be Jelly Cos Jam Don't Shake Like That**. Night shift workers with sleeping problems had our sympathy: there were times when we all wanted to shout **Milkman Keep Those Bottles Quiet**. And there was one number that would raise some politically correct eyebrows now: **Beat Me Daddy Eight to the Bar**. There were raucous numbers like **Pistol Packin' Mama** and the **Boogie Woogie Bugle Boy of Company B,** lively numbers such as the **Trolley Song,** numbers with an uplifting message such as the exhortation to **Accentuate the Positive**. Who could possibly quarrel with that, especially if they were faced with the range of anthropomorphic options offered in **Swingin' on a Star,** featuring life as a pig, a mule or a fish.

But with millions far from home and loved ones, it was the songs about parting that were the biggest hits and the best remembered. The archetypal nostalgia song, of course, was Bing Crosby's **White Christmas,** said to be the best selling 78 of all time. **I'll Get By As Long As I Have You** was a sentiment most would share. Judy Garland promised **No Love No Nothin'** at any rate until **My Guy's Come Back**. Dinah Shore sang of **Long Ago and Far Away,** Frances Langford dwelt on **As Time Goes By** (a pre-war flop revived by the success of the film *Casablanca*). Helen Forrest **Couldn't Sleep a Wink Last Night,** while Doris Day decided to take a **Sentimental Journey,** which proved a lucky choice for her since it set her on the road to stardom. And always Lily Ann Carol insisted **I'll Walk Alone**. Sinatra's **Shoo Shoo Baby,** that had the bobbysoxers screaming in the aisles, was top of the many "goodbye" songs. Any number of singers asked (after the film *Now Voyager*) **Would It Be Wrong to Kiss,** while in a lighter mood it was nice to know **She Smiled at Me In My Dreams Last Night**. Inevitably at times most of us got **Blues in the Night** but if it was the flightiness of women that was your problem you could always buy your very own **Paper Doll**. Of the purely romantic melodies with no war connections **Moonlight Becomes You** is a perfect example. But perhaps the song that resulted in more tears being shed than any other was **I'll Be Seeing You,** sung by pretty well every big-name vocalist during the war. That always brought a lump to everyone's throat.[14]

Real music buffs had a different viewpoint about what they heard on AFN and the AEFP:

Every single time we had any quiet breaks from our duties, I tuned the radio to the AEF Programme . . . this was when swing became an inseparable part of our young lives. The Miller AEF Band was on the air most days and they played tunes like the old civilian band's instrumentals, **String of Pearls, In the Mood, Tuxedo Junction,** plus some wonderful new ones like **Holiday for Strings** using the classic Miller reed sound as well as the huge string section. Also superb ballads with the swoon singer Johnny Desmond and an all-GI vocal group The Crew Chiefs who had a wild close harmony blend with a lead singer who could sing higher than a girl. Johnny Desmond became a favourite with girls in the UK and also especially in France with his very clear diction, smooth phrasing and Sinatra-like swoony sound.

We also heard all the other American civilian bands such as Benny Goodman, both Tommy and Jimmy Dorsey, Harry James, Charlie Barnet, Count Basie, Duke Ellington, Woody Herman, Artie Shaw in programmes recorded in the USA and flown out on transcription discs. In hospital over Christmas 1944 I consoled myself with music on the radio and that was when I became aware of Helen Forrest, as they often played Artie Shaw items like **Say It with a Kiss, Deep Purple, I Poured My Heart into a Song,** and her later vocals with Benny Goodman and Harry James, notably **I've Heard That Song Before** and **I Had the Craziest Dream**, just before she left bands to go solo. I also heard Jo Stafford, both as a band singer on her Tommy Dorsey records and her then current airchecks on the Johnny Mercer Music Shop Shows with the Pied Pipers. Two favourites from that time are still **Candy,** where Stafford is with Johnny Mercer and the Pied Pipers vocal group; and **I'll Remember April**, backed on both by the Paul Weston Orchestra, which also swung mightily when required.

It is what it can do to the emotions which made the music of World War II so memorable. This from a Wren who, at one of the many wartime dances, saw a young RAF pilot who looked somehow familiar:

I didn't know any pilots so it took me some time to realise that he was a young man from home. His father was one of the managers at the factory where my stepfather and stepbrothers worked. I had often admired him from afar but had never spoken to him: I didn't move in his circle. However, there was an excuse-me quick step so I excused his partner and began to dance with him. It turned out he knew who I was. He was very charming, quiet and so handsome in his uniform. When the dance was over the band struck up again, **Don't Sit Under the Apple Tree with Anyone Else But Me**. We danced again and several times more that night. At the end of the evening he asked if I would be there again the following Saturday. The next weekend I was once more standing at the side of the dance floor, looking around for the pilot. I couldn't see him anywhere but at last I recognised another pilot he'd been with the previous week. I asked him if his friend would be there. "I'm afraid he won't be coming." And before I could say anything he told me: "He caught it last week."

My quiet young pilot from home was dead, killed on a night raid over enemy territory. I cried myself to sleep that night. And ever since, whenever I hear **Don't Sit Under the Apple Tree** I think of him.

And a final comment about AFN that sums up the feelings of many: "I still miss it, like so many things. It won't happen again."

Let the very last word go to a listener who risked imprisonment daily for the pleasure of listening to AFN:

We in the Channel Islands were occupied by German forces in July 1940. For a couple of years we were allowed to keep radios but when the tide of war swung in the Allies' favour we had to hand our sets in or suffer the consequences. I along with others made crystal sets which were easy to conceal. But we could only pick up a particular wavelength which happened to be AFN. I remember listening to Glenn Miller who was my favorite band leader. . . . When we went to parties, as we had a strict curfew once we reached our host's place we had to stay all night: German patrols often shot first and asked questions after. We used to sing patriotic songs and tunes like **Swingin' on a Star** and **The Trolley Song** to while the night away. Memories![15]

NOTES

1. *History of AFRTS*, p. 50, quoting interview with Capt. Robert Light.

2. Gorham, *Sound and Fury*, p. 171.

3. Official population statistics: *Whitaker's Almanac 1946*; *Fighting with Figures: A Statistical Digest of the Second World War* (CSO London, 1995).

4. Gorham, *Sound and Fury*, p. 171.

5. BBCWAC, quoted by Briggs, *History*, Vol. III, p. 713.

6. Audrey Johnson, author of *Do March in Step Girls*.

7. Gorham, *Sound and Fury*, ibid.

8. BBCWAC, R52/2 (Memorandum, "The American Forces Network," 30 April 1948).

9. BBCWAC, R34/909/1 (DPP memo, 24 July 1943).

10. BBCWAC (Press release, 28 November 1944), quoted by Briggs, *History*, Vol. III, p. 723.

11. *Yorkshire Post*, 13 November 1943, quoted by Briggs, *History*, Vol. III, p. 720 (the BBC comments are quoted by Briggs from BBC archival material).

12. BBCWAC, R44/11 (New York World Telegram, 6 November 1944).

13. Private letters to the author. The "music buff's" reflections are from Con Holland-Skinner, of Burnham Market, Norfolk, and first appeared in the *MTM* [Music That Matters] *Newsletter*.

14. Because of copyright restrictions, it has not been possible to quote any of the actual lyrics of the songs mentioned.

15. Considering how far the Channel Islands are from the site of the nearest AFN transmitter, it seems likely that that particular listener was confusing the AEFP (whose strong signals he would be in line to receive) with AFN—a common mistake, as noted in chapter 9.

Appendix I:
Transmitters

This list of AFN transmitters is from the definitive list kept by BBC engineers (BBCWAC, R53/8). Each transmitter was given a number as permission was applied to set it up. However, sometimes a batch of applications was received at the same time, so the transmitters were not necessarily approved or erected in numerical order. The numbers therefore indicate only the approximate order in which they were set up and came into operation, and this accounts for various discrepancies in dates. However, it seems very likely (though it has not been possible to confirm it) that the first seven names on the list are the stations that went on the air when AFN began operations on 4 July 1943. In a few cases, one place name has been substituted for another, but it is not always clear whether the transmitter was re-sited or a new site chosen before installation. For instance, in Transmitter 37, "Wem" has been crossed out and "Malvern" written in. But one announcer recalls that he started with AFN at Wem, and since it would be impossible to confuse the two towns there must originally have been a transmitter there. The locations of the transmitters are significant because they pinpointed fairly precisely the locations of U.S. bases and, therefore, were a military secret. Altogether, seventy-five transmitters were planned, and in the event sixty-six were opened, covering much of England (except the northeast, London, and the southeast below the Thames), as well as parts of Wales, Scotland, and Northern Ireland.

Transmitter	Location	Remarks
1. Taunton	2½ m NW of Taunton, Somerset	Closed 2 Aug. 1945
2. Bristol	1½ m from center of Bristol	Closed 25 Nov. 1944
3. Cheltenham	½ m from eastern edge of Cheltenham	Closed 6 Mar. 1945
4. Shrivenham	6½ m from center of Swindon, Wilts	
5. Thatcham	3¼ m east of Newbury, Berks	
6. Tidworth	On edge of North Tidworth, Wilts	
7. Wilton, Wilts	3 m from center of Salisbury	Closed 1 July 1945
8. Bassingbourn	2½ m from Royston, 10½ m from Cambridge	Closed 24 Sept. 1945
9. Chelveston	2½ m from center of Rushden, 11 m N by NNW of Bedford	Closed 13 Sept. 1945
10. Polebrook	1¾ m ENE of Polebrook, 15 m from Kettering, Northants	Closed 28 June 1945
11. Alconbury	4½ m NW of Huntingdon	CANCELLED. Replaced by 51
12. Oxford	2 m E of center of Oxford, 3 m W of Wheatley Hospital	
13. Horsham St Faith	3½ m from center of Norwich	Closed 12 July 1945
14. Bury St Edmunds	¾ m N of Bury St Edmunds, Suffolk	Closed 4 Aug. 1945
15. Great Saling	4 m WNW of Braintree, Essex	CANCELED. Replaced by 52
16. Tavistock	12 m N of Plymouth, Devon	Open 28 Dec. 1943 Closed 18 May 1944
17. Lichfield	15 m N of Birmingham	Closed 15 Sept. 1945
18. Newport	Tredegar Park, Monmouthshire	Open 5 Jan. 1944 Closed 24 Apr. 1945
19. Haydock Park	17 m W of center of Manchester (halfway between Manchester & Liverpool)	Open 31 Dec. 1943 Closed 2 Oct. 1945
20. Warton	9 m W of Preston, Lancs	Open 4 Jan. 1944
21. Glasgow	Crookston, 4 m from edge of city	Open 22 Dec. 1943 Closed 1 May 1945
22. Bovingdon	8 m NW of Watford Junction, 12 m from NW London	
23. Goxhill	5 m S of Hull	Open 12 Jan. 1944* Closed 11 May 1945
24. Whitchurch	Shropshire (originally planned for Chester)	Open 2 May 1944 Closed 7 June 1945

---

*Opening date given as January 1943, but this must be wrong as AFN did not start until July 1943.

Transmitter	Location	Remarks
25. Prestwick	2 m NE of Prestwick, 4 m NE of Ayr	Open 30 Apr. 1944 Closed 7 Oct. 1945
26. Upper Ballinderry	12 m SW of Belfast	Open 29 Nov. 1943
27. Crossgar	¾ m WNW of Crossgar, 4 m NNW of Downpatrick	Open 29 Nov. 1943 Closed 10 July 1944 (later replaced by 57)
28. Market Hill	Gosford Castle, 1 m N of Market Hill, 10 m NW of Newry	Open 9 Dec. 1943 Closed 8 July 1944
29. Fintona	½ m SW of Fintona, 7 m S of Omagh	Open 17 Dec. 1943
30. Ballyscullion House	3 m NW of Antrim	Open 22 Dec. 1943 Closed 24 Oct. 1944
31. Beech Hill (Marine Corps Camp B)	5 m SE of Londonderry	Open 5 Dec. 1943
32. Exeter	Devonshire	Open 13 Jan. 1944 Closed 24 Oct. 1944
33. Fremington	3 m W of Barnstaple, Devon	Open 13 Jan. 1944 Closed 20 Mar. 1945
34. Westbury	Wiltshire	Open 17 Jan. 1944 Closed 22 Oct. 1945
35. Carmarthen	Wales	Open 29 Jan. 1944 Closed 23 Feb. 1945
36. Pembroke	Wales	Open 7 Feb. 1944 Closed 19 July 1944
37. Wem	10 m N of Shrewsbury (relocated at Malvern, Worcs)	Open 27 Jan. 1944 Closed 16 Sept. 1945
38. Watton	8 m SE of Swaffham, Norfolk	Open 22 Jan. 1944 Closed 22 July 1945
39. Metfield	5 m NW of Halesworth, Suffolk	Closed 18 July 1945
40. Bude	Cornwall	Open 2 Feb. 1944 Closed 24 Oct. 1944
41. Bridgend	Glamorgan	Open 29 Jan. 1944 Closed 19 July 1944
42. Marston Magna	5 m E of Ilchester, Somerset	Open 31 Jan. 1944
43. Sunningdale	7 m S of Windsor, Berks	Open 6 Mar. 1944 Closed 19 May 1945
44. Kidderminster	Worcestershire	Open 31 Jan. 1944 Closed 30 June 1945
45. Willingale	8 m W of Chelmsford, Essex	Open 22 Jan. 1944 Closed 4 June 1945
46. Dorchester	Dorset	Open 31 Jan. 1944 Closed 30 Mar. 1945
47. Raydon	9 m SW of Ipswich, Suffolk	Open 19 Jan. 1944 Closed 20 Sept. 1945

Transmitter	Location	Remarks
48. Langar Cum Barnston	9 m SE of Nottingham	CANCELLED. Replaced by 54
49. Bottisham	12 m E of Cambridge	Open 19 Jan. 1944
50. Wrangston	13 m E of Plymouth	CANCELLED. Replaced by 53
51. Sudbury	8 m NW of Burton-on Trent, Staffs	(replacing 11) Closed 30 Oct. 1945
52. Gosfield	8 m from Braintree, Essex	(replacing 15) Open 31 Jan. 1944
53. Stow on the Wold	Gloucestershire (replacing 50)	CANCELLED. Replaced by 56
54. Harlaxton Aerodrome	Grantham, Lincs (replacing 48)	CANCELLED. Replaced by 55
55. Barkston Heath Airfield	Grantham, Lincs	(replacing 54) Open 27 May 1944 Closed 27 May 1945
56. 38th Hospital, Winchester	Hampshire	(replacing 53)
57. Rathfryland	9 m NE of Newry	(replacing 27)
58. Newtownards	9½ m E of Belfast	
59. Stone	Staffordshire	Open 18 Sept. 1944 Closed 29 Oct. 1945
60/62 Foxley	Herefordshire	Open 17 Feb. 1945 Closed 29 July 1945
61. Stoneleigh	Warwickshire	Open 23 Nov. 1944 Closed 19 June 1945
63. High Wycombe	Buckinghamshire	Closed 6 Sept. 1945
64. Debden	Essex	Open 8 Feb. 1945 Closed 24 July 1945
65. 110th Hospital	Gloucester	Open 7 Mar. 1945
66. Yeovil	Somerset	Open 18 May 1945 Closed 4 June 1945
67. Southampton		Open 19 Apr. 1945
68. Cowglen	Glasgow	Open 2 May 1945 Closed 6 Oct. 1945
69. Cambridge		Closed 2 Oct. 1945
70. Braintree, Essex		CANCELLED
71. Seething	Norfolk	
72. Cottingham	(unclear whether Yorks or Northants)	Closed 25 June 1945
73. NOT ALLOCATED		
74. Londonderry		Closed 8 Oct. 1945
75. Bournemouth		Open 28 June 1945 Closed 31 Oct. 1945

The following list of the main London locations of the internal loud-speaker system carrying AFN is instructive as an indication of those places patronized by the American forces:

Rainbow Corner, Piccadilly
Liberty Club, 13 Upper Woburn Place
Washington Club, 6 Curzon Street
Duchess Street Club
Nurses Club, 10 Charles Street
Jules Club, Jermyn Street
Reindeer Club, Clifford Street
Columbia Club, 75 Seymour Street
Victory Club, 15 Seymour Street
Hans Crescent Club, Knightsbridge
Milestone Club, Kensington High Street
Mostyn Club, Portman Street
Prince's Gardens Club, Prince's Gardens
General Devers' Suite at the Dorchester Hotel.

In addition, in the Greater London area there were outlets at the head-quarters of the Eighth Air Force, the London Central Base Command, and various BBC premises.

Appendix II:
AFN Program Schedules

Every week, the *Stars and Stripes*, the daily newspaper in the European Theater of Operations for the U.S. armed forces, published a leaflet giving AFN's frequencies and the programs for the coming week. It was, like *Stars and Stripes* itself, printed by the London Times newspaper as a gesture of Anglo-American cooperation. Here is the schedule for just one week in 1944.

SUNDAY 9 APRIL

0800 Sign On: Hymns from Home; Program Resume
0815 Sunday Serenade
0900 World News (BBC)
0910 Band Wagon
0930 Major Bowes
1000 Morning Varieties
1030 Mormon Tabernacle Choir
1100 Your Town: Radio News Letter from Three American Towns
1115 Harry James
1130 Hour of Charm
1200 News
1210 Barracks Bag and Program Resume
1300 World News (BBC)
1310 Melody Roundup
1325 GI Tommy
1335 Bob Crosby Show
1400 Headlines; Sacred Music: BBC Orchestra
1430 John Charles Thomas: Metropolitan Baritone Sings Popular Favorites
1500 Take Your Choice
1530 Sammy Kaye's Sunday Serenade
1600 News Flashes
1605 Radio Chapel with Chaplain John Weaver
1625 Invitation to Two Towns in the United Kingdom
1630 Andre Kostelanetz
1700 Information Please
1730 South American Way
1800 World News (BBC)
1815 GI Supper Club

1900 Seven O'Clock Sports
1905 Jack Benny Program
1930 California Melodies
2000 News from Home
2010 Fred Waring Program
2020 Fanny Brice
2045 Into Battle (BBC)

2100 World News (BBC)
2115 Great Music
2130 Jubilee
2200 Your Radio Theater
2255 Final Edition
2300 Sign Off until 1100 Monday April
10

MONDAY APRIL 10

1100 Spotlight on Tommy Dorsey
1115 Personal Album (Dyana Gale)
1130 Jack Payne & His Orchestra
1150 French Lesson
1200 Noon Edition
1205 Barracks Bag
1300 World News (BBC)
1310 Melody Roundup
1330 Dinah Shore (repeat)
1400 Headlines: BBC Scottish Orchestra
1430 Visiting Hour
1500 Music While You Work
1530 Off the Record
1630 Family Hour
1700 Rainbow Rhythm & Program
     Resume
1730 BBC Midland Light Orchestra
1755 Quiet Moment

1800 World News (BBC)
1815 GI Supper Club
1900 Seven O'Clock Sports
1905 Red Skelton
1930 Command Performance
2000 News from Home
2010 Fred Waring Program
2025 Leave and Learn
2030 Contented Hour
2100 World News (BBC)
2115 Front Line Theatre
2145 Ranch House
2200 Village Store with Joan Davis and
     Jack Haley
2225 One Night Stand with Bobby
     Sherwood
2255 Final Edition
2300 Sign Off until 1100 Tuesday April
     11

TUESDAY APRIL 11

1100 Spotlight on Les Brown
1115 Personal Album (Nora Martin)
1130 Great Music
1150 French Lesson
1200 Noon Edition
1205 Barracks Bag
1300 World News (BBC)
1310 Melody Roundup
1330 Chamber Music Society of Lower
     Basin Street
1400 News: Leslie Bridgewater Quintet
1430 Visiting Hour: Aldrich Family
1500 Music While You Work
1530 Off the Record
1630 War Commentary
1645 Miss Parade
1700 Gay Nineties Review & Program
     Resume
1730 Southern Serenade

1755 Quiet Moment
1800 World News (BBC)
1810 GI Supper Club
1900 Seven O'Clock Sports
1905 Comedy Caravan with Jimmy
     Durante and Gary Moore
1930 Boxing from Rainbow Corner
2000 News from Home
2010 Fred Waring Program
2025 Calling APOs
2030 Carnival of Music
2100 World News (BBC)
2115 Hit Parade
2145 USO in the ETO
2200 Duffy's Tavern
2225 One Night Stand with Paul Martin
2255 Final Edition
2300 Sign Off until 1100 Wednesday
     April 12

WEDNESDAY APRIL 12

1100 Spotlight on Mark Kinney
1115 Personal Album (Shirley Ross)
1130 Music in Three-Quarter Time
1150 French Lesson
1200 Noon Edition
1205 Barracks Bag
1300 World News (BBC)
1310 Melody Roundup
1330 Andre Kostelanetz
1400 Headlines: Geraldo's Orchestra
1430 Visiting Hour
1500 Music While You Work
1530 Off the Record
1630 Lone Ranger
1700 Tommy Dorsey & Program
       Resume
1730 BBC Midland Light Orchestra
1755 Quiet Moment
1800 World News (BBC)

1810 GI Supper Club
1850 Army Talks
1900 Seven O'Clock Sports
1905 Rhapsody in Khaki
1935 Fibber McGee and Molly
2000 News from Home
2010 Fred Waring Program
2025 Human Interest in Books
2030 Kay Kyser
2100 World News (BBC)
2115 Bob Hope Show
2145 Showtime
2200 Hall of Fame
2225 One Night Stand with Teddy
       Powell
2255 Final Edition
2300 Sign Off until 1100 Thursday April
       13

THURSDAY APRIL 13

1100 Spotlight on Jose Savre Maracin
1115 Personal Album (Pat Friday)
1130 Band of the Queen's Royal
       Regiment
1150 French Lesson
1200 Noon Edition
1205 Barracks Bag
1300 World News (BBC)
1310 Melody Roundup
1330 Jubilee
1400 Headlines: Falkman Apache Band
1430 Visiting Hour: Hospital Theater
1500 Music While You Work
1530 Off the Record
1630 Music We Love
1700 National Barn Dance & Program
       Resume
1730 Albert Sandler's Palm Court
       Orchestra

1755 Quiet Moment
1800 World News (BBC)
1810 GI Supper Club
1900 Seven O'Clock Sports
1905 Symphony Hall
2000 News from Home
2010 Fred Waring Program
2025 This Week in Science
2030 Bing Crosby Music Hall
2100 World News (BBC)
2115 Mail Call
2145 USO in the ETO
2200 Truth or Consequence
2225 One Night Stand with Joe
       Reichman
2255 Final Edition
2300 Sign Off until 1100 Friday April
       14

FRIDAY APRIL 14

1100 Spotlight on Boyd Raeburn
1115 Personal Album with Anita
1130 Curtain Call
1150 French Lesson

1200 Noon Edition
1205 Barracks Bag
1300 World News (BBC)
1310 Melody Roundup

1330 Rhapsody in Khaki
1400 Headlines: Melody Mixture with
      Jack Byfield
1400 Visiting Hour
1500 Music While You Work
1530 Off the Record
1630 Music from America: Don
      Vorhee's Orchestra and Guests
1700 South American Way & Program
      Resume
1730 Midland Light Orchestra
1755 Quiet Moment
1800 World News (BBC)
1810 GI Supper Cub
1900 Seven O'Clock Sports
1905 Combined Operation

1930 Burns and Allen
2000 News from Home
2010 Fred Waring Program
2025 This Is the Army
2030 Kate Smith
2100 World News (BBC)
2115 Serenade
2120 American Commentary: Raymond
      Gram Swing
2135 Charlie McCarthy Show
2200 One Night Stand with Les Brown
2225 Suspense with Margo & Philip
      Dorn
2255 Final Edition
2300 Sign Off until 1100 Saturday April
      15

SATURDAY APRIL 15

1100 Spotlight on Tommy Dorsey
1115 Personal Album with Phil Regan
1130 Yanks Radio Weekly
1200 Noon Edition
1205 Barracks Bag
1300 World News (BBC)
1310 Melody Roundup
1330 Crosby Music Hall
1400 Headlines and Downbeat
1430 Hello India
1500 Music While You Work
1530 Off the Record
1630 NBC Symphony & Program
      Resume
1730 Waltz Time
1800 World News (BBC)
1810 Harry James

1830 Atlantic Spotlight
1900 Seven O'Clock Sports
1905 Chamber Music Society of Lower
      Basin Street
1930 Dinah Shore Program
2000 News from Home
2010 Take the Air
2030 GI Journal
2100 World News (BBC)
2115 All Time Hit Parade
2145 WACS Museum
2200 Xavier Cugat
2230 One Night Stand with Freddie
      Martin
2255 Final Edition
2300 Sign Off until 0800 Sunday April
      16

A Note
on the Principal Sources Used

Since the greater part of this book is about the relationship between the BBC and various American government agencies, it is natural that the source for much of the contents should be the BBC Written Archives. These are situated at Caversham Park, on the outskirts of the Berkshire town of Reading. As has been indicated in the text, once the "American Troop Network" had been set up, the BBC kept a careful watch on it, and there is no shortage of references to it in the files. There is also much about the subsequent establishment of the Allied Expeditionary Forces Program, which again closely involved the Anglo-American relationship. There are clearly gaps in the files, but there is enough to give a good picture of what was happening. All the files I have made use of are indicated in the end-of-chapter notes. I am particularly grateful to the BBC for giving me permission to quote freely from all the many documents in the Archives and for their extremely helpful and well-informed staff under the direction of the BBC Written Archivist, Jacqueline Kavanagh. The BBC program journal, *Radio Times*, was also most helpful and gave me generous permission to quote not only from articles on the announcers who appeared on the AEFP (particularly those by Margaret Foster) but also to use contemporary photographs.

I have not been so fortunate on the American side. The Library of Congress and the National Archives at College Park, Maryland, were as helpful as they could be, given that I was unable to visit the United States to examine the files maintained at the latter. As far as the Allied

Expeditionary Forces Programme is concerned, these consist first of all of the files of the Supreme Headquarters of the Allied Expeditionary Forces (RG331, consisting of 34 boxes 290/8/2/6 covering the years 1944–45). Fortunately, microfilm copies of these were presented by the United States to the Public Record Office at Kew, on the outskirts of London, and they proved a useful source of additional material. College Park also holds the records relating to the history of the Armed Forces Radio and Television Service, 1940–87 (RG330). Of the many files listed, only one specifically refers to an Armed Forces Network in Europe, and no dates are indicated. The Library of Congress says that it has no paperwork relating to the Armed Forces Radio Service during the period 1943–46. The American Forces Network in Frankfurt informed me that it, too, has no archives relating to the war or immediate post-war years, but it kindly provided me with some printed material, an audiotape of the final day's broadcasting of AFN Munich, and a number of photographs. The Armed Forces Radio and Television Service did not respond to my inquiries. The Eisenhower Library at Abilene, Kansas, was most helpful and gave me useful guidance in tracking down documentary material.

Of the printed works, by far the most useful was the official *History of AFRTS 1942–1992, The First 50 Years*, produced for the American Forces Information Service and the Armed Forces Radio and Television Service under the aegis of the Defense Department. Although he is not named in the text, which is also undated, the author (according to the National Archives AFRTS files) was Dr. Lawrence Suid. The work contains some errors, but generally it is a most comprehensive picture of how the AFRTS came into being and developed into a major forces broadcasting organization. The sources quoted are particularly valuable. Traveling much the same path is Trent Christman's *Brass Button Broadcasters*. This he describes, rightly, as "a lighthearted look at 50 years of military broadcasting." The author has a good ear for an amusing anecdote and has generously given me permission to quote some. The work is well illustrated, but there is no index. Mention should also be made of the ground-breaking 700-page study on the history of AFRS up to 1946, written as a doctoral thesis, by Theodore DeLay.

It would be difficult to write about broadcasting in Britain without reference to the monumental work by Asa Briggs, *The History of Broadcasting in the United Kingdom*, published in four volumes. Lord Briggs's chronicle of the BBC story, particularly during the war years, is masterly, and his ability to compress the most complex issues in a few telling sentences can only be admired. The parallel work dealing with the history of American broadcasting by Erik Barnouw, embracing three volumes, is another excellent study; however, as it deals almost entirely with affairs on the American side of the Atlantic, I have not referred to it as much as Briggs.

Maurice Gorham's autobiographical volume *Sound and Fury* gives a revealing insider's view of the BBC in the period before, during, and just after the war. It is an entertaining, often outspoken volume, full of interesting insights. His other main work in the field, *Broadcasting: Television and Radio since 1900* is a more considered piece and also contains much worthwhile material on the development of broadcasting in Britain. In a different vein is *Star Spangled Radio*, co-authored by Colonel Ed Kirby, head of broadcasting at SHAEF. It is for the most part a lively, informative, and often amusing account of wartime forces broadcasting. Unhappily, the chapter on the AEFP—pointedly entitled "How to Develop Anglo-American Friendship Despite the BBC"—is so vitriolic and partisan about Britain's premier broadcasting service that it needs to be treated with considerable caution. Two quite dissimilar volumes, also from the other side of the Atlantic, proved useful. One was John Dunning's *Tune in Yesterday*, first published in 1978 and completely revised and extended as *On the Air: The Encyclopaedia of Old Time Radio*, which looks in informed detail at some 1,500 of the top radio shows from the "golden age" of radio. *Same Time, Same Station*, by Ron Lackmann, is nowhere near as comprehensive or always so reliable but is a useful and enjoyable reference work all the same. On a different scale are two of the remarkably detailed research projects undertaken by Harry Mackenzie: *Command Performance USA* lists every single *Command Performance* show, its cast and musical numbers, as well as those for *Mail Call* and *GI Journal*, while *One Night Stand* does the same for that popular wartime show.

Much has been written about the impact of the American "invasion" of Britain during the war. Probably the two best accounts are *Rich Relations: The American Occupation of Britain 1942–1945* by David Reynolds and *Over Here: The GIs in Wartime Britain* by Juliet Gardiner. The former is an outstanding study that explores the subject in a most readable and comprehensive way. The latter, although not on the same scale, is both detailed and entertaining. Two worthwhile studies look at one particular aspect of the American presence: their stay in Northern Ireland. Audrey Johnson's *Do March in Step Girls* is a vivid personal account by a member of Britain's Women's Royal Naval Service who spent some time at an American naval base in Londonderry, while Mary Pat Kelly's *Home Away from Home* takes a more general look at "the Yanks in Ireland" during the war. Books on life in wartime Britain are legion, but one of the most authoritative and exhaustive accounts is Angus Calder's *The People's War*.

The Glenn Miller story has attracted a great deal of attention. I found the two most useful books were Geoffrey Butcher's detailed study *Next to a Letter from Home* and Chris Way's *The Big Bands Go to War*, which apart from Miller is an absorbing study of the wartime activities of the military big bands of the era. In the music field generally, George T. Simon's *The Big Bands* is an invaluable look at every American band, bandleader, and vocalist during the big-band era, while Frank Huggett's *Goodnight Sweetheart* is an interesting, well-illustrated survey of the top songs of the war years as seen from the British viewpoint. Musical reference works of particular value are *Your Hit Parade*, which lists every hit parade and Top Ten tune and vocalist for every week from 1935 to 1994, while *Pop Hits 1940–54* is a remarkably comprehensive and informative look at the hit-music scene of those years.

WORKS CONSULTED

1. Official Sources

These consisted of the BBC Written Archives, the Library of Congress, the National Archives at College Park, Maryland, the Public Record Office in London, and the official AFRTS history (details of which are given above).

2. Published Works

Anon. *The Royal Family in Wartime* (Odhams Press, 1945).
_____. *Gazetteer of the British Isles* (Bartholomew 9th ed., 1943).
Barnouw, Erik. *The Golden Web* (OUP New York, 1968).
BBC Year Books 1944, 1945 (BBC; various authors).
Bechhofer Roberts, C. E. *The Trial of Jones and Hulten* (Jarrold, 1945).
_____. *The Trial of William Joyce* (Jarrold, 1946).
Belsey, James, and Helen Reid. *The West at War* (Redcliffe Press, 1990).
Briggs, Asa. *History of Broadcasting in the United Kingdom*, 4 vols. (Oxford University Press, 1961–1979).
Brinkley, David. *Washington Goes to War* (Alfred A. Knopf, 1988).
Butcher, Geoffrey. *Next to a Letter from Home* (Mainstream Publishing, 1986).
Calder, Angus. *The People's War 1939–45* (Jonathan Cape, 1969).
Carey, Mike. *I'll Sing You a Thousand Love Songs: The Denny Dennis Story* (Printed for the Denny Dennis Music Society of Derby, 1992).
Charmley, John. *Churchill: The End of Glory* (Hodder & Stoughton, 1993).
Christman, Trent. *Brass Button Broadcasters* (Turner Publishing, 1993).
DeLay, Theodore S. *An Historical Study of the Armed Forces Radio Service to 1946* (privately printed, 1951).
Dundatscheck, Eric. *Sustineo Alas or Keep Them Flying* (Erisys, 1993).
Dunning, John. *Tune in Yesterday* (Prentice-Hall, 1978).
Eisenhower, Dwight D. *Crusade in Europe* (Heinemann, 1948).
Elrod, Bruce C. *Your Hit Parade 1935–1994* (Popular Culture Ink, 1994).
Encyclopaedia Britannica. *Britannica Book of the Year, 1947*.
Falconer, Jonathan. *RAF Bomber Airfields of World War II* (Ian Allan, 1992).
Foster, Andy, and Steve Furst. *Radio Comedy 1938–1968* (Virgin Publishing, 1996).

Gardiner, Juliet. *Over Here: The GIs in Wartime Britain* (Collins & Brown, 1992).

Gorham, Maurice. *Sound and Fury* (Percival Marshall, 1948).

_____. *Broadcasting: Sound and Television since 1900* (Andrew Dakers, 1952).

Hall, J. W (ed). *The Trial of William Joyce* (Wm Hodge & Co, 1946).

Halliwell, Leslie. *Filmgoer's Companion* (Granada, 1984).

Howlett, Peter. *Fighting with Figures: A Statistical Digest of the Second World War* (Central Statistical Office, London, 1995).

Huggett, Frank. *Goodnight Sweetheart* (W. H. Allen, 1979).

Irving, David. *The War between the Generals* (Allen Lane, 1981).

Johnson, Audrey. *Do March in Step Girls: A Wren's Story* (privately printed, 1997).

Johnson, Derek E. *East Anglia At War 1939–45* (Jarrold, 1992).

Jones, Steve. *When the Lights Went Down: Crime in Wartime London* (Wicked Publications, 1995).

Kelly, Mary Pat. *Home away from Home: The Yanks in Ireland* (Appletree Press, 1994).

Kirby, Edward M., and Jack W. Harris. *Star Spangled Radio* (Ziff Davis, 1948).

Lackmann, Ron. *Same Time, Same Station* (Facts on File, 1996).

Leitch, Michael. *Great Songs of World War II* (Wise Publications, n.d.).

Liddell Hart, Basil (ed.). *History of World War II* (Purnell, 1966).

Longmate, Norman. *The Doodlebugs: The Story of the Flying Bombs* (Hutchinson, 1981).

Mackenzie, Harry. *Command Performance USA* (Greenwood Publishing, 1996).

_____. *One Night Stand Series* (Greenwood Publishing, 1991).

Manvell, Roger. *Films and the Second World War* (A. S. Barnes, 1974).

Montague, Ron. *When the Ovaltineys Sang* (privately printed, 1990).

Morgan, Colin. *The BBC's Anti Slush Committee* (privately printed, 1991).

Morris, Eric. *Blockade: Berlin and the Cold War* (Hamish Hamilton, 1973).

Pafford, Wilfred. *Let's Hear It for the Backroom Boys* (privately printed, 1998).

Parker, Derek. *Radio: The Great Years* (David & Charles, 1977).

Parrish, Thomas (ed.). *Encyclopaedia of World War II* (Secker & Warburg, 1978).

Pawley, Edward. *BBC Engineering 1922–1972* (BBC Publications, 1972).

Pelling, Henry. *Winston Churchill* (Macmillan, 1974).

Pimlott, Ben (ed). *The Second World War Diary of Hugh Dalton 1940–45* (Jonathan Cape, 1986).

Plischke, Elmer, & Henry P. Pilgert. *US Information Programs in Berlin* (Office of the U.S. High Commissioner for Germany, 1953).

Raymond, R. Alwyn. *The Cleft Chin Murder* (Claud Morris, 1945).

Reynolds, David. *Rich Relations: The American Occupation of Britain 1943–1945* (HarperCollins, 1995).

Rhodes, Anthony. *Propaganda: The Art of Persuasion. World War II* (Angus & Robertson, 1976).

Rosignoli, Guido. *Army Badges and Insignia of World War 2* (Blandford Press, 1972).

Ruppenthal, Roland G. *Logistical Support of the Armies, Official History of the US Army in World War II* (Center of Military History, 1953).

Sears, Richard. *V Discs: A History and Discography* (Greenwood Publishing, 1980).

Simon, George T. *The Big Bands* (Schirmer Books, 1981).

Smithies, Edward. *Crime in Wartime: A Social History of Crime in World War II* (Allen & Unwin, 1982).

Snyder, Louis L. *Encyclopaedia of the Third Reich* (McGraw-Hill, 1976).

Sperber, A. M. *Murrow: His Life and Times* (Michael Joseph, 1987).

Taylor, Doreen. *A Microphone and a Frequency* (Heinemann, 1983).

Teubig, Klaus. *V Disc Catalogue* (Deutscher Bibliotheksverband, Berlin, 1976).

Thompson, R. W. *The Yankee Marlborough* (Allen & Unwin, 1963).

Walker, Andrew. *A Skyful of Freedom* (Broadside Books, 1992).

Way, Chris. *The Big Bands Go to War* (Mainstream, 1991).

West, W. J. (ed.). *Orwell: The War Broadcasts* (Duckworth/BBC, 1985).

Whitaker's Almanac 1940–1946.

Whitburn, Joel. *Pop Hits 1940-1954* (Record Research Inc., 1994).

Wickham, Dick. *Station 146, Seething Airfield Norfolk (The Story of the 448th Bombardment Group)* (privately printed, n.d.).

Who Was Who, Vol. VII.

3. Newspapers and Periodicals

Los Angeles Times; New York World Telegram; Saturday Evening Post; The Times; Daily Telegraph; Daily Mirror; Sunday Express; Yorkshire Post; Western Daily Press; Bath Evening Chronicle.

Yank; Stars and Stripes; Picture Post; Radio Times; History Today; Transatlantic; Melody Maker; Radio and Television News; Radio Bygones; Radio Days; Goldmine; In Tune; Tune into Yesterday (newsletter of the Old Time Radio Show Collectors Association of England); *Memory Lane; Journal into Melody* (official magazine of the Robert Farnon Society); *Moonlight Serenader* (journal of the Glenn Miller Society).

4. Audio/Visual

Encyclopaedia Britannica (CD rom, 1999 Standard Edition).

Glenn Miller: The Lost Recordings (CD/audiotape set, Conifer Records, London, 1995).

Glenn Miller: The Secret Broadcasts. The Army Air Forces Training Command (3-CD set, Conifer Records, London, 1996).

GI Jukebox 1936–1946 (5-CD set, Michele International, Hainault, Essex, 1993).

Hill, Trevor, and Gregor Prumbs. *Songs and Sounds of War* (2-CD set, privately produced, Cheltenham, 1999).

Lulay, Guenter. *AFN Radio Souvenirs, A Celebration in Words and Music of the American Forces Network in Germany* (4-tape audio compilation, privately produced, Heidelberg, 1999).

Prumbs, Gregor. *American & British Forces Radio Services 1943–1946* (CD, privately produced, Krefeld, 1998).

Robert Farnon. *The Lost Recordings, 1944–45* (CD, Cowtown Publications, Ontario, 1997).

Capt. Robert Farnon and the Canadian Band of the AEF. *Rare Wartime Recordings 1943–45* (CD, Robert Farnon Society, 1997).

World Book 1998 Multimedia Encyclopaedia.

In addition to the above, I listened to recordings of a great many wartime and postwar broadcasts, as indicated in the end-of-chapter notes, and also examined the following German-produced videotapes, which provided interesting and useful information about the history of AFN: *Music in the Air* (ZDF Television), *Happy [40th] Birthday AFN* (Telmax International/ZDF, 1983), *Happy [50th] Birthday AFN* (Hesscher Rundfunk Arte, 1993), *Radio Star, Die AFN Story* (Docfilm, 1994).

Index

Individual broadcasting announcers, musical numbers, orchestras, programs, and vocalists are listed under those general headings except in a few cases.

Adams, Godfrey, BBC Director of Program Planning: AFN, views on, 1, 40; commercial radio, threat from, 14, 140–141; separatism, concern over, 18, 52; U.S. programs on BBC, 3, 9 n.6, 20

AEFP, see Allied Expeditionary Forces Program

AFN, see American Forces Network

"AFN Shrivenham" (Wiltshire), 144

AFRS, see Armed Forces Radio Service

AFRS Orchestra, 67, 73

Alaska, forces broadcasting in, 61–62

Allied Expeditionary Forces Program (AEFP): AFN's contribution to, 97, 99; AFRS/AFN objections to, 87–88; BBC rejection of proposals for, 88; Canadian and British AEF bands, 106; Canadian contribution to, 106; Eisenhower, D. D. [appeal to Churchill, 89–90; tribute by, 124]; first program of, 96–97; and Glen Miller band, 110–111; go-ahead given for, 90–91; Gorham, Maurice, appointed head, 93; negotiations on, 83–86; Niven, David, role with, 98; origins of, 83; "politics and intrigue," 102; preparations for, 94–95; problems [over Glenn Miller, 107–109; over religious broadcasts, 85–86; over title (AEFP of the BBC), 95–96, 99–101]; program(s), 104–106 ["best entertainment program ever," 116; final, and Eisenhower's tribute, 124]; U.S. forces' dissatisfaction with, 113–115; women announcers on, 98–99

American Broadcasting Company (ABC), 65

American Broadcasting Station in Europe (ABSIE), 81–82

American Expeditionary Station (AES), 66–67, 89

American Federation of Musicians, and record dispute, 75, 107

American Forces Network (AFN): announcers on, 35–36; and BBC [help given by; initial opposition to, 11–20; negotiations with, 22–24; problems over news with, 51–56; threat to audience of, "laughable, " 139]; British listeners to, 34–35, 138–140; final program of, 129; Gorham, Maurice, views on, 18, 120–121; Hayes, John, role as head of station at, 25–26, 42, 56, 119–120; hours of broadcasting on, 33–34; opening-day broadcast by, 30; programs on, 35–38; staffing, 26, 31 n.15, 125; transmitters, 15, 24, 27, 32, 33–34, 48, 118; and women, lack of on air, 38

Andersen, Lale, 6–7, 59

Anglo–American relations: AFN, effects on, 50, 141, 145; BBC awareness of need for good, 16, 25; Eisenhower's emphasis on, 82–83, 108, 115; Kirby, Col., unhelpful to, 113; separatism, dangers of, 18–20

Armed Forces Radio Service (AFRS): achievements of, 78; origins of, 62–63, 68 n.9; OWI, disputes with, 64; programs and performers, 70–74; recording techniques pioneered by, 65–66; sounds of home on, 70; wartime expansion and postwar run-down of, 76–78, 130. *See also* Lewis, Tom

Ashbridge, Sir Noel, BBC DDG, 56

Astaire, Fred, 39

Axis Sally (Mildred Gillars), 7, 59, 73, 119

Balkwill, M., BBC News, 55

Barker, Gen. Ray, Asst. Chief of Staff SHAEF: AEFP, role in negotiations over, 83–87, 95–96, 100; BBC, tribute to, 124; and Gorham, Maurice, 95; Kirby, Col., threat of disciplinary action against, 113; and Lewis, Tom, 87–88

"Baron of Bounce" (Ken Dunnagan), 132, 136 n.13

Baruch, Lt. Andre, 67

Baseball: British views on, 42; GIs' desire for, 9 n.6

Bataan, forces broadcasting in, 60

"Battle of the Beams, " 21 n.6

Battle of the Bulge, 119

BBC, *see* British Broadcasting Corporation

Bedell Smith, Lt. Gen. W., Eisenhower's Chief of Staff, 86–87

Benchley, Robert, 4

Bennett, Tony, 133

Benny, Jack: and AFN/AFRS, 28; on BBC, 3, 4, 20, 49, 139; live on AFN Berlin 128; outdone by British comedian Will Hay, 139; sends signed disc to Panama Canal Zone radio, 61

Bergman, Ingrid, 122, 128

Binkin, Syl, AFN, 30, 31 n.25, 80–81, 126 n.23

Blue Danube Network, Austria, 134–135

Boardman, Lt. Col. True, 113–115

Bogart, Humphrey, 67

Boult, Sir Adrian, 109–110

Bracken, Brendan, British Minister of Information, 15, 90–91

Britain in wartime: bombing of, blackout in, 1–2, 80–81; shortages in, 1–2, 41, 81; travel restrictions in, 40

British Broadcasting Corporation (BBC): and AEFP [resistance to, 83–90; rows over title of, 95–96, 99–101]; and AFN [problems with over news coverage, 51–56; relationship with and help to, 25, 33, 81, 129–130, 135, 136 n.5; U.K. listeners of, 48, 138–140]; Allies, demand of for broadcasting stations, 13, 17; Americanization of resisted, 4, 141; British forces' view of, 5–6; music censorship by, 46–47; U.S. forces' views on, 2, 113–115. *See also* Adams, Godfrey; AEFP; AFN; Gorham, Maurice; Haley, William

British Forces Network (BFN), 124, 132, 134

British Royal Family, 108; role of in war, 116 n.12

Broadcasting announcers: AES [Love, Anita, 67; Rudman, Corporal Frances, 67; Smith, WAC Margie, 67]; AFN Germany [Cosgrove, Don, 132; Dunnagan, Ken, 132; Jones, Red, 132; Phillips, Stew, 131; Vrotsos, Johnny, 132; White, Mark, 132]; AFN London

[Binkin, Syl, 30, 80; Crawford, Broderick, 37, 105; Crawford, Dick (Saddlebags), 36; Dudley, Dick, 37, 97, 131, 136 n.5; Jameson, Keith, 37, 105, 106, 121; Kerr, Johnny, 35–36, 40, 49, 82, 142; McNamara, John, 37; Moffat, Ralph Muffit, 37, 131, 143; Monaghan, George, 35–36, 38, 49, 82, 98, 106, 112, 131, 142; Paulsen, Verner, 37–38]; AFRS [Carpenter, Ken, 71; GI Jill, 73–74; Whitman, Ernie Bubbles, 72; Wilson, Don, 72; Zell, Harry von, 72]; Axis [Axis Sally, 7, 59, 73, 119; Tokyo Rose, 73]; BBC/AEFP [Balcon, Jill, 99; Engelmann, Franklin, 94, 96–97, 108, 112, 124; Griffiths, Joan, 99; Hubble, Margaret, 98–99, 136 n.5; McLoughlin, Betty, 99; Metcalfe, Jean, 99; Murray, Pete, 37; Samson, Charmian, 98–99; Waldman, Ronnie, 97, 136 n.5; Wilmot, Gerry, 106]

Brophy, Murray, U.S. War Department, 30 n.1

Brown, Joe E., 61–62

"Brownouts"/dimouts, 8 n.3

Canada: AEFP, contribution to, 96, 102, 106; Britain, troops in, 17; Maxted, Stanley, Arnhem broadcast, 104

Capra, Frank, 62

Carlos Place, London, first AFN studio, 28, 52, 56, 81

Carroll, Wallace, OWI, 50

Censorship, 4, 23, 46–47, 51, 53

Churchill, Winston S., British Prime Minister: AEFP, role in, 89–91, 101, 103 n.22; **Lili Marlene**, intervenes over, 6–7; Operation Domino, views on, 21 n.6; Roosevelt, F. D., talks with, 27–28

Clark, J. B., BBC Controller, Overseas Services, 83

Cleft Chin murder case, *see* Jones and Hulten

Clooney, Rosemary, 133

Coca Cola, 46, 74

Collins, Norman, BBC Gen. Overseas Service Director, 86

Columbia Broadcasting System (CBS), 17

Command Performance, 111; and AFRS, 64; appearances on, most frequent, 70–71; on BBC, 3–4, 20, 22; *Dick Tracy Wedding Special*, 77; introduction to, 71; origins of, and "sounds of home," 69–70; and OWI, 64; popularity of, with U.S. forces in Pacific, 77

Commercial advertising: American forces' attitude to, 142; BBC/British views of, 16, 46–47, 140–142; U.S. programs, deleted from, 24, 46–47, 66

Connor, Tommie, 9 n.17

Cox, Pfc. Freddie, AFN, 38

Crawford, Broderick, AFN, 37, 105

Crosby, Bing: on ABSIE, 82, 92 n.4; British troops, popular with, 3; Dick Tracy, role as, 77; impromptu London blackout concert by, 105; live programs, insistence on, 65; Shelton, Anne, sings with, 105; Sinatra, Frank, rivalry with, 34, 39, 40, 143; voted U.S. forces' most popular singer, 40

Crosby, Gary, with AFN, 133

Daily Mirror, 19

Daily Variety, 77

Dalton, Hugh, U.K. government minister, 20

Davis, Gen. Benjamin, 72

Davis, Elmer, OWI, 22

D Day, 82, 96

Della Cioppa, Guy, OWI, 17, 24, 49, 52

"Desert Rats, " 7, 9 n.18

Devers, Lt. Gen. Jacob, 25

Dick Tracy Wedding Special, AFRS, 77

Dietrich, Marlene, 6, 37, 122

"Dixieland Duke of Deutschland" (Don Cosgrove), 132

Donahue, Sam (U.S. Navy Band), 110

Doolittle, Gen., Commander U.S. Eighth Air Force, 102 n.2, 107

Duffle Bag: Kerr, Johnny, presented by and details of, 35–36; postwar, 132; shot-down airmen listen in to, 82; *Sound Wave* magazine praises, 35; voted top AFN program, 36, 77

Eagle Squadron, 95

Eisenhower, Gen. (later President) Dwight D.: AEFP, involvement in, 82, 89–90, 101, 103 n.22, 124; AFN, discusses plans for, 11–12; Anglo-American cooperation, views on, 82–83, 141; appointed C.-in-C. ETO, 8; BBC News, high opinion of, 51; Henry, Leroy, intervenes in case of, 19; Miller, Glenn, asks for in ETO, 107

Engelmann, Franklin, BBC: in AEFP, 94; co-host of Independence Day broadcast, 112; decorated at war's end, 124; Miller, Glenn, views on, 108; Monaghan, George, reproves, 112; opening-day broadcast, 96–97

European Theater of Operations, U.S. Army (ETOUSA), 87, 119, 121

Evans, Bernard, BBC News, 53–54

Farnon, Capt. Robt, Canadian Band of the AEF, 106, 136 n.5

Federal Communications Commission (FCC), 33, 61

Fields, Gracie, 9 n.17

Foot, Robert W., BBC joint DG, 44 n.34

Forces Broadcasting: AES, formation of, 66–67; and Alaska, 61–62; and BBC Forces Programme, 3, 59–60; and Far East, 60; and Panama Canal Zone, 61; and Russia, for German forces in, 59; Spanish Civil War, role in, 58–59. *See also* AEFP; AFN; AFRS

Forte, Pfc. John, AES, 67

Frankfurter Rundschau, 137 n.15

Gale, Lt. Gen. Sir H. M., British Army, 84

Germany: AFN network in, 124, 127–128, 135–136; Allied nonfraternization policy in, 129; Berlin blockade, AFN valued during, 133–134; British Forces Network set up in, 124; chaos in at war's end, 127; and German listeners to AFN, 132–133, 135; venereal disease in, 129

GI Jill (Martha Wilkerson), 73–74

GI Jive, 73–74

Gilbert, Morris, U.S. Embassy, London, 12

Gillars, Mildred, *see* Axis Sally

Goebbels, Josef, Nazi propaganda chief, 7, 51

Gorham, Maurice: and AEFP, 102, 116; and AFN, 18, 120, 121, 139; on

American newsreading, 99; and Barker, Gen., 95; difficulties faced by, 93; and Kirby, Col., 93, 101, 120–121; and Miller, Glenn, 107–108

Green, Benny, 34

Gurney, Col. Charles H., first head of AFN, 25

Haley, William, BBC DG: AEFP, involvement in, 88–91, 93; AFN, expresses thanks to, 56; Americanization of BBC, concerns about, 4, 141; appointment of as DG, 44 n.34

Halperin, Marty AFRS, 68 n.11

Harlan, Capt. Bob, AFN, 132

Haw-Haw, Lord, (William Joyce), 4–5

Hay, Will, 139

Hayes, Col. John, head of AFN: AEFP, role in, 83–84, 96; AFRS, relationship with, 119–120, 125; role of as head of network, 25–26, 31 n.25, 47, 127

Henry, Leroy, U.S. Army courtmartial of, 19

Hodges, Gen. C. H., 124

Holiner, Mann, producer of *Jubilee*, 72

Hollywood Victory Committee, 70

Hope, Bob, 28, 90; AFRS, reduces commitment to, 130; on AFRS/AFN, 28; on BBC, 3–4, 20, 49; in *Dick Tracy Wedding Special* and *Chrismas Command Performance*, 70, 77; Trinder, Tommy, compared with, 80

Hucko, Sgt. "Peanuts," AEFP, 110

Hughes, Gen., 11

ITMA (It's That Man Again), BBC, 49, 113

Jameson, Keith, AFN, 37, 105, 106, 121

Joint Army-Navy Committee on Welfare and Recreation, 62

Jolson, Al, 4

Jones and Hulten, trial of ("Cleft Chin" murder case), 20

Joyce, William (Lord Haw-Haw), 4–5

Jubilee, 28, 72

Kennedy, George, 133

Kerr, Johnny, AFN: background and broadcasting style, 35–36; banter on air with WAC, 40; heard by shot-down airmen, 82; ITMA, views on, 49; U.K. listeners, popularity with, 142

Kirby, Col. Edward M., Head of Broadcasting SHAEF: AEFP involvement in, 90, 100–101, 113, 120–121; BBC, attitude to, 86; *Command Performance* and *Army Hour*, role with, 102 n.2; and Gorham, Maurice, 93; and Miller, Glenn, 107, 108; and "talent for rapid-fire action, " 93

Landis, Carole, 70

Lewis, Tom, Head of AFRS: AEFP negotiations, involvement with, 87–88, 93; appointment of and policy decisions by, 62–64, 69; OWI, battles with, 64; and "victory thru air power" speech, 78

Light, Capt. Robert, AFN: AEFP, views, 101, 103 n.23, 113; audience for AFN, estimate of, 138; Paris AFN, set up by, 121; Patton, Gen., Munich brush with, 127–128

Lilli Marlene, 6–7, 59, 105

"Lord Haw-Haw, " *see* Joyce, William

Los Angeles Daily News, 70

Louis, Joe, v. Buddy Baer, 70

Love, Anita, American Red Cross, 67

MacArthur, Gen. Douglas, 60

Macgregor, J. C. S., BBC Assistant Controller News, 53–55

McKinley, Sgt. Ray, AEFP, 110–111

MacMurray, Fred, 72

McNally, Sgt. Jim, AFN, 121

Madden, Cecil, BBC: AEFP, role in, 94, 105, 109; Miller, Glenn, anecdote on, 109, 116 n.18; Niven, David, views on, 98

Magnetophon (audiotape recording system), 123, 125 n.19

Mail Call, 4, 20, 28, 47, 71, 77, 97, 111

March, Frederic, 67

Marshall, Gen. George C., U.S. Chief of Staff, 8, 11, 62

Maxted, Stanley, AEFP, 104

Melachrino, R.S.M. George, British Band of the AEF, 106–107

Melody Maker magazine, 74, 110

Miller, Glenn, and orchestra: ABSIE, broadcasts on, 81–82; band's achievements, 123; BBC, difficulties with, 107–109; and Boult, Sir Adrian, 108; and Engelmann, Franklin, 108; and "ETO morale booster" description, 107; multiple microphones, anecdote of, 109; Paris, proposes band move to, 122–123; reported missing, 123; V-bombs, driven from London by, 80–81

Monaghan, George, AFN: on AEFP, 98; background and broadcasting style, 35–36; banter in *Canada Show*, 106; delight on air at promotion, 38; vs. Franklin Engelmann, 112; heard by shot-down airmen, 82; ITMA, views on, 49; live show in U.K., 131; popularity with U.K. audience, 142

Montgomery, Douglass, 106

Morgan, Brewster, OWI, 21 n.14, 22–23, 30 n.1

Morgan, Frank, 4, 77

Morley, Royston, BBC/AEFP, 94, 104, 124

Murray, Pete, 37

Murrow, Ed, 28, 137 n.18

Musical numbers, 145–148; **Amor**, 40; **Bell Bottom Trousers**, 38; **Besame Mucho**, 40; **Dark Eyes**, 124; **Drinking Rum & Coca Cola**, 46; **I'll Be Seeing You**, 40, 74; **I'll Get By**, 40, 74; **I'll Walk Alone**, 38, 40, 143; **I Love You**, 40; **It Must Be Jelly**, 112; **It Had To Be You**, 40; **Lilli Marlene**, 6–7, 59, 105; **Lily of Laguna**, 82; **Long Ago and Far Away**, 40, 74, 81; **McNamara's Band**, 37; **My Guy's Come Back**, 110; **Near You**, 131; **Opus One**, 35; **Oranges and Lemons**, 95; **Out of My Dreams**, 132; **Paper Doll**, 40; **San Fernando Valley**, 40; **Sentimental Journey**, 39; **Sgt. Mac's Git Along Song**, 110–111; **Sinatra, Sinatra, Clear From Rangoon to Sumatra**, 39; **Somewhere on Via Roma**, 67; **Sur le Pont d'Avignon**, 82; **Swingin on a Star**, 74; **Trolley Song**, 40; **Undercurrent Blues**, 132; **Volga**

Boatmen, 124; **What Is This Thing Called Love**, 35; **When I Got in the Army**, 136 n.5

National Broadcasting Corporation (NBC), 37, 61, 65
New York World Telegram, 112, 142
Niven, David: AEFP, role in, 98, 114; co-host of Independence Day broadcast, 112; decorated at war's end, 124; Miller, Glenn, directive to, 109
Northern Ireland, 2, 12–13, 40
Nussbaum, Major, AFN, 53–54

Ockner, Sgt. George, 110
Office of War Information (OWI): British, given helpful information by, 144; AFN, role in, 15, 17, 22–23, 26, 50; AFRS, strained relations with, 63–64; origins of, 11–12
On the Record AFN, 35–36, 82, 105, 142
Operation Domino, 21 n.6
Orchestras: AFRS, 73; American Band of the AEF, *see* Glenn Miller; Andre Kostenlanetz, 132; Artie Shaw, 30, 38, 109–110; BBC Symphony, 109; Benny Goodman, 38, 73, 110, 132; British Band of the AEF, 106; Canadian Band of the AEF, 106, 136 n.5; Francis Craig, 131; Fred Waring, 41, 97; Glenn Miller, 41, 80–82, 107–109, 122–123; Harry James, 30, 38, 41, 49; Jimmy Dorsey, 40; Kay Kyser, 38, 41; Les Brown, 39; Louis Prima, 38; Ray Noble, 30; Tommy Dorsey, 35, 49, 106, 109; U.S. Navy Band, 109
Osborn, Brig. Gen. Frank, 62

Panama Canal Zone, forces broadcasting in, 60–61
Parrish, Sgt. Pete, AFN, 121
Patton, Gen. George S., 67, 124, 128
Performing rights, problems over, 47
Performing Rights Society (U.K.), 24
Philippines, forces broadcasting in, 60
Portland Place, London, AFN studio, 81
Powell, Staff Sgt. Mel, AEFP, 110
Programs: AES [*Barracks Bag*, 67; *Mediterranean Hit Parade*, 67]; AFN (Germany) [*Bouncin' in Bavaria*, 131; *Dancing Round the Baltic*, 134;

Dixieland Duke of Deutschland, 132; *Duffle Bag*, 132, 137 n.15; *Hot-Hot House/Cool Castle*, 132, 136 n.13; *Lunchen in Munchen*, 131; *Melody Go Round*, 137 n.15; *Merely Music*, 137 n.15; *Midnight in Munich*, 131; *Music in the Air*, 132, 137 n.15; *Off the Record*, 132, 137 n.15; *Personal Album*, 131; *Stickbuddy Jamboree*, 132; *Vocal Touch*, 131–132]; AFN (London) [*Barrack Bag*, 36; *Combined Operation*, 41; *Concert for Chowhounds*, 33; *Duffle Bag*, 35, 40, 77, 82, 105, 142; *GI Tommy*, 41; *Invitation*, 41; *Learn on Your Leave*, 41; *Miss Parade*, 36; *Off the Record*, 36; *On the Record*, 36, 82, 105, 142; *Repeat Performance*, 143; *Rhapsody in Khaki*, 37; *Smash Hits*, 38; *Strictly on the Record*, 105; *Visiting Hour*, 41; *WACS Museum*, 41; *Weekend Leave*, 41]; U.K./AEFP [*AEF Ranch House*, 37; *AEF Special*, 105; *American Eagle in Britain*, 95; *Atlantic Spotlight*, 106; *Background Hour*, 49; *Canada Show*, 106; *Combat Diary*, 104; *Family Favorites*, 99; *Farewell AFN*, 129–130, 136 n.5; *Forces Favorites*, 99; *Into Battle*, 28; *ITMA*, 49, 113; *Mark up the Map*, 104–105; *Monday Night at Eight*, 97; *Rise and Shine*, 97, 105; *A Soldier and a Song*, 110; *Strings with Wings*, 110; *SwingShift*, 110; *Uptown Hall*, 110; *Variety Bandbox*, 106; *War Commentary*, 28, 50]; U.S. (AFRS) [*AFRS Magic Carpet*, 73; *Army Hour*, 102 n.2; *At Ease*, 73, 77; *Command Performance*, 3–4, 20, 28, 64, 69, 71, 77, 102 n.2, 111, 140; *Downbeat*, 77; *GI Jive*, 73–74, 77; *GI Journal*, 72, 77, 78; *Hometown Highlights*, 66; *Jubilee*, 28, 72, 77; *Mail Call*, 4, 20, 28, 47, 71, 77, 97, 111; *Melody Roundup*, 72, 77; *One Night Stand*, 74; *Personal Album*, 72, 77; *Remember*, 72; *Showtime*, 74; *Spotlight Bands*, 74; *Yank Bandstand*, 74; *Yank Swing Session*, 77; *Yarns for Yanks*, 72]; U.S. (commercial) [*Bing Crosby Music Hall*, 30, 77; *Bob Hope Show*, 4, 38; *Dinah Shore Show*, 30, 97; *Edgar Bergen–Charlie McCarthy Show*, 4, 28, 30; *Fred Allen*, 49, 69; *Guy*

Lombardo, 77; *Information Please*, 41; *Jack Benny Show*, 3, 4, 37; *Kate Smith*, 28, 97; *Lone Ranger*, 28; *Radio Chapel*, 85; *This Is London*, 28; *Your Hit Parade*, 39, 40, 67, 74–75]

Queensberry All Services Club, London, 105–106

Radio in the American Sector (RIAS), 134
Radio Arnhem, 119
Radio International, 59
Radio Luxembourg, 35, 43 n.13, 123
Radio Times, 29, 43 n.16, 99, 103 n.18
Rainbow Corner, 27
Religious broadcasting, 85–86
Roosevelt, President Franklin D., 22, 27, 37, 62
Rudman, Corporal Frances, AES, 67
Ryan, A. P., BBC Controller News, 51–52

Separatism (Anglo-American), dangers of, 18–20
SHAEF (Supreme Headquarters Allied Expeditionary Force), 81, 83–91, 95, 99–101
SHAPE (Supreme Headquarters, Allied Powers Europe), 134
Shelton, Anne, 7, 105, 109
Shore, Dinah: on ABSIE, 82; favorite AFN singer, 40; *the* female vocalist, 38; on GI Jive, 73; presents *Showtime*, 74; special performance for two GIs, 105; as Tess Trueheart in *Dick Tracy Wedding Special*, 77
Sigmon, Loyd, AFN, 26–28, 34
Sinatra, Frank: Crosby, Bing, rivalry with 34, 40, 143; in *Dick Tracy Wedding Special*, 77; *Your Hit Parade* makes his name with troops, 74
"Slush" Committee, 46–47, 56 n.2
Smith, WAC Margie, AES, 67
Song lyrics, BBC censorship of, 46–47, 56 n.2
Song titles, *see* Musical numbers
Sound Wave magazine, 35
Special Service Division, U.S. War Dept., 28, 62, 78 n.14, 86
Stars and Stripes:; and AFN [helps with news, 29, 52; publicizes, 120; start

headline news in, 29]; correspondent on bombing raid, 121; origins of, 31 n.24; reports on AES, 67, 68 n.15
Start Point, Devon, site of AEFP transmitter, 93
Sunday Express, 14
Sweden: AES heard in, 67; and AFN, 134

Thiel, Brig. Claude, 136 n.5
Tokyo Rose, 73
Transmitters: AEFP, 93, 120, 124; Aircraft beacons, use as, 21 n.6; BBC transmissions, effects on, 15, 24; installation program, 26–27, 32, 118; London area, ban on, 27; problems over, 12–13, 33; signals more powerful than expected, 34, 48
Trinder, Tommy, 90
"Twelve, Twelve," Allied deception radio station, 119

United Service Organizations (USO), 62
U.S. Armed Forces: AEFP, criticism of, 113–115; airfield building program for, 32; BBC, dislike of, 2, 113–115; black troops [and Henry, Leroy, court martial of, 19; Jubilee program aimed at, 72; morale of, 72]; buildup of in U.K. and morale, 1–2; legal position of, 19; listening habits of, 9 n.6; numbers of in U.K., 27, 118; recreational clubs for, 27
U.S. Navy Band (Sam Donahue) and Melody Maker's views on, 110
U.S. radio stations: KMPC Los Angeles, 26; WHTH, Hartford, Conn., 36; WPIC, Ashtabula, Ohio, 36

V-bombs, 80, 82
V discs, 75
VD (venereal disease), 129, 136 n.4
Vincent, Capt. George, author of V-disc program, 75
Visiting Forces Act, 19
V mail, 44 n.26
Vocalists: Andersen, Lale, 6–7, 59; Andrews Sisters, 46, 77; Brent, Gloria, 109; Carless, Dorothy, 109, 131; Carol, Lily Ann, 38, 143; Carpenter, Paul, 106, 131; Crosby, Bing, 3, 34, 39, 40, 65, 70, 74, 77, 82,

92 n.4, 105, 143; Dallas, Joanne, 106; Day, Doris, 39; Dennis, Denny, 106; Desmond, Johnny, 82, 110, 122; Eberle, Ray, 40; Eberly, Bob, 40; Edwards, Joan, 74; Forrest, Helen, 38, 74; Green, Paula, 109; Haymes, Dick, 40, 74; Horne, Lena, 40; Langford, Frances, 38, 41, 70; Lynn, Vera, 109; Powers, Jack, 105, 110, 131; Rogers, Roy, 72; Shelton, Anne, 7, 105, 109; Shore, Dinah, 38, 40, 70, 74, 77, 82, 105; Simms, Ginny, 38, 40; Sinatra, Frank, 34, 40, 74, 77, 143; Wain, Bea, 39, 67, 70
Voice of America, 134, 137 n.18

Way to the Stars (feature movie), 106
Weaver, Pat, AFRS/NBC president, 78
Welch, Rev. J. W., BBC Director of Religious Broadcasting, 85–86
Werner, Mort, 73

Western Union boys, 70
Whitney, Major, 12
Why We Fight (documentary film), 62
Wigan, Tony, BBC News, 52, 54
Wilkerson, Martha (GI Jill), 73–74
Willson, Meridith, AFRS, 73
Wilmot, Gerry, Canadian AEFP, 106
Winant, John G., U.S. Ambassador to Britain, 18, 42
Wireless Telegraphy Board (U.K.), 25, 33
Women announcers: AES, 67; AFN, lack of in, 38; BBC/AEFP, 98–99
Women's Army Corps (WAC), 38, 67, 94
Women's Royal Naval Service (WRENS), 2, 39, 40
Woodey, Lt., AFN, 53

Yank magazine, 39, 44 n.27, 125 n.18
Yorkshire Post, 141
Young, Loretta, 63, 71
Your Hit Parade, 39, 40, 67, 74–75

ABOUT THE AUTHOR

In a journalistic career extending over 40 years, Patrick Morley spent ten years with some of the leading English provincial newspapers before joining the BBC. He held senior news posts with that organization for over 30 years and after a spell as editor of New Zealand Television News ended his broadcasting career as Head of News for the BBC West Region in Bristol. After retiring from the BBC he lectured on broadcasting journalism and operated an antiquarian book business specializing in true crime.